A PERFECT EDUCATION

A
PERFECT
EDUCATION

by

Kenneth E. Eble

THE MACMILLAN COMPANY *New York*

COLLIER-MACMILLAN LTD. *London*

For my students

CONTENTS

PART ONE

IN DELIGHT AND WONDER

CHAPTER I

THE SENSE OF PLAY

To LEARN is to love. Any sound education must grow from this principle—which doesn't permit itself to be a principle, but is instead an understanding. Children bring the understanding with them. Adults must try to regain it. Education as a formal enterprise tries to accommodate this simple truth to many ends. The result is about what one could expect. Everywhere buildings, bond issues, curriculum studies, principals, schools of education; somewhere love and learning.

Education is personal. At its best, it is intensely personal. Our shortcomings in recognizing this fact are revealed in the way we make a joke of pupils falling in love with teachers. It is no joke—it is the way of learning. That is the advantage of live teachers and live books. They can be fallen in love with, possessed, and since love requires continuity, they can be dwelt upon, in a way that more immediately powerful influences—television, for example—cannot. Teachers and books, then, and someone to love them, to use them, to cherish them, these come first.

Learning begins in delight and flourishes in wonder. Surely the greatest gift a parent can give a child, once heredity has done what it can, is to let that child experience the delight of learning. Response is everything. Parents worry too much, and probably the more educated they are, the more they worry. No parents could be more concerned with the education of their children than American parents. And yet that very concern often discourages the delight in which all learning should begin.

The more educated adult Americans are, the more they must unlearn as parents. They must unlearn some of the secondhand strivings that consciously and unconsciously push their children into formal educational patterns without much regard for the children's aptitudes or society's needs. They must unlearn the habit of being nervously involved in their children's education—subjects and teachers and schools—and yet uninvolved in learning themselves. They must unlearn their fears, shake off the habit of excessive worry.

More positively, they must laugh greatly. For children, solemnity is like a whole pane of glass in an abandoned building. Solemnity invites shattering—not just destructive shattering but the kind of creative shattering that out of Victorian solemnity gave us *Alice in Wonderland* and *Huckleberry Finn*. In a sense, the Victorian Age enriched posterity by producing such rebels as Lewis Carroll and Mark Twain. But a system of education that deliberately tries to educate everyone cannot be built on the hope that contrary genius will prove superior to the system. And parents, too, cannot rely just on the learning that comes from the clash between their own seriousness and their children's rebellion.

But why laughter? Because laughter is giving and recognizing. It forces a physical giving that releases for a moment the very self. And if we did not recognize some ragged corner of ourselves, some flawed reality, we would not laugh. Such giving is necessary to prepare the self to learn. Such recognizing acknowledges the delight in learning that encourages one to learn more. Parents can hardly do better than respond to their children's sense of absurdity, to let physical ticklings grow into wit, to let wit grow into a sense of the world as it is and as it should be.

Furthermore, if a person is laughing, he can't be talking. Consider life's greatest moments, in youth or age. Are they not moments when talking stops, or is inadequate, or is inappropriate? Speech is one of man's most glorious abilities, but life at its highest pitch is nonverbal—silence or the shriek, the moan, the gasp. There is a lesson here, particularly when one considers that although the child's immense task is to become a talking animal, he will probably spend a great deal of his life regretting it. Laughter is "laughing with" and "laughing at." Talking is too much "talking to." People can laugh together, at the same time, with a shared sense of understanding, but they cannot profitably talk at the same time.

It is what laughter stands for, what it forces us to be, that makes it a first principle for learning. It means a genuine giving in of one's self to a shared understanding. It offers the highest kind of security: that of finding value in the same particulars and on the same terms as another. Since it is pleasurable, it affords the highest kind of motivation. Since it is freeing, it opens pathways to the discovering spirit.

Laughter and love have much in common. They exist together, each both object and image for the other. Surely both are intrinsic to learning, but laughter has particular virtues. It is freeing rather than confining. It is critical in distinguishing and relating, whereas love inclines toward accepting and generalizing. It is inclusive more than exclusive. And it encourages far fewer sins in its name. I suspect laughter demands more of the intelligence than love and makes just as many demands on the imagination. And, like love, it demands response.

Laughter, love, and learning are most closely and ideally related in play. The energy of mind, spirit, and body that a child gives to play far surpasses the energy he gives to his formal education. Although adult Americans work hard, they sometimes do it as if they wanted to make up for the loss of play. One might do worse than ask that the basic meaning of "school" be restored to public school education. The Greek word σχολή, from which our word "school" derives, means "leisure." The activities characteristic of a school are those in which leisure is employed. Such learning is closer to play than to work, to the pursuit of knowledge for its own sake than to training for either jobs or democracy, and is motivated by a sustained feeling of love and delight in learning rather than by the sense of necessity and duty that is the chief support of our schools. "Recess" probably comes closer to the real meaning of "school" than what goes on during the rest of the day. And, recess is also the only part of the school program that, for both teacher and pupil, is an unqualified success.

Where does education begin? Surely it begins in play and continues in play for all our lives. Yet no sooner does education become formalized than it becomes solemnized. The current debate over education is largely between two solemnities: education for adjustment to life versus education for the development of the mind. Behind both is the pragmatic premise that education, like play, is worthless in itself. It must have some use, which is always something other than either education or play. So regarded the purpose of education is to create the good society or the democratic man or the intellectual man or the well-rounded man. The purpose of play is to develop the spirit of cooperation or the sense of sportsmanship or the strength of mind and body (so that they may be employed in important tasks).

One of man's most unfortunate patterns of thinking is the harsh opposition of work to play. For the ancient Greeks as for the early Christians, work was a necessary evil because man no longer lived in the Golden Age or because he had been banished from Paradise. In modern times, the word "work" has expanded to include a great many activities beyond the mere struggle for subsistence. During the greater part of this country's history, Americans have regarded work as man's proper activity and have looked upon play with hostility and suspicion. Play is for kids, and adults who play must pay for such pleasures with some measure of guilt. Play probably would have been made a juvenile offense long ago had it not been recognized as such a good preparation for work.

Progressive education has been damned most heartily because it has permitted the child to play his way through school. Much of this has been what Huizinga calls puerile play, the kind of mindless make-believe that is neither fun nor education. But what the reformers have offered in its stead has been little more than a grim certainty, since Sputnik I, that we play around at our peril, that Russian students don't play around and neither should we. Yet the most successful magazine in years—even during the Sputnik years—is *Playboy*, aimed at America's educated males—recently graduated college students, young executives, missile engineers, and those who man our far-flung first and last lines of defense. Is this what we have worked so hard for at PTA, to find our sons carrying keys to the Playboy clubs and our daughters wearing bunny tails?

The sense of play will manifest itself. If it is driven out of formal academia by current solemnity, then it will crop up somewhere else, like *Playboy*. Whether or not we can fix direct responsibility on the public schools for the hedonism that persists in a time of grave concerns, we must look at play with more respect than we have till now, with less prejudice against it for the companions it has kept.

Obviously, play is the way all children learn the majority of their preschool lessons. It trains muscles and senses. It refines judgment. It involves the individual in society. It both shapes dreams and presents realities. And although we tend to see it as primarily a child's activity, it is a lifelong education. It is unencumbered by formal structures, yet has its ordering and its discipline. Seemingly random, a child's play is never quite that. Free as it may appear, it is in itself a compulsion to activity. Put a normal child in any setting and one thing is certain: he will not sit idle. He will play and inevitably he will learn. It is obvious, then, that if a parent is to speculate about education, especially about a perfect education, he must learn all he can about play and apply all he learns to the formal structure that seems necessary to education on a large scale.

The child's world is made almost entirely of play. It seems to be the only activity that never palls. A specific kind of play, any one game, may pall, particularly under the scrutiny of overattentive parents trying to make sure the child has fun. But play in itself does not, either for the child or for the adult.

What is it that gives play its enduring fascination? To begin somewhere—not necessarily at the center of the question—play is "free activity." It is probably of the same physical order as any activity that gives looseness, freeness, to muscles: the horse rolling in the dirt, the morning stretch and wriggle, the deliciousness of free motion in swinging a bat or a tennis racket or rushing head-long to an orthopedic ward on skis. It must be unfettered. Freedom is as essential to play as restraint is antagonistic to it. Children always come *from* play and always move from freedom to restraint, from the glorious dirt of outdoors to the less glorious, less dirty confines of a house.

Closely allied with freedom, perhaps part of the same thing, is the sense of control, of mastery, that play brings. The child try-ing for the seventeenth time to build his house of dominoes is seeking mastery, and over no trivial thing. Long before he might be a Newton, the child is contending with man's most elemental antagonist, gravity itself.

So it is with less fundamental contests. A spinning top, a car that will roll, a dish that will break—all give a sense of mastery, of initiating a motion or of opposing an existing one, a sense of being a subject rather than an object. Considering how much a child is forced into the position of object, it is no wonder that play is so attractive. Perhaps too that is why play, as perceived by adults, always seems to be on the edge of wrongdoing. The environment, including adults, *is* hostile. Only the child in his play challenges them head-on.

Consider how little of play is not antagonistic. Play, even silent, lone play, is a putting of the self into relation with something else. To cover all possibilities, we might call that something else the environment, though it probably takes the form of a physical object, another person, even one's own fingers or toes. And though "mastery," "antagonism," and even "control" may be too strong terms, yet it seems fair to say that play does essentially involve a kind of contest with the vast outside, with the child winning a share of the encounters.

What else can we say? Play is, of course, investigative, curious, seeking. Its freedom is used in exploring, and its seeking of control is the basis of the learning it provides. Whether we look at play as a means by which a complex biological species learns or as a retracing of the racial experiences of the species, the various scholarly theories agree that "finding out" is much of what play is. Groos' investigation of play as the basic learning of animals and the basic and more prolonged learning of superior species and G. Stanley Hall's anthropological explanation of play as repeating the universal activities of man through all his history both focus on the learning aspect of play. The surplus-energy theory of Schiller and Spencer, in which play is explained as a response growing out of the essential excitability of the nerve cells, is a physiological explanation of the freedom we have been discussing.

In these theories, play and learning are bound together. The human organism has a compulsion to free its movements, to feel its way, to explore its environment. Learning is pleasurable, as Aristotle said, or, one might say, learning is play.

There is another characteristic of play that deserves our attention: its tendency to fall into patterns, to seek structure. What we have been talking about thus far is play at a very simple level: the movement of an infant in a crib, the amused babble of a slightly older child, the poking into everything of a crawling baby. But beyond the earliest responses, very little play is random. As play becomes more than muscular and sensory activity, it seems to move more and more toward organization. For example, an observer watching children play will be struck by the repetitiousness of the activity. What, one wonders, is the child seeking in going back over, again and again, the chase of cops and robbers, the day-after-day preoccupation with a swinging rope or a bouncing ball? What ancestral lesson is being learned? What anticipation of the future is hidden in the purposeful abandon of the games children play? Surely something more than is apparent is necessary to justify the maddening repetition of children's games, or children's stories, or children's talk.

It is, of course, not entirely repetition. No two games of cops and robbers are exactly alike. They have large differences as well as small: changes in the cast, changes in the locale, changes in the outcome. But more than that, they all have constant changes in the attitudes—of dying, of being shot, of escaping, of resisting—and although even these are defined by the accepted patterns of the game, the child has freedom to imagine within them according to his mood of the moment.

The point here is that the freedom of play is given definition both by the context of games and by the child's own desires. Although parents sometimes complain that all their children want to do is play, children do get bored, and they do say they want something, not something to play, ordinarily, but something to do. The need for freedom, reaching out, clearly runs into another need, a need for definition, for pattern, for regularity. Thus the "freedom" and "discipline" that Whitehead points out as central to education are also the chief concerns of play itself.

Perhaps here lies the answer to a most puzzling question about play, one that needs answering before we can go much further. Why is play so pleasurable? Johan Huizinga admits at the outset of his book *Homo Ludens* that "the *fun* of playing resists all analysis, all logical interpretation." But in a sense, as I have just noted, the question answers itself. The organism seeks freedom and reasserts that seeking in defining itself in terms of its relationships with the environment. At a more primitive level, the movement of the organism is in itself pleasurable, the pleasure increasing as such movements broaden and intensify contacts with all that lies outside. Becoming more complex, life's essential movements become play and, in turn, are facilitated by play, which gives direction and pattern to movement and so affords the organism satisfaction.

Yet it seems to me that this is a partial answer. Physical stress and release, sensory satisfactions, even when organized into loose patterns, are not yet play as we think of it, although they may be basic to the satisfaction play brings. One realizes that the physical, sensory aspects of play, which perhaps may be explained in terms of physiological satisfactions, are not all there is to it. The mind is as involved in play as the body—more involved as the organism grows older. And it is fully involved, in a way that an adult's rationality finds hard to admit. Even when an adult acknowledges the involvement of the mind in play, he will usually feel that a precious resource is being squandered, just as the word "play" suffers for its numerous pejorative uses. "In acknowledging play," Huizinga writes, "you acknowledge mind, for whatever else play is, it is not matter." From the earliest time that we can distinguish play, we are involved in the mind, in the remembrance of previous play, in the remembrance of previous motion, in the planning and expectation of future similar action, in the relating of object to object, and ultimately in the shaping mind as it constructs the elaborate imaginary world in which fully developed play takes place. Play is highly rational in the sense that it calls, very early, upon those acts of relating, distinguishing, and judging that are rational acts. That the entire context may be irrational or suprarational does not diminish the fact that play is as essentially mental as physical. The full commitment of mind as well as body has much to do with the satisfaction play brings.

Huizinga, having begun as we have by regarding freedom as the first main characteristic of play, cites as the second main characteristic play's separation from "ordinary" or "real" life. Play stands outside real life in definite limits as to time and to space. It flourishes in secrecy, imposes its own world of law and movement, beginning and end.

Summing up the formal characteristics of play, we might call it a free activity standing quite consciously outside "ordinary life" as being "not serious," but at the same time absorbing the player intensely and utterly. It is an activity connected with no material interest, and no profit can be gained by it. It proceeds within its own proper boundaries of time and space according to fixed rules and in an orderly manner. It promotes the formation of social groupings which tend to surround themselves with secrecy and to stress their difference from the common world by disguise or other means.

The removal of play from the demands and restrictions of the real world is an essential part of its freedom and further accounts for its appeal. Within the removed world of play, the child commits himself in the way that adults commit themselves only to the most intense of their pleasures. The great advantage of play in this respect is that, however like life it is, it is not life and affords the player more of a chance for experimentation, a wider scope for the realization of his imagination than life itself.

These observations about the nature of play have obvious implications for education and are central to the idea of a perfect education. The function of play, Huizinga writes, "can largely be derived from the two basic aspects under which we meet it: as a contest *for* something or a representation *of* something." Both, of course, are aspects of formal education. Contests, whether football, spelling bees, or beauty pageants, seem to be the most effective form American education finds for its many concerns. The representational aspect of play is similarly and as firmly embodied in American education's emphasis upon making the schoolroom "like real life." Right now, the utility of play may be that of tempering the swing to vigor, to discipline, to demands, which in themselves are no better than the slackness that has given rise to such an emphasis. Almost as immediate is the need for recognition that play—call it leisure, call it free time, call it anything but work—is now and will become even more a part of an American's adult life.

The public schools should not abandon the positive gains that have come in recognizing the value of play and in taking education out of the hands of the Gradgrinds who could conceive of it only in terms of discipline. Freedoms won should not be relinquished. What is needed is more application of mind and imagination, from the designing of schoolrooms to the developing of teachers to permit freedom to be the animating force that moves the child toward the disciplined acquiring of skills and the growth of knowledge.

School should be a natural outgrowth of a child's developing patterns of play, and everything possible should be done to make the child's zeal for play serve the purposes of formal education. Any good elementary teacher knows this and uses the child's enthusiasm, without losing control of the direction the child's interest takes or giving up the teacher's necessary role as leader and guide. The Montessori method is currently gaining attention because it so well uses the natural inclinations of children to play and to learn.

But play precedes formal instruction—precedes it and flourishes for five invaluable years for most American children. It seems to go on in full delight and wonder in the most squalid of neighborhoods, the most restricted of environments, and, conversely, it can find its dissatisfactions, its boredoms, in the most privileged. Because individual human development is so complex, perhaps parents may do as well letting their children grow as laboring over their development—but parents are not inclined to do so. Assuming that parents must or will take a hand in that period of pre-school learning, that period most distinguished by play, what should they do?

Before confronting that question directly, let us exercise some caution—by way of example—in setting up guidelines for an individual's learning. Whatever is said about education must be said with maximum allowance for the great variety of ways a person may learn, any one of which may work well or badly. The educations of Montaigne and John Stuart Mill are instructive examples.

Montaigne's education came to him under conditions of maximum freedom and with wise provisions for making learning pleasurable. His father, "having made all possible inquiries among men of learning and understanding with regard to a perfect system of education," arrived at a number of free and effective means of learning. For the learning of Latin, he placed Montaigne, before he could talk, in charge of a German who knew no French. The inviolable rule of the house was that no language but Latin would be used. "It is wonderful," Montaigne later wrote, "how much they all profited by it. . . . In short, we became so Latinized that it overflowed to our villages around, where to this day may be heard several Latin names of artisans and tools, which through frequent use have taken root. . . . And so, without any artificial means, without any book, without grammar or teaching, without any rod and without tears, I learned a Latin quite as pure as that of my schoolmaster."

Montaigne's father also attempted to have his son taught Greek by a method, artificial but new, that made a game out of much of the routine learning. His objective was not to force, but to whet desire, "to train my mind in all freedom and indulgence, without rigor or constraint." So intent was he in carrying out his aims that he had his son awakened to the sound of a spinet. One has to add that the Greek lessons—and, it is implied, other unconventional methods—did not work. This, Montaigne says, was not because of any defect in the lessons but because of the sterile and unsuitable soil: the heaviness, softness, sluggishness of mind, slow wit, tardy apprehension, weak initiative, and incredibly deficient memory with which Montaigne charged himself.

Unfortunately, his father turned to more conventional modes of training, a mistake Montaigne describes as "being sent to school." There his readings in Latin continued, not under strict discipline, but as stolen diversions, which a wise tutor not only let him continue but also permitted him to carry on in secret. Montaigne concludes "Of the Education of Boys," one of the best short treatises on education, with the observation that "there is nothing like alluring the appetite and affections: else we shall produce only asses laden with books."

John Stuart Mill's education differed greatly from Montaigne's. Each father was intensely concerned with his son's education. Each made formal education an integral part of his son's daily life. But there was nothing of freedom, nothing conducive to play, nothing left to a child's natural inclinations in Mill's education. He began Greek at five. He began his daily walks with his father, daily catechisms on all learning, at six. He became and stayed a prodigy of learning. Yet there is a sincere and infinite melancholy in Mill's backward glance that gives more warning than Montaigne's self-depreciation. "I never was a boy; never played at cricket: it is better to let Nature have her way."

One might make some ambitious conjectures from these two examples alone. The discursive, wide-ranging, curious mind of Montaigne seems to rise naturally from the kind of education he received. Yet it is doubtful that the father had in mind Montaigne the essayist when he looked so carefully to his education. It was just that such an education, like that given in the more liberal of liberal-arts colleges, prepared him for no more useful task.

By contrast, James Mill's education of his son seems to have been an unqualified success. Mill became a saint of rationality, building his reputation in formal philosophy in logic and showing that same formidable logic in his great social essays. And yet, Mill not only had to go through a considerable emotional crisis in his twenties before he could really assert himself as a thinking man, but he ended up as a thinker somewhat entrapped in the thought he was able to express.

Of the two, Mill's education is much closer to our own present system and practice of education. His education was unusual because of his formidable intellect and the ambitions of his formidable parent, but otherwise it is quite in keeping with the current emphasis on intellectual excellence. Given Mill's potential, few American children of educated parents would escape some similar kind of forced feeding. And although Mill was undoubtedly a great man, perhaps his greatness lacked the humanness, the urbaneness, the breadth, and the style of Montaigne's. A technological civilization may find these virtues superfluous, but a perfect education cannot pass them by.

Certainly we need to guard against our current compulsion to begin learning under discipline at the earliest possible age. The question is not whether a child can be taught to read at two, but whether he might be more gainfully employed at other matters at that age. No one can tell us. Common sense, observation, respect, and a sense of play may be better guides than pedagogical texts or experiments.

However we judge them as models, the educations of both Montaigne and Mill remind us that a child's education cannot merely be turned over to the public or private school. It is a father's responsibility as well as a mother's. And the responsibility of parents gets too little public exposure. In the current debate on education, it gets almost no attention, chiefly because the schools provide such large and assailable targets.

Unfortunately, most men and many women do not find the actual education of their children to be their most engaging interest. Granting this, what are the modest demands every parent might make upon himself as an educator before he can turn the whole thing over to the public schools—too often defying them to make something out of his bad job?

First, laughter, even before love—because putting laughter first may keep love from smothering, from cloying, from ultimately thwarting. We give in laughter in ways we do not always do in love. And if we laugh, it seems to me, we are bound to love. Laughter is freeing ourselves, giving ourselves a freedom without which those we love and are responsible for cannot have their own freedom. Man, Aristotle said, is the laughing animal. We too often forget how fundamentally true such a statement is.

The burdens of bringing up children are great and fall upon all parents, except those both rich and callous enough to pay someone else to assume their burdens. One has to admit how much time parenthood takes, how it reduces one's developed intelligence to babble, how it destroys the girl one has married and replaces her with a creature who bears, always and sufferingly, one's children. One has little choice but to laugh. For laughter makes parenthood bearable—and it creates the very air in which learning thrives.

And that is the point about laughter. If it is not linked with learning in the home, the connection is not likely to be made at school. Formal education is still a solemn enterprise. Surely the thing that drives hundreds of bright, laughing college students out of the colleges of education is the solemnity of their utterances as well as their behavior. There is nothing quite so solemn as a textbook on *The Foundations of Education* or on *The Administration of the Public Schools,* unless it be professors of such subjects or the future principals and superintendents to whom they lecture.

Next to laughter, and assuming love, I would ask for responsiveness in parents willing to take an active part in educating their children. The child at play or in school needs someone to come home to, someone to tell things to, someone to respond. Like laughter, responsiveness is not as easy to provide or as commonly found as is often believed. Good teachers are almost infinitely responsive. Boys and girls become good students for teachers who provide, often for the first time, a response to what they feel most deeply.

It is not easy for parents to be responsive. Reading the evening paper is commonly—and often unjustifiably—judged to be more interesting than reading a paper in spelling or arithmetic. Children's games are commonly more fascinating to the children themselves (or to visiting relatives or friends, or to researchers in educational psychology) than to parents. Very young children's play is, for adults, silly, pointless, and even maddening. The course of the game is always the child's course. Although the time will come when Parker and Brothers will provide written rules for games and children will sometimes obey them, most preschool games have rules that come into being one instant and change the next. The adult involved must submit to whim, infantile sadism, and an illogic far stronger than his own rational processes. Why a grown man not only must suffer being shot, but must be shot in the exact right place (a place that may change without notice), must experience the exact shades of mortification, and must die in the right place and the right attitude is something only the playmaster, usually between three and six, can explain, and he won't. He will only insist upon it. And then all games, all types of play, seem to end in "one more time." Often they end in children's tears or anger and father's (mother gets out of games by staying in the kitchen) mighty assertion of adult rights and masculine dignity.

I dwell on these far from appealing details to indicate some of the difficulties of being responsive and of remaining so. I would also challenge the comforting rationalization that children don't really want adults in their play. Of course they want them, if only to humiliate them. What they don't want is adults running the show and expecting *them* to be responsive. It is difficult, but once the right balance between joining and intruding is found and once easy rationalizations have been discarded, responsiveness—and most often in play—is an incitement to learning that any parent can provide. A child gets only a limited response from raw environment. Falls bruise, glass breaks, animals yelp or run or bite. Parents should provide a superior environment, one capable of laughing, crying, galumphing, sympathizing, and stomping the floor in righteous indignation.

Parents would be well advised to listen to themselves as their children hear them, to sit down before a primer for parents, as it might be prepared by a polite but perceptive child:

A is for *after,* as in *after supper, after I read the paper, after your nap.* Fathers are always going to play *after.*
B is for *before,* as in *before you come to supper, before you get any dessert, before you go out to play.* Mostly things you don't want to do but have to.
C is for *can't,* as in *Can't you stop that singing? Can't you turn down the radio? Can't you ever come in when you're called?* Means you can and you darn well better.
D is for *don't,* as in *Don't let me catch you doing that again, Don't come in the house with those muddy shoes, Don't expect me to do it for you again, Don't talk to your mother like that, Don't you ever hit him again, Don't lie to me.* Most sentences begin with *don't.*

The willingness of parents to play, to listen, to answer questions, to direct investigations, to enter in when invited and to stay out when asked, are all educational experiences that a child should not have to wait until school to find. What I am getting at is that play should be taken for what it's worth, and it is worth a great deal. Robert Frost said that the figure a poem makes is the same as for love—each "begins in delight and ends in wisdom." The figure, it seems to me, fits learning as well. Parents need to laugh at their vexations, to respond more and reprimand less, and to enter fully into the spirit of play, which too much of their own learning and too much concern for their children's learning may have taken from them.

CHAPTER II

THE SENSE OF DISCOVERY

ALL EDUCATION is an opening out. The miracle of children is their delight in all the unfolding. The tragedy of growing old is the tightening back into the withered bud that marks the end of life. How wonderful—and how brief—is the time when the infant is growing into the child, the child into the adolescent, and eagerly, unashamedly, exposes himself to all the world. For it is then that delight in discovery is most intense. What sadder time is there than when there is nothing new under the sun.

A perfect education is one that proceeds by surprises and the promise of other surprises, one that offers most opportunity for discovery. We don't seek what we already know or even what we almost know. We seek what we know not at all. A man measures himself by the heights he has gained. A child charts more unknown seas, maps more continents, than any explorer since man first ventured out beyond the horizon.

Educators should worry less about articulation between levels of learning and more about fostering the imagination that leaps over gaps. Education should concern itself more with heights to be gained and ranges lying beyond, and less with four-abreast walkways heated in winter and sheltered from snow and rain. Is it worthwhile arriving anywhere if we have not had an experience along the way? Ideally, learning should be hidden away from children, awaiting their seeking it out. Teachers should play the sphinx—speak seldom, and then in riddles. A school is an unhealthy place insofar as it subverts the sense of wonder.

Parents are always worrying about what their children are "up to" and forcing them to get "down to" business. Our language is wiser than our fears. All discovery is a rising up to, just as business is almost always a going down. A parent cannot, you say, stand idly by and watch a child totter off a precipice. No, nor should he.

Yet he cannot remove cliffs or trees or rocks or stairs. At best he can pick up the broken glass beneath the fence, cut down the rotten branch, be quick of eye and swift of foot, and pray.

If processes beyond our control had not forced us erect, we would seek out the horizontal always and remain there forever. If it were not for the stars, our heads would always greet our feet, and nowadays, we spend too many of our nights indoors. Everywhere we level. Bulldozers remove hills and trees and rocks to make room for houses that lie flat on the land, no longer a second story to roam, an attic to find. Our highways are marvels of maintained grade, our farms of sustained yield, our rivers of controlled navigation. Our schools, except in the most backward areas, have beaten grass into asphalt. Having achieved widespread mediocrity, our schools now build for uniform excellence.

What proverbial unwisdom that curiosity killed a cat, as if we cared more for cats than for learning. The sense of life as open-ended, of growth as change, of change as discovery, of discovery as life itself, is one we need not so much implant as to keep vibrantly alive.

What do we do to enhance the sense of discovery? Chiefly, I think, we treasure a child's curiosity and seek out ways to lead it on and to satisfy it. The playpen is a parent-saving device for which we should be properly thankful in a society and at a time in which nannies are not plentiful. Television is a superior kind of playpen, particularly useful for children who are old enough to crawl over the sides of the playpen but who still need to be restrained without being physically tied. Some zealous mothers, models of planned parenthood, are both playpen and television, and many fathers are that which the children are penned off from.

Parents should be good providers, not just in the common sense of providing food and clothing and shelter but in the uncommon sense of providing opportunities for and incitements to discovery. Such providing consists both of doing enough and not doing too much. A closet full of toys is hardly as fascinating as a closet full of almost anything else, a drawer full of pots and pans, a shelf full of cans and jars and boxes. For all the fussy tidiness that seemed to be a part of child raising fifty years ago, the houses of that day had more nooks and crannies, more closed doors and hidden treasures than today's houses. There is a terrible openness (one could in moments of exasperation call it a vacancy) about modern housing.

The family room is the whole house, and with everything immediately exposed, little lies hidden to be discovered. Music rooms and libraries, rolltop desks, dumb-waiters, attics, basements, outhouses, sheds, and separate garages are not to be found in suburbia. It is not nostalgia alone that makes one view their passing with regret. It is the sameness of what is left, the expectedness of it, its functional and definable quality. One longs for homes where something remains to be discovered and for parents able to make the most of such discoveries.

But if a house does not appeal to the sense of discovery, much can still be done. Play itself is almost always curious, investigative, and parents can encourage that spirit as they can encourage the nonsense that fosters laughter. Questions can be asked and answered. Live questions and answers can be brought into the home from gullies and lawns and trees, from newspapers, maps, pamphlets, from garages and workshops and junkyards. Reference books—a dictionary, an atlas, a bird book, an animal book, a plant book—are easy to acquire. Encyclopedias can be purchased in the supermarket. Among other blessings of living in an affluent society is that of having so many means of discovery close at hand and at a cheap price. What is wanting is parents who make use of these means themselves and who encourage their children to explore them.

For a parent does need to seek ways to enlarge the restricted area in which many children grow up. Consider the size and variety of the child's world outside the home in the middle-class urban and suburban civilization that now dominates American family life. A child's world is likely to be about one block's scope, the area that can be explored without exposure to the real dangers of crossing a busy street.

Within that world are houses to see, sidewalks to race on, some trees, many fences. No stores, no sheds, no vacant lots, no open fields, a few dogs (probably on leashes), a few cats, wagons, tricycles, bicycles, cars and garages, parents, and children. Neighborhoods vary only slightly in the number and variety of things available to the exploring child. Furthermore, human society is almost exclusively that of children and mothers. The fathers leave while all the children are watching cartoons, and they return while all the children are watching other cartoons. Sometimes the fathers have done something in between. Sometimes the children have.

On Saturdays fathers are more or less at home. Good fathers play with the children. Bad fathers play golf. Mediocre fathers play a little, work a little, grumble a lot and wait for Monday. Mothers shop, grumble, and wait for school to begin in the fall.

What is wrong? What is missing? One thing missing is a strong sense of the variety of life. Without becoming overly nostalgic about the small town or the country, let us make the contrast. First, what kind of world did the child have? He undoubtedly had a more spacious one. Although the business section of a small town may have been off limits to the child, large areas of the town were accessible from an early age. The possible discoveries had more variety than is to be found in a suburban block, and what's more, they could be discovered beyond the watchful eyes of mother. Mothers have always been watchful, some neglectfully so, many overbearingly so. In the suburban neighborhood, watchfulness is inescapable, and in urban areas it is necessary to survival. Although there may be much to discover, the child's curiosity is necessarily confined to a limited, controlled space. The limits that parents in any setting are likely to place on their children's explorations are much more restrictive when the parents must worry about the child's safety and can turn the child loose on his own only in a very small physical area.

Furthermore, the small community of the past was not so over-poweringly feminine as modern suburban and urban communities. Fathers did, at times, make an appearance at lunch. Town was not a shopping center occupied almost entirely by women, but a place for loafers and workers and shoppers, male and female. Nor were the houses emptied early in the morning and filled again at night. Life was closer to the infinite variety of nature, and was ruled by nature rather than by television programming and supermarket specials. Children could find mud, and larvae growing in rain barrels, and frogs and toads in many a garden, and weeds, rank weeds of many kinds, and musty vacant sheds and outbuildings filled with machinery and rope, and big trees, and chickens and rabbits and ducks and cats by the thousands.

All this is very well, you say, but we cannot have back the world we once knew, even if it was a world that better fostered our growth. We have our own time and must live and work within it. Our children, too, will live and work in theirs. Why, one might ask, go to the past for lessons when today itself will be very far from tomorrow? But we are going neither back nor forward. We are, rather, looking at the present in one kind of mirror, which seems to show the loss of certain qualities of home and community that might encourage the sense of discovery.

A child's incitements to discovery might be divided into the categories of nature, machines, people, and books. Of these, nature seems to be the one in which our urban civilization is most deficient. Even though our tremendously rich, tremendously mobile society gives far more people access to the more spectacular areas of nature than ever before, nature is not an important part of daily experience. The small community, the farm and open range, *were* closer to nature—and not necessarily to an Emersonian nature that teaches all lessons and urges the highest morality. It must often have been Mill's nature, a nature guilty of every crime that men are hanged for. Yet it was nature, and it, above all, was to be discovered, bounteous, mysterious, unmindful, neither judging nor cautioning nor limiting, but mostly, for children at least, infinitely inviting.

We try, of course, to keep from losing this aspect of the past. A museum of natural history has a greater abundance of nature than any block of rural America, however glowingly it may exist in the mind of a nostalgic lover of nature. Yet that nature is secondhand, capable of being looked at but not really discovered, not handled, not made one's own. Like the official days of discovery provided by conscientious city parents, museums are both too easy to discover in and too difficult, too much something provided, too designed to guide learning, and too overpowering. Zoos and public parks are as wonderful as museums. All are inviting places, necessary places, to be enhanced by careful planning and sound management. Yet for discovery one needs some things unmanaged, undesigned until a child's eye imposes a pattern. The area reserved for the discovery of nature shrinks by the year. And with it shrinks some of a child's opportunity for learning.

Far more than anything else, nature stimulates our sense of discovery. The first crocus in spring, the first bird in the birdhouse, the first melon on a vine, the first worm lying on the sidewalk after a rain—all of these have an appeal that few adults can deny, however often they recur. The bug in a child's hand, a bee sting, a frog jumping through the weeds, and the sun firing a piece of paper to flame through a magnifying glass are discoveries of magnitude.

Every day brings them anew, from new clouds building up in the west to the first snowfall to dandelions or mushrooms poking up in the lawn. The variety that seems one of man's strongest pleasures is furnished in abundance, awaiting only the inquiring eye, the alert ear, the keen nose, the reaching hand to have itself discovered. But along with variety, nature furnishes extraordinary examples of pattern, too: the seasons themselves, the cycles of life of all growing things, the symmetries and asymmetries in all plant life.

Nature does other things as well. Surely our first incitement to philosophy is the question raised by the apparent purposelessness of nature against the evidences of design. If it does not answer ethical questions, it at least raises them. It provokes the mind to relate, to compare and contrast, to distinguish, and to see similarities. It never ceases to play upon our senses, arouse our sentiments, inspire feelings. All of these must be part of a child's education. Nature asks hardly more than space to put on its display, but it must have that. Too many adults prize nature as mere evidence of their regard for property values in the neighborhood they occupy. How dispiriting to see the contest between the child and growing things, the desire for a green, carpet-thick lawn ruling out the child's need to learn.

As nature has decreased as an invitation to the growing child to wonder, so the mechanical marvels around him have probably increased. We are too inclined to oppose the natural to the mechanical. Children recognize the contest, but accept it as a part of their growing sense of life and are as delighted with machines as with growing things. The adult response to anything mechanical is too often a fashionable hostility or bewilderment. Yet a wrecking ball is as awe-inspiring as lightning striking an oak, a giant earthmover as terrifying as a dinosaur.

The very young child may be more responsive to a mechanical object than to nature itself, the inorganic superior here to the organic. The messy guts between the fingers afford no hint of an answer as to what makes a worm crawl. A dismembered toy, on the other hand, reveals many parts, implies relationships, and may provide the challenge to put back this piece here, another there, thus restoring life to a thing but recently dead.

Again, one might make comparison between the rural past and the city present. On the farm there were always mechanical objects close (often hazardously close) at hand. The exposure, it seems to me, was a good one for the child, sharpening his senses, developing relationships, establishing connections with a physical, mechanical world larger than the play world, but recognizable and explorable. Surely there is a relationship between the vast expanse of rural land and people and the fecundity of American inventions in the nineteenth century.

Machines, unlike nature itself, have increased marvelously in the twentieth century, but not without some loss. Nowadays there is a passion for concealment of all working parts, which probably bears some occult relationship to our attitudes toward sex. Perhaps our continued undraping and exposure of the human body has forced us to a compensatory concealment of machines that were once gloriously exposed. Perhaps our attitude toward machines has not evolved as far as our attitude toward sex, at least in the matter of concealing the working parts. Because we seem destined to insist that man has other, more important, functions than sex, we may always keep that function, the act itself, hidden and somehow shameful. But the machine's excuse for being, particularly for critics of the machine, is its function, and we are more rigid than in our attitude toward sex in our insistence on immaculate function. Nor can such concealment be defended upon aesthetic grounds, except if one argues from the false sense of beauty left over from the nineteenth century that values prettiness, cleanness, and piety above everything else.

When we concern ourselves with education, we cannot afford to disdain machines, first because they excite and satisfy curiosity in a somewhat different way than does nature, and second because it is desirable to create at an early age a respect for machines and working with machines. This respect is necessary to the machines upon which our society increasingly depends and useful to the many young men and women who are ill suited to an academic education. The city provides much in the way of watching the more spectacular machines: cranes and piledrivers and pneumatic hammers and streetsweepers and sandblasters. Wherever something moves with the clanking and vibrating and shrieking associated with immense power, children (and adults) will flock. At the other extreme, the smaller mechanisms, an exposed alarm clock, a food grinder, a typewriter, an eggbeater, are of a size and kind to invite manipulation and discovery—although most of these machines are now electric and conceal their secrets.

People are the third of the categories of discoveries children make. In speaking of the children's world as I have been doing in these introductory chapters, I am in danger of seeming to encourage that modern kind of isolating that shows up in modern retailing with its worlds within worlds: kiddies, subteens, teens, young moderns, and so on. As a perfect education would have it, the children's world must be our world too. We may have to ask our way in, and we may be impolitely and properly asked out, but we must be there, if only to be looked at and puzzled over.

Although we have a superabundance of people in the world, education today probably consists less of knowing people than at any other time. Once the education of a prince, as Telemachus' education in the *Odyssey,* was (after proper tutelage in the use of arms) an education in appearing before his elders. On the one hand he was expected to develop manners, in the broadest and most significant sense, and on the other to observe his elders and profit from his observations. Many later examples can be adduced, from the training of the Renaissance courtier to the proper education of a British gentleman. As democracy has attempted to erase the distinctions between one class and another, one man and another, it has discouraged this kind of education. The consequence may be a diminished sensitivity to manners, a comfortable and general assessment of the people immediately around us, and a not very intense interest in those beyond that immediate circle.

The sense of family is probably not as strong as it has been in the past—certainly not as strong as that evoked by Dylan Thomas' memories of his uncles and aunts in his "A Child's Christmas in Wales." I will not argue that aunts and uncles should be provided where nature has made an omission or even that aunts and uncles are worth the premium children place upon them. Yet the family gives the child well before school age the raw material of a drama: a limited but varied group of people to whom the child is sufficiently exposed to arouse curiosity and to make him ponder relationships. A child *is* privileged, I think, to have different people moving in and out of the family circle: different in ages, occupations, places of residence, temperament, even in morality. A child is underprivileged for being underexposed.

In view of the weakening of family ties, the increased mobility of American families may be an advantage. The need for security, in children as in adults, should be considered in relation to the contrary need for change, variety, difference. The family itself provides the stable center, and the family's mobility provides the chance to see other people living different kinds of lives in different places. The family vacation may be deserving of the scorn heaped upon it by suffering adults, and yet if it involves a child's excited curiosity about "Who was that?" and "Why does he talk that way?" and "What's he doing?" it's worth a good deal of manly complaining and womanly forbearance.

Surely one of the factors that contributes to our crucial racial problems is the comparative immobility of the white South and the sullen forced immobility of the Negro family, which may move, but only from one urban ghetto to another. Conversely, one of the immense advantages of the great city, if it were possible for children to live decently and to move freely within it, would be the exposure to people of every origin, of many languages, of immense diversity in occupations and interests. As it is, many living in the city or outside it must wait until they are adult for full access to its immense variety. The experience is, even then, exhilarating and a very important education. Enabling children in isolated, restricted localities, whether urban slums or rural backwaters, to discover people outside their confined environments might be a major aim of that part of a perfect education for which parents are responsible.

Finally, books are part of what a child should discover, and they, in turn, become the means of further discovery. The commonplaces here are like the commonplaces about the discoveries to be made in nature or machines or people. My own bias might make me argue their case too vigorously or force me to defend books against the seductions of television, the movies, and the spoken word. I hope not to make this argument, for I think that books are not only *not* life but are not as important as life. Nor have I anything to add to the obvious truths that television can be a remarkable educational device (particularly outside the school), that it falls far short of what it could be, and that it is, whatever its excellence, still a device. It should not be confused with life any more than books should be.

There may come a time when reading and writing are no longer central to learning. Writing, as a matter of fact, is urged on American education in something other than complete honesty. Although it is often useful to be able to write, although writing affords a kind of mental discipline and, perhaps, training valuable outside itself, although being totally unable to write would be a decided handicap, technology has reached a point where one cannot assert that the ability to write is a necessity for an educated man. The various devices for recording and playing back language have a rather short history. Their increasing utility, availability, and ease of transport and operation have, in the last ten years, made changes as consequential as the development of the typewriter. There is really no question that we will continue to move further and further and very rapidly in this direction and that the time is not far away when almost all of what we might call purely "utilitarian" writing ("communication," as it is often called) will be oral and mechanical. Secretaries will be preserved, if they are preserved, for other reasons than the necessity of providing a permanent record of verbal transactions. The electronic revolution, as it can properly be called, has already had a powerful impact on the acquiring of language skills by children. Even reading and writing are being approached through typewriters that give the child the sense of creating language on the spot.

But despite what seems to me an obvious development in the practical world of affairs, there are some reasons for urging books now, and in the future. (In the back of my mind is the possibility that books have a limited span of existence, that the age of the printed book will reach no further into the future than it reaches back into the past.) The chief reason is, paradoxically, part of the reason writing has become less important. Books—writing itself— require more of an individual than some are able and than many are willing to give. For communication, if that is all we are interested in, writing is inefficient, inaccurate, unnecessarily time-consuming, and not very effective. A face-to-face conversation is still the best way to do business, and the easiest.

But if we put business, and ease, aside, books and writing have more to say for themselves. James Mill's maxim is still a sound one for learning: "A pupil from whom nothing is ever demanded which he cannot do, never does all he can." First, reading makes demands that in themselves are as important as what is read. Second, reading and writing are still the chief means by which one can look at thought, and by so looking, reflecting, experimenting, can help develop his own thought processes. Third, and this is the major point in this context, reading is still the major means to self-discovery, the means by which a child can leave everything else aside and all on his own find access to everything that man has been able to express in writing. It is arguable whether books are superior to the full visual and oral re-creation of whatever portion of the world the movie or television camera focuses on. In some ways—in showing people and places, for example—they obviously are not. In others—dealing with ideas, chiefly—they as obviously are. But there need be no pitting of books against the other media. All contribute greatly to the growth of the discovering child. Books are still a large part of the way modern man expands his world, opens himself up to experience. Giving the very young child the opportunity to hold a portion of that experience in his hand, to conduct the magic transaction of making symbols on a page become pictures in his mind, giving him the means to move freely and naturally in that vast land of book learning, is what books are rightly prized for.

These are some of the ways of looking at the sense of discovery that, like the urge to play, the child brings to school with him. If we do not fence off the world, we can leave much to the child. If we are willing to expose and risk the child's exposure, what he discovers and how he discovers it become the base from which formal instruction proceeds.

What is left for the schools? Primarily, the experience itself. There are few experiences to match going to school for the first time. Once gone and lost to memory, one must wait years to find it again. Even being driven there in a station wagon with a mother alongside is not bad, if one can keep from being run over by other mothers in other station wagons. But best by far is some distance to walk alone, short enough to keep one from turning back, long enough to allow a backward glance, or several, to allow dawdling, but not too much, since the fear of being late is as pressing as the fear of getting there. It is nice, certainly, to have a brother's hand, or a sister's if worse comes to worse. Fear and reluctance and a leaving behind, but the world to be gained. All those other children, all that sun or wind or rain on a clean face, all those neat new clothes, all those things to carry and to look at in the hands of others. A street to cross. There should be that, or vacant lots, and a central walkway to which all the students finally come. Milling about, one shares the sense of everyone's being *in* something now, something they can't get out of and don't really—even the youngest—want to.

Whoever planned these matters planned right for the beginning of school. Fall is the right time. Spring would be too much. How could one savor his own growth when all nature was springing up at every step? No, spring is better savored later, when winter's dullness has rubbed off the first memories, and school and life can take on that firstness of spring together. Then one can feel again what was so overpowering in fall, the excitement of beginning, and this time without the fear of what is to come. Now there is even time to loiter before the bell, and to somehow express without quite shouting it out, "I've done it! I'm doing it! I'm here!"

All this is what I mean by discovery. The school can sit there, ugly, brooding, impassive, so long as it provides space in which discoveries can be made and children and teachers to make them. Schools, of course, should do better. Ugliness is no virtue. The prison is no model for the schoolroom. Nor does age mellow a school. If any major city ever searched its collective conscience it would reflect how zealously it reconstructs itself—all but its schools. The shame of New York is the shame of private enterprise wrecking and building and leaving the schools untouched. A community should tear down its schools every forty or fifty years. If they must be used, then use them as final homes for the aged rather than as the first places of learning for the young.

The difference between what is done and what should be done can be measured by looking at American cities. Thirty-five percent of the school buildings in the forty-three largest cities of this country were built before 1920. "A majority of these buildings," a specialist in classroom buildings writes, "are traditionally formal in design, using heavy masonry construction with load-bearing walls throughout, small classrooms, and permanent seating. When these buildings were designed and constructed it was not unusual to place the school in the center of the site and leave only small play space." A tour of school plants in any major city is a disorienting experience, as it forces comparisons between the new and the old. One responds with awe to the ingenious and satisfying ways architects have recently solved the problems of urban schools by erecting buildings on stilts with play space beneath, by taking advantage of roof space, by building to overlook existing parks, by giving new schoolrooms inside and out an air of shutting out a part of the city as well as of expanding the enclosed areas within. It is as exhilarating to walk through a flexible, open and brightly lighted new classroom, often with windows opening out on a green-splashed courtyard, as it is depressing to walk through a soot-begrimed elementary school fifty or more years old.

Buildings are, nevertheless, secondary. They are receptacles into which children will pour life. Parents are primary and teachers are primary. Thus far I have been directing my remarks toward parents, for learning and fostering a desire to learn begin long before the child enters the classroom. If a sense of play and a sense of discovery are to be encouraged, they cannot wait for school to begin. Parents and teachers must try to match the curiosity of the child with a curiosity of their own, the discoveries the child is making with discoveries of their own.

* If I were to ask one thing above all others of elementary teachers, it would be imagination. Not intelligence (though it is hard to think of one without the other), not kindness (though that, too), not even formal instruction in a school of education, but the kind of mind that is playful, fanciful, odd in the relationships it perceives, that actively connects things as they are with things as they might be, that always pokes into corners and comes up with that which excites laughter or wonder.

Unfortunately, imagination is what teacher training, educational administration, and the conditions of elementary school teaching most discourage. Begin with the attractions of elementary teaching to the college student. Low in status, often low in standards, promising lowly rewards, elementary teacher training attracts few males and a disproportionate number of girls with safe, unilluminated intelligences and calm dispositions that make them "good" with children. This is not condemnation of elementary teachers nor of those who prepare them. It is a recognition of the basic difficulty of getting highly imaginative people into a profession whose attractions are so often negative: The future teacher does not have to pursue a specific major, can avoid a foreign language, will have a safe local occupation at the end.

Proceed to educational administration, a subject and a profession that imagination has touched even less than intellect. The order of common sense operating there is too often that of the school-board president who barred from the school those who wished to bring their own lunch and would not pay for the hot lunch they did not eat. Isolated and exaggerated as such a case is, it does indicate how far administrative actions can be from the education that administrations are supposed to serve. A study of the written compositions of elementary school principals provides more of a basis for a sound generalization. The sample of writing consisted of various compositions done by 137 men and 95 women, representing elementary school principals from different geographical areas of the United States. After a formidable array of objective indices describing the language of these principals, the author permits herself these subjective observations:

A literate individual reading through a set of compositions, all of which have been written to complete the same assignment, can sort the papers into several "graded" stacks even though he may know relatively little about "gross errors," vocabulary level, or subordination index. In a given set of papers some are outstanding because of their efficiency of expression, their sincerity, or an originality that imparts a kind of freshness to a subject that seems already to have been beaten into staleness by so many others. . . . As the present writer reviews her "reaction" comments to the principals' compositions, she finds that her most frequently used adjectives are: banal, unclear, plodding, disorganized. Verve is conspicuously missing. Remarkably few of the papers rise above a kind of dreary mediocrity. The compositions are so similar both in content and approach that one begins to feel that the whole set might have been written by the same person.

The study appears to have been fairly conducted and judiciously analyzed, and its conclusions support the notion that imagination is not a primary quality to be found in elementary school principals.

Finally, there are conditions of public school teaching that are against attracting and holding imaginative teachers. These conditions are probably worse at the elementary level, despite the fact that the shortage of teachers is greatest there. To name them is to sink into the slough of despond: low salaries, low prestige, limited advancement, uncongenial training, overcrowded classes, parental interference. If imagination is a conspicuous quality in an elementary teacher, surely its first use will be to consider employment elsewhere. Already the junior highs and senior highs draw teachers away from the elementary schools, just as the junior colleges and colleges draw them away from the secondary schools.

Were we to make imagination a requirement for certification, we would have even fewer teachers to choose from than we have now.

And yet, one does not quite despair—at least one freely speculating on a perfect education. A trip to an elementary classroom helps dispel much of the gloom. It may be the little chairs one sits on, but one begins to feel a visceral response that leads to lumps in the throat and tears in the eyes. There is so much to be witnessed in the open display of children's discoveries: the self-portraits, the first stories, the table covered with rocks and plants, bugs under glass and in jars. One can imagine many worse fates than committing oneself wholly to the teaching of young children. The best elementary teacher I ever saw was a young man—an art teacher, by training—who used everything he could imagine to get response from his pupils. He bombarded them with music, paintings, natural and mechanical objects of all kinds, and he drew from them stories, drawings, and other responses startling in their inventiveness. It is rare to see a talented and imaginative adult commit that talent and imagination so wholeheartedly to children day after day. But if it can be done it is a glorious experience for both teacher and pupil.

Imagination or the lack of it distinguishes the best from the worst of elementary teachers. The best, when working with the very young, find their attention fully absorbed, their imagination racing, as they try to keep pace with the imaginative pupils, try to draw out those whose experiences have created fears or whose curiosities have been dulled, and try to direct those whose highly charged being would scatter sensations everywhere. At the other extreme is the teacher whose presence is dutiful, whose only rod and staff is the daily lesson plan, and who makes even show-and-tell an uninspiring experience.

For all the affection American society lavishes on its children, for all that good parents love their children, for all the elementary teachers who are joyfully and imaginatively devoted to their work, the difficulty of devoting a career to the concerns of children has been badly underestimated. That underestimation most critically appears in the conditions I have mentioned, in the absurd assumption that because elementary teaching involves the youngest of children it deserves the lowest of recognitions. The truth, that assumption seems to say, is that it can be done by almost anyone willing to read a roll book, pass out the colored paper, watch for raised hands and dancing feet, and keep a supply of Kleenex on the desk. And yet, by such standards, college teaching is easier, requiring neither Kleenex and colored paper nor the ability to lead a rhythm band.

In a very real way, elementary teaching should provide more for the self-development of the teacher instead of less than at any other level of teaching. Sabbaticals should be a commonplace, and it should be possible to vary teaching, to alternate it with periods of study or with other kinds of occupations. We have at least diminished our hostility (largely an economic one) toward married teachers, which greatly improves the likelihood of getting good teachers who can remain alive as persons. But that should not work against those who make teaching a career, or against elementary teaching becoming the kind of career the best of teachers, male or female, can enter into and give their full commitment to.

Ideally, certificates for elementary school teachers should be granted about as stingily and after as rigorous a training as those for registered nurses, if not for physicians and surgeons. Training should include courses that require a positive display of imaginative work, in painting, writing, dance, or music, or in the sciences, or in the verbal disciplines. It should demand a single interest sufficiently developed so that the teacher has something in which he can join the students in discovering, working at his level while the children work at theirs. It should not be merely a general preparation in a variety of subjects, which leaves the teacher with nothing to work on at his own level and with little of the excitement of having the children's imaginative creations reflect on his own work. It should challenge the teacher at the most difficult point in elementary teaching: how to commit a fully trained and active adult intelligence and sensibility to the minds and hearts of children. This last is the most difficult of all, and until the public recognizes fully the difficulties and amply rewards those teachers who transcend them, the pupils' own imaginations will remain the chief hope of lower school learning.

CHAPTER III

THE SENSE OF ORDER

ALL ART, ALL LIFE, all education is a search for order. A developed sense of order is our one means of confronting the multiplicity of the world, whether we examine a part of its structure and comprehend its design, whether we take the given and transform it into art, whether we give contour to the meaninglessness of existence, or whether we recognize order as both means and end of education.

As has been pointed out, even play, that freest of all human activity, is not lacking in form. The essential rhythm of physical activities is but an aspect of order. Language is an imposer of order. Numbers are order themselves. The aesthetic sense is based on perceptions of rhythm, proportion, harmony. The liberal arts might be defined as those freeing studies that enable a person to perceive order and to impose it.

If modern education makes too much *use* of play, uses play without respecting it, without being playful, it misses the nature of order. Order in the schools is tidiness, order at home is coming to meals on time, order in the church is learning the books of the Bible in proper order. Order is everywhere opposition, at worst antagonism.

When one enters a schoolroom, one is struck by how orderly everything is. Here is the office of the principal. Here is the daily attendance record. Here is the teacher. Here are the pupils. Here are the bells that ring. Here are the orderly water fountains (at times sending disorderly streams of water on the orderly floor). Here are the coat racks. Here are the coats and jackets and rubbers underneath. Here are the lost coats and jackets and sweaters and lunch buckets, heaped testimony to the child's resistance to order.

Everywhere order—and fussing. Fussing to get the letters within the line. Fussing to keep the desks neat. Fussing to keep the schedule. Fussing to arrange the PTA program, to regulate the temperature, to render an orderly pupil personnel accounting. Fussing to see that boys have the right cut of hair, girls the right cut of dress. Fussing with the curriculum, and with teacher training programs, and with auxiliary services, all devoted to arriving at the perfectly orderly school system.

Everywhere order, the home as much as the school. Here is the carefully edged front lawn. Here is the living-centered back lawn. Here is the cement-floored patio. Here is the barbecue grill. Here is the playground equipment. Here is the redwood sandbox. Here is the perennial border. Here is the annual area. Here is the vegetable plot for tiny tots. Here is the lawn edger and the power mower and the electric hedge trimmer and the dandelion digger and the crabgrass killer and the pushbutton insecticide.

Everywhere unwholesome order. Outside and inside. The case against ourselves as adults—and it is always against the prevailing part of us—is devastating. Our lives, necessarily run by pattern, are regulated by the clock, or if not that, by the rhythm of physical needs or the outer rhythm of the world. We may measure the necessity of order by the discontent we feel in being wholly deprived of it. A day spent without plan is refreshing, a week possible, a year deadly, a life impossible.

And yet that is not the whole story. Human beings range from those who seem to fatten on disorder to the fussy ones who can stand nothing out of place. Pushed too far in either direction, one arrives at some form of madness. And although people tend to think of order as far up the scale of good and disorder as far down, they may do so to assure themselves that they enjoy being up there rather than sinking so invitingly down.

The great dualities by which we describe the dynamics of human beings—the Apollonian versus the Dionysian, the rational versus the irrational, the intellectual versus the emotional, the spiritual versus the material—all have order on one side. Philosophy is little more than repeated attempts to reconcile these opposites. Philosophy turned psychology seeks reconciliation within the psyche. Philosophy turned social science seeks reconciliation within the society. Philosophy as an individual's reflective thought process opposes chaos, checks compulsions, encourages patterns.

No child can long escape an awareness of these dualities. That being so, perhaps one aim of education at its very beginning is to work against the opposition of order and disorder, to go against the grain and not let the child be forced into seeing work as the opposite of play, home the opposite of school, cultivation of the mind the opposite of involvement in the physical world. Everywhere, then, we should make an effort, not to harmonize precisely, but to capitalize on the saving fact that the two sides of our nature are not sides at all but warp and woof, and to lead children into perceiving a pattern in life as free, as organic, as patterns observable in nature, in the weather, the growing plant, the movement of the winds or the sea.

Discovery, not only of the physical world but of the mind itself and its activities, is a linkage between the freedom of play and the restraint of order. The "sweet disorder" of Herrick's poem ends in the order of art, which makes the poem possible. A perfect education, then, would be mindful of the order in play, the passion in thought, the thought in physical action, the freedom in constraint. In accepting such notions, we come close to advocating an education in paradox. Such an education would not be very false to life. It should prepare one for the great paradoxes—that the tree of knowledge is of both good and evil, that surfeit follows close upon satisfaction, that we perfect our physical skills only to have age take them away, that we fall in love at too young an age to appreciate it, that the wisdom of old age is poor compensation for the lost ignorance of youth, that the pursuit of happiness is one way of being unhappy, that all our pursuits lead to the grave.

But in less portentous ways, paradoxes engage the mind, stimulate thought, sharpen perceptions. The child is constantly exposed to the smaller paradoxes of his own existence—that punishment often follows pleasure, that what appears fair may be foul, that school, for all its being what he most likes to stay home from, is also what he most eagerly goes back to. The solving of a paradox, whether by disproving it, by rationalizing about it, or by reconciling oneself to it, is an assertion of stability or order. It provides an existence that gives us little more than, to use Robert Frost's phrase, a momentary stay against confusion.

Nevertheless, we do seek an "orderly" education. What are we striving for that organization can help us gain? To make little ladies and gentlemen? No, that idea went out at the turn of the century. To make good citizens? The idea is still embedded in American education. To develop the whole child? Of course, but that is merely a fashionable and fuzzy way of disguising all aims. My argument here is that a perfect education would seek to implant certain senses as necessary to the development of an educated man or woman. And not so much implant them—the senses of play, discovery, order—as to acknowledge their natural presence, endorse their value, perceive their primacy, and encourage their early growth so that they have some chance of remaining a lifelong possession. The emphasis is upon the acquiring of skills and habits and feelings rather than knowledge, on learning fewer things but acquiring a surer sense of what they do and how they do it, on relating what is learned to a central developing sense of order in the things of the world as in one's life.

But before considering how we might develop a sense of order in the growing child, let us consider how the idea of order is reflected in the larger goals of education. Order, as seen in the public schools, is almost always in the context of administration: the place of this subject in the total curriculum, the place of this grade in this school in the total school system, the regulation of the hours of the day and the places of instruction and the personnel who instruct future citizens to prepare them for an orderly place in an orderly society. Administration is indispensable. Yet educational administration often seems to reason backward or not to reason at all, but to assume that it proceeds from a clear idea of what kind of society we want and what kind of schools and curricula and teachers will, properly administered, bring it about. American philosophy has steadily opposed such a static conception of education, although it may be a good one by ultimate standards if ever the ultimate standards ultimately display themselves. Plato's *Republic*, the best example of beginning with the kind of society one wants and arriving at the kind of education that will achieve it, is almost exactly opposed to the drift of American education, if not to its formally stated philosophies. The society of the *Republic* is static, the education is constraining rather than freeing, and the emphasis falls heavily upon order, specialization, harmony of parts, and control.

All of this is in sharp contrast to American beliefs in a dynamic society. Truth in our place and time is pluralistic, and education is regarded as fundamentally liberating, providing the way to the higher and better, and is vigorously democratic rather than aristocratic. Only in a fondness for management techniques is American education similar to the theories of the *Republic*. In educational administration we do find a similar penchant for order, specialization, and harmony of parts, and even some sympathy for exercising authoritarian control. This is surely more because the formalizing of education, whatever the philosophy behind it, demands an emphasis upon order rather than because the Spartan ideals of the *Republic* and American ideals of education have much in common. It must be acknowledged, however, that if American education ever becomes more concerned with realizing the greatest possibilities for society than with the development of the individual, the *Republic* affords an attractive design. For all the emphasis upon education for citizenship, I still feel that America is more committed to the Athenian ideal than to the Spartan, to the "open" rather than the "closed" society. The open society permits a democracy to change, to develop or strengthen one particular while discarding or deemphasizing another. We have been made increasingly and uncomfortably aware of how a society's ability to change is related to its capacity for physical survival. One might say of the social fabric as of the physical universe that motion—change—is the fundamental condition and that stability is only a temporary stand or disposition of moving parts.

Consequently, it seems reasonable to say that education for citizenship, even education for democracy, is not as accurate a description of American goals as education for participation in an open society, that education in social utility is not as vital an aim as is education for each according to his potentiality, his bent, and that education as the exclusive property of the schools is far from the philosophic ideal, however practical considerations and human shortcomings may make it seem so. The hope of achieving stability in the midst of change is the hope of developing within the individual a sense of order superior to the circumstances in which he will find himself. Thus without discarding the vocational objectives, and even retaining (though with less enthusiasm) the social objectives, an education should seek above all to give the individual at an early age maximum chance for self-development in the years to follow.

By this limited excursion into the broadest of territories, I return to the main point: that order, in itself, is but a part of the dynamics of a perfect education, and that the fact that things stick so tightly, compactly, invisibly together only increases our delight

when they all blow apart. I am not advocating anarchy in education, but I think anarchy might be more desirable an element than
formal education ever allows. Public education on the scale
America is attempting it is always in danger of substituting order
and management for learning itself.

The sense of order as something worth consciously developing
throughout the years of formal schooling is another matter. The
very young seem to see the duality of order and disorder as more a
part of the nature of things than their elders. They seem, in fact,
to attach most value to disorder, to breaking things apart, to
jumping from this activity to the next, to living according to immediate physical needs rather than according to some larger design. Nevertheless, one of the great discoveries children make is
that there is an essential order even in things that they have pulled
apart when they realize that they can be put back together. As
chaos preceded the ordered universe, so the chaotic impulse seems
to precede the sense of order. The sense of order develops later than
the sense of play or discovery, and yet it is closely related to them.
"The typical child prodigies," Aldous Huxley writes in "Young
Archimedes," "are musical and mathematical; the other talents
ripen slowly under the influence of emotional experience and
growth." Elsewhere in the story, Huxley has his central character
discovering that the square on the hypotenuse of a right-angled
triangle is equal in area to the sum of the squares on the other two
sides. He does it, Huxley tells us, not in Euclid's way, but by a
"simpler and more satisfying method which was, in all probability,
employed by Pythagoras himself." This description follows:

He had drawn a square and dissected it, by a pair of crossed perpendicu-
lars, into two squares and two equal rectangles. The equal rectangles he
divided up by their diagonals into four equal right-angled triangles. The
two squares are then seen to be the squares on the two sides of any one
of these triangles other than the hypotenuse. So much for the first diagram. In the next, he took the four right-angled triangles into which the
rectangles had been divided and rearranged them round the original
square so that their right angles filled the corners of the square, the hy-
potenuses looked inwards and the greater and less sides of the triangles
were in continuation along the sides of the square (which are each equal
to the sum of these sides). In this way the original square is redissected

into four right-angled triangles and the square on the hypotenuse. The four triangles are equal to the two rectangles of the original dissection. Therefore the square on the hypotenuse is equal to the sum of the two squares—the squares on the other two sides—into which, with the rectangles, the original square was first dissected.

In very untechnical language, but clearly and with a relentless logic, Guido expounded his proof. Robin listened, with an expression on his bright, freckled face of perfect incomprehension.

"In a moment," Guido implored. "Wait a moment. But do just look at this. *Do.*" He coaxed and cajoled. "It's so beautiful. It's so easy."

Trying to reconstruct this demonstration by following the verbal directions is as laborious and as lengthy as the directions themselves. But sketching it out as Guido did, as we have in the diagram, shows immediately how simple, how beautiful, such a discovery can be.

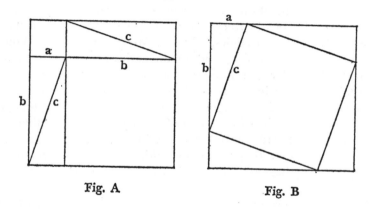

Fig. A   Fig. B

Thus, the square in Figure B obviously equals the two squares in Figure A, or $a^2 + b^2 = c^2$

The pleasure one has in confronting this demonstration for the first time arises, I think, from the comprehension of relationships between forms. H. D. F. Kitto describes a similar experience with numbers:

It was with great delight that I disclosed to myself a whole system of numerical behavior of which my mathematical teachers had left me (I am glad to say) in complete ignorance. With increasing wonder I worked out the series $10 \times 10 = 100$; $9 \times 11 = 99$; $8 \times 12 = 96$; $7 \times 13 = 91$ . . . and found that the differences were, successively, 1, 3, 5, 7 . . . the odd-number series. Even more marvelous was the discovery that if each successive product is subtracted from the original 100, there is produced the series 1, 4, 9, 16. . . . They had never told me, and I had never suspected, that Numbers play these grave and beautiful games with each other. . . .

I take it that developing these recognitions, in terms of actual physical forms and numbers, is part of what the new mathematics is striving for: to see how numbers relate, how they form patterns, how, before long, they can be visualized as having the orderliness of the physical world itself. It is a great feeling when one gets into analytic geometry with sufficient sensibility to recognize that the numbers do, in fact, represent constructs of a physical kind. Ultimately, the satisfaction from mathematics is probably as aesthetic as the response to art, and it is purer perhaps because of its dissociation from humanity itself.

Poincaré discusses this sense of mathematical order, of mathematical beauty, as it applies to mathematical creativity. It is, he argues, a special aptitude. A person so gifted follows the syllogisms of a mathematical demonstration because of "the feeling, the intuition, so to speak, of this order, so as to perceive at a glance the reasoning as a whole." Such feelings, such intuitions, are aesthetic feelings aroused by "the harmony of numbers and forms, of geometric elegance." Poincaré asks: "Now, what are the mathematic entities to which we attribute this character of beauty and elegance, and which are capable of developing in us a sort of aesthetic emotion?" And he answers: "They are those whose elements are harmoniously disposed so that the mind without effort can embrace their totality while realizing the details. This harmony is at once a satisfaction of our aesthetic needs and an aid to the mind, sustaining and guiding. And at the same time, in putting under our eyes a well-ordered whole, it makes us foresee a mathematical law."

I am not saying that the precise sense that Poincaré is discussing can be developed in children or adults—although if it can be developed, such development is more likely in children, to judge from the early age associated with mathematical achievements. I am saying that the sense of order may be capable of being de-

veloped in modest ways, that it would be pleasurable in its development, and that it is well worth postulating as a basic goal of
learning. If a sense of order is kept in mind in the planning and
teaching in elementary schools, it might provide a wise measure
for what should be included in the curriculum and a creative
force for shaping teaching and learning, whatever the specific
subject.

Very early, in simple but effective ways, the aesthetics of numbers should be introduced, and the study of numbers should be
animated by the pleasure of discovering their beauty as well as the
satisfaction of applying their utility. For surely while arithmetic is
showing its usefulness in dividing up apples and buying candy and
encouraging small feats of memory, it is also developing the child's
sense of form, of arrangement, of order. Relating and differentiat-
ing and arranging, whether with physical forms or abstractions,
are fundamental ways of contending with the multiplicity of experience. Out of such activities of the senses and intellect comes
what order can be made of the world around and within us.

By such reasoning, music might be given a large place in the
curriculum, not only for the practical value of learning to play
an instrument and for the development of the feelings, but for the
rich possibilities music offers toward developing a sense of order.
For it is, after all, in music that an exposure to the patterns of
rhythm and sound sharpens the sense of relationships within the
apparently disordered world of sensations.

It strikes me that some attention might be given to the formal
ordering of music without detracting from the immediate pleasure
that music brings. An exceptional teacher who possessed a sure
sense of the basic structure of music might be able to point out the
order in music without becoming entangled in terminology and
without going beyond the child's power of comprehension and
response. Musical training is, of course, already part of the early
years of primary school, but it seems to ignore the larger implications of music. That is, music is used to improve children's co-
ordination, to sharpen their senses, and to involve them in group
activity. Later it is acknowledged for its usefulness to other aims:
to arouse emotions, to accompany paintings and stories, to add to
the children's information about great men and their achievements.
All of these are worthy, but not very often does such activity lead

to consideration of the necessary and complex order that underlies all music.

Mathematics and music might fruitfully be developed side by side. The music of the spheres is one of the most durable of figures from classical antiquity, uniting in it what one hears in the inner ear, what one sees in the sky, and what one constructs in the mind. The numerical properties of music not only offer opportunities to introduce, illustrate, and amplify mathematical relationships, but introduce a dimension of feeling into studies ordinarily associated only with the mind. Far from being mere dilettantism, a "fun" activity, such conscious bringing together of music and mathematics could be the kind of pleasurable learning that invites the learner into further exploration on his own.

In a larger sense, what I am speculating about is the place of art in the lower schools, and what I am obviously asking for is an education that is more aesthetic than social. Art activity is, of course, as central to elementary education as reading. At times, to teachers and parents and pupils, school must seem to be nothing but coloring and cutting and pasting. I do not know how the aims of art are described in the literature of the elementary schools, but it seems obvious that in addition to the training of the muscles of hand and eye, art is developing both the mind and the senses. Whatever the student is working with, he is relating and manipulating shapes and colors, line and space, with some idea of design. As a child who is given a set of oddly shaped blocks will find ways of piling them up into more or less stable constructions, so he learns to deal with shapes on a sheet of paper, cut squares and triangles and trapezoids, and to fashion forms of his own devising that have no names. Modern art has had this beneficial effect: It has enabled teachers to permit, even to encourage, the child to deal with forms freely under the guidance of a developing sense of relationships and design rather than under an adult's ideas of reality.

Another basic subject that relates to a sense of order is language. It is a great—and laborious—undertaking to learn a language with a complicated structure like Latin or Greek. The rewards are not only the ability such study gives but the feeling of awe that wells up when one at last sees all the parts of the language fitting together. But I doubt that one can expect such a feeling to arise in the elementary schools or even hope that language study can proceed there without a large amount of rote learning, drill, and frustration. Perhaps all one can do in teaching a foreign language is to introduce it early enough so that some of the rudimentary skills are acquired before the mind becomes resistant to them.

Given that early introduction, it might be possible to turn the attention of some students to the structure of language, of their own as well as of a foreign one. Much would depend on the language teacher, who should have a skill comparable to that of the music teacher who can deal with the essential order of music without detracting from music's sensory appeal and the listener's pleasure in it. By beginning early, proceeding slowly, and unfolding the nature of the language itself as well as teaching the use of it, one might give the child more quickly a sophisticated awareness of language that will encourage him to ponder upon the order that language itself imposes upon perception and thought. Such an emphasis might help justify foreign-language study, which, with difficulty in the large expanse of America landlocked between the Alleghenies and the Sierra Nevadas, argues its case on purely pragmatic grounds.

In the study of English language and literature—reading and writing in the early grades, English as it later comes to be called— I would have an emphasis as frankly aesthetic as the present one is social. It is paradoxical—more than that, it is irritating—that "language arts," the term professional education has fastened upon English, has so little to do with art. Its attention to language is almost entirely in terms of use: speaking on the phone, writing letters, conducting business, copying from encyclopedias. What a dreary approach to literature is that stale leftover from the late nineteenth century: that literature is life. Dreary, that is, unless one's life is a good deal more like literature than the average man's. Stripped of the breadth that the name "literature" gives it and treated as "language arts" that ignore art, English in the elementary school too often plods along with dullness on one side and morality on the other.

The proper study of literature in the elementary schools is one that begins at the point of the child's interest and proceeds on the premise that what is most worthwhile in literature is as much a matter of sensing as of intellectualizing or moralizing. The best way to begin is through poetry, for here one starts with an ordering of words that provides both delight and learning. What child would not respond to a poem like:

Ooery, onery, ickery, Ann,
Fillacy, fallacy, Nicholas, John,
Quivy, quavy, English Navy,
Striggle-um, straggle-um. Buck.

And when has "Tell me a story" ever ceased to appeal? And yet, many teachers fail to make the most of a child's pleasure in poetry, forget that the appeal of a story is not what is merely *in* the story but what it creates in the mind of the listener. In both poetry and stories worth the telling, the writer's ordering of language in sound as in sense is crucial to the effect.

Much more could be done than is now commonly done to impart the feeling of poetry to very young students, to show the poet's insistence on form, on order, and yet his unwillingness to be overwhelmed by it. The poet's struggle is the young schoolchild's struggle: a battle of desire against necessity, of freedom against form. By exposure, by wise guidance, by encouraging the student to express first in speech and later in writing his own wrestling for control over both experience and language, one begins to get at the sense of order I am stressing here. Literature as one of the fine arts seems best for the elementary school. Soon enough English will become identified solely with correctness of speech. Soon enough discipline will impose itself. There is time at the beginning to build on the sense of play that creates counting rhymes, riddles, and puns and on the sense of discovery that gives such point to new words and forbidden words, and to the strengthening of the sense of order in looking closely at how the writer achieves what he has aimed for. Admittedly, there is a danger that such an approach may be narrowly formalistic, may detach itself, in its zeal for focus and analysis, from everything else in a poem or story that gives it worth and interest, including the poetry itself. But there are dangers in any approach. The great shortcoming of language arts in the schools is that their diffuseness allows no approach. Above all else, in English as in all other subjects, I would ask that the subject be kept alive. And that, I think, requires both a specific interest in what is being taught and a recognition of larger aims to which all studies are directed. In language and literature, trying to perceive how the writer imposes order on both language and experience would serve both ends.

Science and the social sciences are the last group of subjects I will specifically mention. Science, in what might be called its mechanical as well as its natural aspects, almost exactly illustrates a movement from play through discovery to order. From the fascination with things that click and whir and sputter, seemingly at the urging of mysterious, playful forces, the child moves to trying to find out what is behind them. Inevitably, then, he becomes acquainted with the ordered explanation of a machine's workings. Beyond that, he may be brought to see simple laws at work that seem to govern motions regardless of the mechanism. It strikes me, as I have mentioned before, that our humanistic, moralistic education has created an unfortunate hostility to the machine. How many Elementary classes visit the public library, the zoo, the dairy, the police station, but how many visit the machine shop? If we are to be users and devisers and controllers of machines—as increasing numbers of us must be—then science in terms of mechanics needs to win a large place in the lower schools. The natural sciences have already a large place, chiefly, I suspect, because our fundamental sympathies are as invested in nature as our antagonisms are directed against the machine. The schools are full of toads and butterflies and birds' nests and sea shells, as they should be. Without detracting from the sense of wonder that living things arouse, both the study of nature and the study of machines can be directed toward perceiving design, toward developing the sense of order we have been discussing.

In what has been said, the social sciences have been somewhat passed over. The exclusion was deliberate, for I do not see much of a place for the social sciences in the lower schools except in terms of exposure to the social world, which is already much a part of primary schooling. The experience of learning to work together may be gained regardless of the subject being worked at. The actual study of social institutions requires too much in the way of experience and judgment to be very fruitfully explored in the lower grades. History can hardly be made to show a design to the seasoned historian, much less to students just being introduced to the facts. The social sciences need more of experiencing, of living, before the person can bring enough to them to be rewarded by something other than bare facts. Historians, social scientists, philosophers, develop later, and I think the kind of possible grounding that might be given in the facts of these disciplines is much less important to children than fostering in them a sense of order through means more within their youthful powers. It is probably a fact that the social sciences as they are introduced in the lower grades now are comprehended by the students more through feelings, affections, and sympathies than through intellect. That, it seems to me, is as it should be, the young acquiring a sense of the importance of great men and great deeds, a sense of the social fabric around them, a sense of their fitting into some part of another part and that part into other parts of a complex social and historical design.

I am now, hopefully, at a point where what I have written can stand as testimony of a sort to the workings of a human mind toward order. What began as delight, free thought, a faith that one might make discoveries along the way, ends in an orderly arrangement of words on the page directed toward seeing education in terms of a few fundamental principles. At this point, too, a suggestion of a design for a curriculum seems to have emerged. Mathematics, language, and basic science are the trivium, moving the classical trivium—grammar, logic, rhetoric—in the direction science has taken the world. As the ultimate goal, I would choose the acquiring of knowledge toward the development of wisdom. For the immediate aim, I accept the objective implied in the classical trivium of teaching the child to think, and I offer the fostering of the senses of play, discovery, and order as a means to that end.

Such a design leaves much out—or more accurately it places the emphasis in the elementary schools not upon the acquisition of knowledge but upon the development of attitudes, responses, and recognitions that foster learning at any period of life and that make the most of the natural inclinations of the child. The varied course of study common to elementary education seems to me a gain from which a perfect education should not retreat, but the course of study must be seen in relation to somewhat more central objectives of learning than finding out about the world around us or getting along with our fellow man. These objectives, of course, are important, but like physical education they are attainments that a child might be expected to acquire as a matter of growth and through informal exposure. The nature of the healthy child is to run, to jump, to kick, and body mechanics and similar concerns can justifiably be set aside to make room for that which can less afford to be neglected. Not all children, of course, are in good physical health or free from mental and physical defects, but the special education such children require need not have an undue effect upon the objectives of the non-special education that is the school's largest responsibility.

There is no perfection built into any pattern of courses toward any educational goal. The emphasis I place upon form may arouse some justified fears. A teacher might easily substitute a preoccupation with form for a proper wrestling with thought. Literature might be more badly taught if elementary and secondary teachers were encouraged to *teach* literature through its elementary forms and subforms. Similarly, the teaching of the fine arts could easily miss fulfilling its larger aims by becoming wrapped up in formal considerations. Even the new mathematics could be treated as rather elegant trifling with form by a teacher out of touch with the reality of numbers. These cautions, however, do not dissuade me from contending that the development of a sense of order is a fundamental, achievable goal for the lower schools. Given this development in the context of mathematics, language, and basic science, the student might gain both a grasp of facts and an awareness of the relationships that make facts meaningful.

PART TWO

SEEING THE WORLD
FEELINGLY

CHAPTER IV

SENSE AND INTELLECT

THE HEART of the matter of teaching and learning is the
compact entered into between the teacher and the learner
by which both bend their minds to tasks they would rather
avoid. The mind is both fractious and lazy, and though by itself
more than sentient, not necessarily possessed of sensibility. Though
intellect may not be the villain that romanticism would make it,
intellect alone is not enough. Without the motivation that comes
from desiring, learning would hardly take place at all.

We know we are often driven to learn from both inner and
outer compulsions. In the best of times, we may feel ourselves not
driven at all, but caught up in learning, borne aloft toward some
higher plane. At the worst, we may feel like rats in a box, trying
to comprehend what it is that gives us a pellet instead of a shock.
For all the investigation of learning, how we learn is still a mystery,
explainable only by partial yet sweeping theories such as those by
which the Marxist explains history or the Freudian explains man
himself.

Today, the conditioned reflex is again offered as the basis for
all learning. Learning is explained in terms of stimulus and response. Convincing as the many experiments in conditioning are,
they still seem to fall short of a satisfying explanation of a complex human process. Skinner's *Walden Two* strikes me as a good
deal less promising than Thoreau's *Walden,* because as easy as
conditioned learning is held to be, how could many men work
up sufficient fervor to commit themselves to it? And as difficult
as Thoreau's commitment to self-learning may seem, when will
the time ever come when men do not emotionally respond to this
commitment?

If we want to build a sound educational system along the lines
of behavioral psychology, we should simply incorporate the feed-

ing process into the programmed learning of whatever skills and subjects we deem important. Parents would refrain from feeding their children at home, thereby making available large sums of money for support of the schools. The children would arrive before the teaching machines not only hungry to learn, but hungry. Mastery of one lesson would mean shredded wheat, of two lessons milk, of three lessons sugar. A fourth lesson mastered and one would get a box top to send in. Over the course of study a hungry student would receive a balanced diet at a fraction of what it now costs and mastery of all the rudimentary skills as well. But of course we are not going to institute or accept a system like that, and not because parents are inordinately fond of caring for and feeding children. It would be cheap and attractive in other ways, but we would hold back because education, for our own children or someone else's, involves feeling as well as muscular or mental response.

More than that, intellect compounded with feeling moves toward the highest kind of learning: toward wisdom, the goal for all education. It is what Shakespeare had clearly in mind when in the sweep of *King Lear* he arrives at the blinding of Gloucester and the realization toward which the play has been tending. "Yet you see how this world goes," Lear remarks in his madness. And Gloucester replies, "I see it feelingly."

As I have posed the development of the senses of play, discovery, and order as both means and ends of preschool and elementary education, and have suggested that helping students discover order in the various subjects under study might be the chief function of the lower schools, let me pose "seeing the world feelingly" as a high aim of teaching and learning as the student moves beyond the primary grades.

At all ages learning is a great delight, but it most clearly appears so in the primary school. The later part of public school education takes place under the worst of circumstances: the adolescence of the students themselves. For probably a majority of students for a majority of their secondary school years, learning must compete with more pressing matters: concern for status, worries about money, troubles with parents, fascination with cars, to name a few. Sex is probably the greatest preoccupation. The adolescent's involvement with sex and the difficulties such involvement poses for the teacher will help explain why I think that "seeing the world feelingly" should be a major aim of secondary education.

Paradoxically and usefully, the student expends most of his imaginative powers on sex—in fantasies of desire and conquest, in creating of situations, actions, plans necessary to courting, in looking at himself and others in the often agonizing terms of attraction and repulsion. And oddly but typically, the public schools have taken the fantasy and romance from sex and made it part of a humdrum world of facts: marriage and the family, courtship, sex education.

Do not mistake me here. I am mindful of the number of high school pregnancies, of dropouts resulting specifically from sexual behavior, of the many effects on adolescents of the "revolution," as it keeps being called, in sexual conduct. I am willing to grant the need for public school education to face these often disturbing facts. But I would ask for imaginative understanding of what the boy and girl are experiencing and of the larger implications that sexual preoccupations have.

The adolescent probably sees the world more feelingly than he will at any other time, except perhaps for the second adolescence of reckless males and females at the beginning of middle age. The teacher, likely as not, is the one who seems most opposed to feeling. And yet that same teacher at that time easily becomes the object of crushes and infatuations. Moreover, it is the prime moment when such attractions begin to shape students toward future attainments.

During adolescence, the teacher is looked upon as being more than a person expertly informed in a subject matter, as one side of the academic argument goes, or as a person particularly skilled in methodology, as the other side has it. He or she is a personality the students see with increasing acuity and personal responsiveness. Central to that personality is feeling, something the teacher does not necessarily incorporate into the lessons or teach with or create a climate for—although these are worth keeping in mind—but something he or she has, like red hair or slim legs or a ready smile or a pleasing voice, capable of being consciously projected but proceeding in large part from the character and personality of the individual.

The one teacher I remember best from my own high school experience was a young English teacher who left us abruptly in the spring and ran away with a man—whether to get married or not, no one seemed sure. The act was mildly scandalous to the adults in my small town and the subject of a great deal of talk among the students, not much of which was moralistic. What interested the students most was that here was an actuality that had hitherto been merely theoretical: that people could and did do such things, and more, that a schoolteacher turned out to be such a person. I am not advocating that all nubile teachers of English or any other subject desert their classrooms as a means of enhancing the teacher image. Nor am I advocating that teachers should substitute personality for the basic task of enlisting the student in the mastery of a subject matter or a skill. (It seems to me a mark of this teacher's excellence that she had *not* given to the class details of her personal life that might have prepared us for her departure.) I am rather using the experience to say that in the act, in the felt response of a teacher to his material and to his students, the most vital educational transactions take place. If the teacher shows no feeling there—whether he teaches biology or mathematics or English—learning has probably not begun. It is that display of willingness to see the world feelingly, to show the kind of emotional commitment to things that the teacher prizes, that comes closest to the deep, if transient, emotional commitments the adolescent is involved in. Although my example involves sexual behavior, it need not have even that much direct relevance to what the student is most concerned with. What the teacher must show is a corresponding depth of feeling and a respect for the worth of feeling even as he or she goes about tasks that are irrelevant to the emotional concerns of the students and that are much more involved with the mind than with the body.

The ideal teacher is the man or woman of feeling, of sensibility, whose emotional commitment to his or her profession adds to personal attractiveness. Perhaps the best way of keeping emotionally alive and still in touch with the daily tasks a teacher must perform is to strive to be a practitioner of what one teaches. If a teacher's subject is English, he should write, and if not that, read, and above all live, feeling deeply and not being afraid to put that feeling into his teaching. If he teaches art or music, he should continue to be a painter or a musician and, forgetting his vanity, let the students be a party to his own efforts to capture some part of reality in an enduring form. If he is a scientist, he should find some part of his avocation in laboratory science or in collecting and classifying. This is not to feed the weevil of discontent that eats away at the dignity and worth of teaching itself. It is to feed teaching with the kind of commitment that feeling calls forth so that teaching will reveal imagination as well as a factual grasp of subject matter.

I should also add, lest I be thought to be giving sanction to an unbridled romanticism, that the practice of one's discipline always places the dreamer against the realities, faces him with the conflicts that the student is going through himself: the conflict between aspiration and attainment, between vision and the realizable form, between the inner strivings and the world in which those strivings have to be fulfilled or checked. If I emphasize the romantic side—that of feeling—rather than the intellectual, it is not because I think the one more important than the other, but because I think the one is even more neglected than the other. The development of the intellect is, however critics disparage the intellectual climate of the secondary schools, still the focus of the teacher's efforts.

Here, then, is what I mean about sense and intellect in the encounter of the teacher and the taught. The "sense" of a thing, the "feeling" for it, must come from the teacher, or else the intellect of the taught will have no reason for working and will not work, will have no imagined direction in which to go and will not go, will have no large design and will always work within the small pattern.

The most obviously successful teacher, I suppose, is he or she who gains disciples. He may be a false prophet or no prophet at all, but to gain disciples he must have somehow shown a large and attractive vision to his students and suggested a reasonable possibility of attaining it. We should worry less about false prophets and more about having no prophets at all, less about the scarcity of well-trained graduates of certified teacher education courses with proper credentials and more about the scarcity of attractive personalities with developed sensibilities as well as intellectual skills.

I have mentioned previously that elementary teachers should possess, above all else, imagination. It is hardly less important in the secondary schools. If it is not everything, it is almost everything. It is a guarantee against dullness, and without dullness, almost anything is possible. The teacher must constantly imagine.

Facts can be looked up patiently the night before or the day before, and even a poor sort of mind can make a show of competence, even brilliance, in setting them forth before he forgets them. Lesson plans can be made out under the supervision of teachers of methods in summer sessions at the university and will last almost as long as the teacher. The school itself will give the unimaginative teacher the framework of daily classroom operation. Discipline, of a sort, may be maintained with little more than strength and inflexibility. The problems that all public school teachers have with discipline, however, underscore the primary place of imagination. For it is imagination that makes enough order out of chaos to make learning possible. It is imagination, in fact, that uses the undisciplined character of students to foster learning.

Imagination is like water on parched ground constantly seeking out the cracks that will take it down into the soil. For the teacher, imagination endows what is being taught with the maximum possibilities of nurturing the ideas that may spring up. Much of the formal content of various disciplines might be set forth by a machine: periodic tables, algebraic formulae, rules of grammar, biological classifications—these are as routinely teachable as the names of the parts of the body. But the relationship between parts, the guesses as to cause and effect, the hazard of creating a hypothesis and going deeply into its possibilities—these are the harder tasks of learning and the ones only an imaginative teacher can deal with.

Imagination is a quality that teachers freely excuse themselves for not having, justifying the deficiency as something denied them at birth. Few will as airily claim to be lacking in common sense. Yet common sense strikes me as a very necessary attribute of the ideal teacher, although by itself it may be a dubious possession. It must have something, like a person's soaring imagination, to operate *against*. Imagination will fill the mind, animate the teacher to the delight and edification of his pupils. Common sense will get him to class somewhat on time.

Common sense is, I think, the sanity of being grounded at numerous points—not tied down, not cemented in, but touching earth firmly at many points to insure stability, and only touching so that one is ready to rise on the right kind of wind. For a teacher, such grounding points are the practical details of the formal structure that seems necessary to educate a large number of individuals, and I would not find an education perfect that would not attempt to work on a large scale. But also they are the countless commitments one has to the common humanity we share. They are recognitions of how difficult, for anyone, some things are to learn, how variously each student faces any day's task, how clumsily we all proceed, how drudgery must be borne, fools suffered, and aims compromised, how theory constantly bows to practice but how practice is inspired by theory, how there's more than one way to skin a cat and more than cats to be skinned.

As for teaching, common sense is useful in keeping teachers from accepting flashes of human insight as divine wisdom. No man of common sense easily becomes a zealot, although he may have great zeal toward many things. All complex matters invite simple explanations. The man of common sense preserves that necessary awareness that everything can't be that simple, even as he may be searching for a simple answer.

Common sense, as I describe it here, is not mere reflex behavior, not merely wearing rubbers when it rains and buying fresh fruits in season. It is not mere practicality. Rather it is a response to and anticipation of situations and of other people, which tempers exact judgment with consideration, which suspends absolutes in favor of immediate actualities, which avoids the precious and the banal alike.

Possession of common sense in teaching is a mark of the teacher's adaptability, of his being willing to relinquish generally workable methods in favor of what will get a lesson across to a particular student in a particular situation. It is knowing when to bear down and when to ease up, when to laugh and when to be laughed at, when to stop talking and when to stop someone else's talking, when to give assistance and when to withdraw it. It is having a disrespect for facts, a disaffection for learning, a distrust of schools, without really disparaging any of them. It is not expecting too much but not expecting too little. It is recognizing that grades, for example, and class hours and schedules, and lesson plans, are flimsy constructs having only provisional worth, only a modest place in anyone's education. It is not making a pupil's mistakes seem to be evidence of bad character. It is knowing that one seldom, if ever, gets the work from students he would like, the assignments fulfilled, the ground covered, any more than one gets the books read. It is cosmic justice tempered with cosmic optimism in a quite uncosmic day-by-day routine.

In short, it is very uncommon sense. Thoreau remarks, "Why level downward to our dullest perceptions always, and praise that as common sense? The commonest sense is the sense of men asleep, which they express by snoring." Common sense is not the dullest perception but the finest of coarse perceptions, for there is something in the coarseness that prevents too fine a judgment, too fixed a stand.

Teachers are not notorious for their common sense. Their persistence in the face of the difficulties bespeaks some want of common sense for which we can all be thankful. Yet we can go on wishing that they had more. It is easy for the teacher to think either too much or too little of himself (or *her*-self, as is more often the case), to assume the martyred idealist's stance on the one hand or the suffering servant's on the other. Common sense could tell him that he is neither, that he is rather a person engaged in a difficult and honorable profession in which the material rewards are small and the satisfactions great. What the teacher does, what he is, has consequences that, like the sharp sensory impressions of childhood—the feel of road dust between the toes or the smell of a stove's heat in a cold room—keep on asserting themselves in small but important ways throughout the lives of those who have been his students.

Common sense might help a teacher maintain a right relation to intellect, the last of a teacher's necessary qualities I will discuss. Intellect is of prime importance to the teacher. To put it bluntly, who wants a dumb teacher? Yet the public school often gives support to the anti-intellectual elements of a given community's culture. Special programs for the gifted student, for example, have had to work against hostility from within the school as well as from without. Though "egghead" is a term somewhat affectionately attached to a college professor, it is more a term of contempt as applied to the public school teacher.

It can be argued that the public schools need such a large number of teachers that by standard measures of intelligence, the population will have a difficult time furnishing enough bright, not to say brilliant, teachers. But that does not mean the intelligent teacher should hide his intelligence in a sham good-fellowship with all men, or neglect his intelligence by sinking into routine, or become either defensive or servile toward intellectualism.

The public schools have a very difficult time trying to figure out what to do with "intellect." "All too often in the history of the United States," Richard Hofstadter writes in *Anti-Intellectualism in American Life,* "the schoolteacher has been in no position to serve as a model for an introduction to the intellectual life." Mr. Hofstadter's full discussion of "Education in a Democracy" is almost overpowering in its account of the difficulties public education faced in the past and still faces today in trying to maintain a satisfactory intellectual climate for elementary and secondary school teaching. Always there are the cruel differences between the dull and the bright, asking for the teacher's compassion toward the one while inclining his intellectual attention to the other. Among the teachers themselves, those with marked intellectual interests constitute a minority in almost any public school. Intellect cannot be kept healthily alive by itself. It needs daily converse, confrontation, challenge, and a healthy debunking that only secure individuals can give it. Little of this is available to the public school teacher.

There are other reasons why intelligence is not looked upon with more favor in the public schools. But among those that specifically relate to teaching, the chief one is surely the almost closed door that awaits the intellectually able schoolteacher. A recent survey, conducted by the National Association of Secondary School Principals, reports that fifty-six percent of the principals had once served as coaches. Since advancing into administration is almost the sole way of moving to a higher position and higher salary, little need be added about what this shows in terms of rewarding intellectual achievements. Starting salaries of teachers are bad enough, but the small range between one teacher's salary and another's and between beginning salaries and salaries for the best teachers at the peak of their careers is even more discouraging. It is no wonder that intellect thins out in the public school. With the growth of higher education and its own enhanced prospects, increasing numbers of bright students will pass up high school or elementary teaching in favor of careers in colleges or universities.

I have passed over a good many valuable qualities that the ideal teacher should have—kindness, compassion, charity, patience—not because they are unimportant but because they are too often used to excuse a lack of other qualities. A kind, compassionate, charitable, patient secondary teacher may do great good. She would do more, I think, were she also sensitive, imaginative, bright, and, for all that, blessed with common sense.

But one quality I would add, and that is style. I will say more about the sense of style in a later chapter of this book, but here I must add it to the teacher's qualifications, for it is, in one respect, the disposition of all that the teacher possesses in the way of sense and intellect. He is or she must be *someone,* because a student's response to a teacher is more for what he is and does than for what he knows—which, however, should be part of his being and doing. Style can be defined as a way of being or doing. A person's carriage, dress, walk—manners, in the large sense—are his style.

And although a person's style may depend, in part, on the accidents of what birth has given him, another part, and the larger part, is what he does with it. I would have some *élan,* some dash, in public school teachers, some eccentricity in many, some developed sense of one's own particular style in all. I would like some attention to style in the selection of prospective teachers, and further attention as a part of the aim of practice teaching. Some good might result, in preparing a student in his discipline, from paying attention to the style of the best representatives of the discipline. Writers and artists are not the sole possessors of style. Historians have style, as do scientists, mathematicians, and educators. I suspect that in life as in writing a creditable style has something to do with largeness of soul. Surely a teacher needs that.

But how, one might ask, do we bring such teachers as I have been describing into existence? The demands I have made upon feeling, imagination, common sense, and intellect seem to ask more than birth often gives or training can accomplish. Can we afford to assume that public school teachers are such special people? I cannot see how we can afford to assume otherwise.

When we confront the actual situation, however, our idealism falters. Gifted teachers are always few, our needs are staggeringly great. More than one and a half million teachers are employed in the public schools. The most disturbing part of Dr. Conant's *The Education of American Teachers* is the appendix in which he faces what seems to be limitations on the supply of teachers in terms of obtaining them from among the top percentages of high school graduates. He surmises that it is out of the question now to talk of recruiting enough teachers from the top ten percent. And although with a larger age group and more graduating from college in 1970 it might seem possible then to get teachers from at least the top thirty percent, the attractions of other professions will also increase and prospective teachers will still include about seventy percent women. And these calculations use only the rough measure of the most capable high school students as measured by grades. Consider how much smaller the possible group becomes if we ask for such attributes as sensibility, imagination, common sense, style, *and* intelligence.

Whether we face the facts as Conant has them, or even as they might be if our efforts to recruit teachers are greatly increased, we still must enhance teaching as a career. We may select teachers from a wider range of intelligence, we may even rationalize the place of intelligence in teaching, but we are not likely to strengthen teaching that way. Our best bet is to increase the percentage of the very able who go into teaching and to improve the training they receive.

I think the most effective measure would be to make teacher training more selective, as I imply in my emphasis on treating the teacher as a special person. Something that has to be sought after, that cannot be for everyone, has a great attraction for citizens in a democratic society. One might guess, and be borne out by the history of medical education, that increasing the difficulties of admittance does not diminish the number applying. Given other favorable conditions that accompany such selectivity—the high level of compensation that comes with scarcity—the number might be expected to increase.

The selection of students for teacher training should not be based solely on high performance in high school, though that undoubtedly must and should play an important part. We must try to identify the sensitive and the imaginative and to woo them into teaching. Ideally, teachers should be selected and admitted to training with as much care as is taken by the professional schools. The grounds for admission would be different, just as the course of training would be. But somewhere a process of selection should take place similar to that by which a Renaissance father chose a tutor.

Selection of teachers is closely related to the favor teaching enjoys as a profession. Public school teaching has a very great attraction in offering three months of freedom. Obviously salaries must make it possible for teachers to avoid working in creameries, roofing firms, Dairy Queen establishments, and motels (though these at least offer free time and some possible stimulation). And teachers themselves must not give in to those who would find work for them safely within the school's administrative system. At most, the school might sponsor, during the summer, teachers who want to incorporate their own imaginative vision into the year's program or who want to do special work with students who are willing to give up a summer to engage in studies not available during the regular year. The nine-month school year, as anachronistic as it is in terms of its origin and as economically wasteful as it is from one point of view, needs defending as a very important part of a perfect education, however easily it might be sacrificed for an economic or efficient or useful education. Unfortunately, much of American education hangs between two less desirable alternatives: the nine-month year at a salary that makes certain the summers will be largely wasted and the twelve-month year that forgets what should take place in the summer.

Teachers are not to be regarded as privileged any more than students for having the summer off. The teacher's school year, as befits a professional commitment, does not restrict itself to the eight-hour day, the forty-hour week, if we must count it that way. Teachers must have time to have the kind of experiencing—travel, reading and writing, study abroad or on another campus—that an imaginative teacher dreams of during the school year. What he brings back to his pupils is worth far more than the savings envisioned in the twelve-month year.

The benefit of such efforts is always at least twofold: the immediate benefit to the community, and the enhanced attractiveness of the profession to prospective teachers. Any perfect education must have as its first objective the enhancing of teaching as a life work if it is to gain any share of this country's young men and women who are capable of seeing the world feelingly. Money is involved, and greater interchange between higher education and the public schools, between the public and the public schools. In moments of feeling, both the college professor and the influential member of the community seem to respond most typically to public school needs by simply sending their own children to private schools.

How much better for both to work with the schools to provide the kind of profession where a sensitive, imaginative, and intelligent individual could exercise his sense and intellect to the fullest extent of his abilities. It really does not matter where one starts, whether with the selection of teachers or with giving the teachers now in the school the kind of life that would foster their crippled imaginations. Obviously, everything needs attention in the American public school, in any school, if we are to strive for the education our desires seem to say we can have.

In the selection process, then, we must evaluate more than mere ability to learn and interest in teaching. These are both useful and good qualities, but we also need to incorporate some way of evaluating the imaginative quality of the future teachers' work. Can they write poetry or fiction, can they compose a piece of music, can they act or direct, can they put together a historical hypothesis and work it out in detail, can they see and disclose the beauty of mathematics? If not, then I suggest gently encouraging them into fields where the financial rewards are greater and where the demands on their minds and feelings will be less.

As to improving the training of teachers, that has been the subject of too much recent and continuing criticism to require extended discussion here. It strikes me that both the colleges and universities and the schools of education are responsible for the discouraging fact that teaching in the public schools is the only profession that is repudiated by those who train the practitioners. English departments, about which I know most, will furnish an example, though I think they are no worse in this respect than many departments. Very few members of a college English department will voluntarily interest themselves in the teaching of English in the public schools. Fewer still will take on an assignment that involves high school or elementary school English. The methods classes in a department most often fall (like the selection of teachers themselves) not to the best-trained, the most imaginative, or the most creative professors but chiefly to those with (1) some past experience in the schools and (2) some interest in doing it. Beyond the methods course, the English department does little to acknowledge its students' future position as teachers while they are in college and even less afterward. And although conditions are improving somewhat, the separation of college professor from public school teacher does more to explain the condition of English teaching in the schools than all the research expended in answering separate aspects of the problem.

I assume that it is not far different in other departments and institutions. At best, teacher education confines itself to the practical matters of school administration, to past history and educational psychology, to theory in the form of philosophy of education, and to methods and practice teaching. The rest of a secondary teacher's training is in subject matter and is gained in separate classrooms, a separate college, often almost a separate world. The separation is harmful to both sides. A subject matter's appeal to the intellect and to the feelings, which attracted the student to this interest in the first place, is to some degree pitted against the deeper feelings supposedly to be aroused by actually teaching a subject to live pupils. But forced to deal abstractly with what is best demonstrated concretely (practice teaching is the most widely respected of all teacher education courses), the education teacher finds himself dealing with material that has little appeal to either the intellect or the feelings. The result is often the creation of an artificial subject matter, the laboring of the obvious, and the deadening of the imagination.

Let me give an example. Here is a passage, not picked at random, but representative of the content of one of the most respected texts in methods for English in the secondary school. Its author is a member of the staff of one of the major graduate schools of education. The publisher is a major textbook publisher. I preface it in this way to point out that this text is about as good as one could expect in methods. It is an excellent text, as textbooks go, but this paragraph, like the book itself, is marked by a kind of condescension, observable in teachers themselves, that arises from viewing the public school teacher as a good deal less than the special person I insist he must be. Its manner assumes that the prospective teacher has very limited powers of perception, little imagination, and little ability to reason from general statement to specific application. The author of the text is amplifying a previously quoted passage referred to in the first paragraph. I have made one small cut in the interest of brevity:

> Perhaps no word is used more loosely in the high school classroom than "rhythm," and all because teachers are resisting too hard the use of the terminology of poetry. If the word must be used, teachers should make it mean something definite, as Professor Louis Martz of Yale does.
>
> "Rhythm ties the common words of the poem more closely together than they usually are found in common speech; rhythm helps the words to cohere in a special form that gradually lifts these words out of the flux

and routine of the ordinary. . . . But at the same time both poet and reader have a large measure of freedom; no two readers will ever read this poem in precisely the same way, nor will the same reader ever read this poem twice in the same way, for the simple reason that, by the time he has got around to reading it the second time, he is no longer quite the same as he was. . . . Thus every reading of a poem is a unique experience, both in rhythm and in total meaning, despite the 'sameness' of the stanza-form. Stanza-forms are only the bones of a poem—upon which our reading puts the flesh."

The statement makes clear the advantage of *hearing* the poem, and, for this reason, it seems to me that most of the reading of poetry in the classroom should be done by the teacher or by particularly able youngsters who have had a chance to prepare the reading of a particular poem. Impromptu reading by tone-deaf students will destroy a poem and lose the patience of the class. A great boon to teachers of poetry in recent years has been the recording of poems, in most cases read by the poets themselves. A number of high schools now have fairly comprehensive collections of poetry records, in the same way that they have films and film strips. If the school has not yet made such an investment, the teacher should try the local public libraries, or nearby college and university libraries. The teacher may be able to interest the PTA in a record-purchasing project or convince a departing senior class that records would make an excellent class gift. When the money is appropriated, the teacher and a committee should select the records carefully, *purchasing only after listening*. Some poets are not the best readers of their poetry, and some read much too dramatically, so that the students have a tendency to laugh.

The writer has sufficient judgment to pick a literate statement by a literate man about the nature of poetry, but not enough to let it speak for itself. And this is precisely why I pick this passage. Those engaged in secondary education almost invariably assume a lower level of comprehension, intelligence, and imagination in their students than the subject-matter specialists. I will not go into the latter's faults here—my purpose is not to find fault, but to get at a basic cause of discontent with teacher education and a grave fault that it fosters in teaching in the secondary schools.

Professor Martz of Yale is not addressing himself to poets, other professors, secondary school students, or teachers, but to any reader with some knowledge of poetry. What he says here was doubtless taught to undergraduates and grasped by English majors with widely differing capacities. Yet here our English methods teacher, himself a college professor, imposes himself as an imperfect amplifier, justifiably choosing to emphasize the important points Professor Martz makes, but unjustifiably blurring what might have caused the student to take off in an imaginative direction, might have drawn him into considering poems that sound upon the ear, into hearing the syllables of his speech and of his pupils, into composing poems in which the freedom works against the form—a hundred and one departures intrinsically related to poetry itself, fired by the imagination of the reader, stimulating a similarly imaginative response in the student. Instead, this writer takes the student by the hand, if not by the ear, and immerses him in commonplaces: one can buy recordings of poems, some high schools have them and some don't, libraries might, a record-purchasing project is worthwhile, and when the money is appropriated the teacher and a committee should select the records carefully, *"purchasing only after listening."*

This seems to me the worst kind of writing, the worst kind of thinking, and the most insulting kind of advice to give to students presumably bright enough to be soon teaching our children. Its approach is partly the fault of the textbook, an artificial growth that secondary schools might well look at more critically, but more than that, it is the fault of an attitude that seems to characterize teacher education. As writing, one could compare this with the standard technique of newswriting, the inverted pyramid where all the big important facts come at the beginning and those of descending importance taper off at the end. The shape of a newspaper story is dictated by the necessities of the composing room: the compositor must be able to lop off paragraph by paragraph at the end without destroying the sense of the story. There is a similar pyramid here with no compositor to throw things away. The whole passage tapers alarmingly into the banality of the final paragraph, from which the reader is not easily going to be rescued.

The result of such writing, such teaching, such an attitude is to inflate the obvious to a degree that would make an inflexible principle out of such a common-sense suggestion as "poetry should be heard." It entangles every invitation to imaginative thought in the encumbrances of procedure. In this passage, unless a reader is wary—and students are too respectful of textbooks to be so—a concern for poetry slides into the senior class gift, the teacher and the

PTA, and the gathering of funds. It is easy for this kind of solicitude to become a habit of mind that makes the intelligent student lose respect for what is specifically being taught in the education classroom and for the profession itself. Although it is a habit firmly attached to the training of teachers for the public schools, I think there is some hope that its effects are not permanent, that actual teachers, facing live pupils, will often prove superior to their training.

I think what I have said here can fairly be related to the primary qualities I have asked for in teachers and in those who prepare teachers. A sensitive person, an imaginative one, would not put up with such prose or be friendly toward the attitude behind it. He should not have to. It is only because teacher education has attracted and catered to the docile, the undecided, the uncommitted and the transient—and women in overwhelming numbers, to boot—that generations of students have put up with it, have come to think like that, and to write such textbooks for the next generation.

This chapter has focused on the teacher because it is largely through the teacher that a student makes the bond between sense and intellect, which nourish learning as sun and water nourish plants. Much of what the teacher does is a matter of what he is and how he conducts himself. If a student sees learning in an attractive context, he is half begun in the task before him. The high turnover of young attractive unmarried teachers is not so lamentable as the low turnover of those who are unattractive, in marriage or out. At least our senses respond to physical beauty, and although the senses can be a distraction to learning, they are more likely to endow teaching, the exercise of intellect, with value in terms of feeling as great as can be gained by logic.

Physical beauty, feminine beauty, is, of course, not the only way of bringing a student to see the world feelingly, and a perfect education would surely not turn over the education of boys and girls from kindergarten to college so completely to women. The fact that American education has done so has interesting implications for the whole question of sense and intellect. There are many reasons why American schooling is so decidedly unmasculine, but one is the tendency to assume that women feel more deeply than men, are more concerned with feeling, and are therefore more attuned to the tender feelings of children. Art, music, literature, in terms of audience, are still regarded as feminine concerns, despite the fact that men continue to be dominant as painters, composers, and writers. Loosely speaking, one explains it in the obvious ways: Because men's muscles are needed for the physical tasks of the world—even though those requiring crude muscle power have diminished rapidly. Because, in a society that emphasizes the practical, men will turn to the practical tasks—although women's work as housewives and mothers is far more practical than the occupations of many husbands. Because motherhood necessarily arouses the affections and because, for want of other specific reasons, women just are more emotional, which seems to imply that they are more religious, spiritual, and artistic. And because, perhaps, women have more time to indulge their feelings.

All of this sounds reasonable and yet leaves a great deal out. For in the arts it is, after all, men who somehow, for all their physical strength, their practicality, their want of maternal affection, manage to refine their sensing apparatus, develop their powers of feeling, and discipline themselves sufficiently to thrill the ladies of the land assembled for concerts or book reviews or art exhibits. Perhaps any artist, male or female, is a freak, but that is not to say that a masculine interest in the arts is freakish. Nor should the domination of public school teaching by women support the notion that teaching is effeminate or that feeling is for mothers, wives, and mistresses.

The modern temper in this country very much rules against the unguarded expression of feelings and the development and refinement of ways to express feelings. The schools are preoccupied, as they seldom have been before, with the development of the intellect. The money and energy going into education incline every subject to the objective method characteristic of science, arousing in its students a distaste for the sterility of intellect alone and frustration over a lack of sanctioned expressions of feeling. Science itself, in the name of defending with science the civilization that the instruments of science so threaten, sets feeling aside to deal with the grim realities close at hand.

A perfect education would, I think, confront these distortions head-on. It would bring an increasing number of men into public school teaching, in the elementary schools as in secondary ones, in the arts as in the sciences or physical education. It would steadily work to develop feelings as well as manual and mental skills. It would be as interested in the feel of a thing as the facts about it. It would break down the attitudes that separate feeling and intellect and strive to strengthen both. Its energies would be as directed to the development of the whole self as to the pursuit of partial, objective truth. It would stand against any subject that could not generate a sense of its worth and against any student who could not express a feeling for his subject. With luck, such an education might bring its young pupils far enough along so that they might begin to see the world feelingly before the world's grimness forced that knowledge upon them. As preparation for further learning, it might establish in its students a pride in man as a being not only capable of learning but of deriving from learning intense feelings of worth and pleasure.

CHAPTER V

THINKING, KNOWING, DOING

SCHOOLTEACHERS spend far too little time in thought, far too much of their own education in trying to know, and the most time of all in doing what little thought and some knowledge has prepared them for. In that respect, they differ little from other people. There is the difference, of course, that they profess to encourage, if not teach, thinking in their students. At least that is the highest claim I hear teachers make: that they are trying to teach students how to think.

"Thought" is respected in our society, but not revered. It should be held in awe, not necessarily because it leads to mastery over the physical world, but for the sheer mystery of it. For although we can be satisfied in a limited way with modern explanations of how thought works, we are, so to speak, always on the outside of it. How account for the leaps it takes? How account for the selectivity it exercises over the millions of impressions flooding in? How explain the effect thought has on the physical body? How master any portion of the complex phenomenon that we describe as learning? How, indeed, teach people to think?

Certainly one of the ideals of any education, perfect or not, is to get people to think. We should probably be more humble in the face of such an ideal than we are, less presumptuously confident that anyone can teach anyone else or even himself to think. The great energy our age has expended in investigating how we think, in pointing out the traps into which thinking can fall, in making us aware of what we use instead of thought, has moved us only a short way toward understanding the process. In schoolroom practices, we are not much further along than the ancients, and in some ways we have slipped back a step or two.

Principally we have retrogressed in making school much less a dialogue than it should be. Teachers, for the most part, love to talk. Given large numbers of pupils per class, most of whom have a built-in conditioning to being talked at, and aware that it is easier and safer to keep talking, the teacher always inclines to too much teaching and too little regard for learning. Teaching of this kind can stimulate thought, although such thought is likely to be a narrow attention to following another's order of presentation or a disconnected chasing after this arresting idea or another. Placed within an institutional context with a high degree of constraint—the fixed number of hours and days, the units to be covered, the accepted book list, the inner and outer pressures from principals and parents—the teacher and student are not likely to force each other into active thought. Operating under the principle that the teacher's function is to train pupils in useful skills and to convey to them quantities of information important to their development as citizens, the schools foster a disengagement from thought itself in favor of improving physical and mental competencies, the latter more in terms of an approved content to be mastered than of a mind to be either exercised or trained.

The Socratic method, dialectic, is one of the inheritances from the classical past that is essential to maintaining the dynamics of learning. Basically a method for arriving at a firm answer through a series of focusing questions, it rests on an even more basic assumption that thought must be active, must be exercised, in order to develop. It also implies that answers to questions are best arrived at through this strenuous kind of questioning. As a part of our cultural background, it embodies thought in the compelling figure of Socrates, who, even at the point of death, would not curb his power of thought, and who, like Jesus, placed the spiritual, his world of ideas, above the material.

The Socratic method is still basic to education, from the elementary school on. It is a demanding form of teaching—demanding of both teacher and student. The ability to ask questions is hard enough, but to control them and direct them toward a goal without arriving at the goal in advance or tipping off the student that that is what the teacher really is doing calls for the skill of an actor, the command of language of a rhetorician, and the mastery of logic of a philosopher. Done properly, it is also an expensive form of education. It requires the rare kind of teacher I have suggested, and at most only a handful of pupils can be taken through the very experience of thinking one's way to an answer. For these reasons and a third—that the Socratic personality is not a popular one in our society at large or even among those engaged in public school education—the Socratic method is much less a part of modern education than I think it should be.

The Socratic dialogue—and that education *must be* a dialogue —is worth emphasizing now because we have seldom been in such danger of losing the personal impact of teacher upon student. The effect of rising enrollments, in the elementary school through college, is always to increase the number of students per teacher. The effect of economic pressure, at all levels, is similarly to increase the number of students per teacher. The effect of a wide range of technical aids to teaching, from television to teaching machines, is also to increase the number of students per teacher. Considering these forces all moving in one direction and the present parlous state of educational research, which can provide experimental data to support the effectiveness of almost any teaching method, one fears that the Socratic method may be completely abandoned.

As I have argued in the previous chapter, education must be personal. There is no way of achieving this except with a living presence. The beneficial effect of having the best teachers in the country brought into the classroom by television is hardly more than what the student has already gained at home from this close but impersonal spectator's view of the great men and women of our time. A book has more intimacy. Television in the classroom is one more example of the school's taking on or using what the home can and usually does provide. What is necessary is not more of what is already available, but live teachers capable of questioning and by so doing bringing into relation with thought some of the unavoidably educational experiences that the average child gets from his greatly enlarged exposure to the world by television, by travel, by the freedoms this century freely gives.

Nor is the kind of intellectual fare television offers—the panel discussion, for example, which is as constraining to educational TV as situation comedy is to commercial TV—any substitute for discussion in which the student is actually involved. The need for dialectic grows as the population becomes more and more exposed to new information, ideas, and experiences and rests content with that uninvolved exposure. American education seems at times to have committed itself to creating spectator intellectuals to match the spectator sports fans who have moved their Sunday devotions from the stadium to the television screen. For such spectators, the intellectual life is not something that a man participates in but rather something that can offer the educated man an hour's diversion when displayed within a sufficiently simpleminded format by someone else.

Dialectic is important in that large range of subjects whose factual content is—even for secondary pupils—the stuff, not of proof or exact demonstration, but of informed opinion moving toward judgment. Literature, history, the social studies, the arts—the list could be extended to all those studies that ask more between teacher and student than the exchange of information. In the many studies which have a large verbal content, in which exposure to the larger context is important, and in which more than demonstration is involved, dialogue is almost the sole means of stimulating thought.

Teaching and learning in the sciences depend somewhat less upon personal interchange. The exactitude required is probably greater. The ability to follow a logical pattern and even the judgment that sets off in one direction rather than another are as much requisites of the sciences as of the verbal disciplines. Yet the student is in more need of clarification than confrontation. The challenge lies in subjecting the physical materials to inquiry and in arriving at quantitative answers that bear out or apply the truth of larger theories. The circular progress of scientific method—the close examination of particulars permitting a generalization, which generalization in turn can be applied to a particular lying outside those actually observed—is an exercise of great value, giving thought a pattern to follow to arrive at highly useful ends. The inductive and deductive logic learned and practiced in the sciences should carry over not only to other academic disciplines but to the rational conduct of life.

Scientific studies also develop, or aim to develop, the power of abstraction, which is necessary to all thought. To move from the manipulation of the physical objects of the world to the manipulation of signs and symbols to arrive at the same end is a great step forward in one's thinking. The realization that such thought is not confined to mathematics or physics or chemistry, but is as necessary to the composition of lyric poetry, is something that might well come in adolescence. The basic ability to work with abstractions is largely responsible for the excitement generated by the new math in the primary grades as in the secondary schools.

The minimum necessity, whether it be for fostering dialogue in the humanities or for disciplined guidance in the sciences, is for a sufficient number of able teachers with few enough pupils to give each pupil continuing opportunities to follow through actual thought processes. The content matters little, except that it must not be trivial and that it must either begin with or catch up the student's interest. But the process matters a great deal. The difficulty of achieving some form of dialectic training in the secondary schools is great; not so much because of the diversified student body of the comprehensive high school as because of the failure to provide either the teachers or the conditions that might make live discourse between student and teacher possible.

Dialectic is no more a panacea for education's ills than it is the only way of learning. Still, I think it comes closer than any other method to getting at the central fact of learning as learning takes place between one person and another. For it is very often the personal, involved confrontation of teacher and pupil that inclines one to learn. The curriculum can go unattended and the requirements go hang, and even though we are aware of only part of *what* is being learned and much less of *how,* if the teacher and pupil are there, locked in on each other's discourse, both are learning a good deal of what can be learned through formal instruction. Metaphorically, one could extend such discourse to the books—not many in number—that have the ability to provoke a dialogue between writer and reader. One can converse with the past and with the greatness of the present. Though the language is figurative, the experience is actual.

Man cannot always be thinking, and who would want him to be? The time we have for education is not a matter of years but a matter of moments of intensity that press us into thought. We ought then to consider what might be in a curriculum that would provoke thought and be worth thinking about. What of philosophy, the discipline that not only defines itself as a love of wisdom but that is concerned with all aspects of thought? Could it be brought down from the heights, and could a place be made for it if it were? The absence of philosophy from the public school curriculum is odd, even if one is willing to grant that public school philosophy is unphilosophical. What philosophy once considered its major province, logic, has lost favor throughout education, except in the resurgence of symbolic logic in advanced studies. What formal logic remains has worked its way into English composition and is sometimes touched upon in speech and debate. Rhetoric has wholly passed over to speech or to English. Metaphysics and ethics were long ago given over to the church. There is little left—politics, physics, psychology, and natural philosophy having passed over into specialized disciplines—except epistemology, and that is too big a word for the secondary schools.

But the fact that philosophy has lost its inclusiveness, has seen its total subject matter taken over by one branch of study and another, does not explain its total absence from the public schools. Indeed, such a fragmentation underscores the need for some place for reflective thought in any period of education beyond the primary school. In secondary education, such a subject could and should be frankly and directly philosophical. It should confront questions of choice with which other learning is not greatly concerned and not get sidetracked into philosophy's separate interests. Its aims should be that of exposure and practice in ways of thinking, and its content should be the major questions about which men think.

Here one might find dialectic practiced as an oral confrontation between student and teacher, as it was when Socrates first perfected its use. Methods of thinking other than dialectic might be examined and practiced as well, from the collection and classification of facts to brainstorming. The very question of what method is most suitable to what kind of learning could be raised within the context of what man knows and how he knows it. All of this seems to me to be capable of capturing a secondary school pupil's interest, for such a concern bears directly upon the student's need to learn a great deal in the separate subject matters. Done imaginatively, demandingly, it could in this aspect alone be the most exciting course in a high school, both for the teacher and the taught.

By the mid-teens, the wonder of where one is going has probably been replaced by an anxiety about possible outcomes. What choices have men made, what alternatives are peculiar to this place and time, what has given value to man's existence, how has he groped his way along and where has he arrived or where does he think he has arrived? These are the kinds of questions that would fill the course. Projected out into their own lives, such questions would to some degree match the students' personal questions about their own desires and possibilities. Such a course would be full of questions with no pat answers. Content aside, the very indeterminate character of method and its aims would usefully oppose the acquisition of facts and skills with which schooling is almost exclusively concerned. By such means, students might be brought early to considering thoughtfully the uses of learning, might find their own insistent questioning about the worth of the course they are on—dominated by compulsory schooling to age sixteen—respected, considered, and if not answered at least not permitted to grow silently into a rejection of learning itself.

Such a course would not be easy to add. It could not be done cheaply, in great lecture halls or on television. It would have to create its body of teachers, few of whom are now in existence. It would have to find its adaptation to track programs, or it just might be one of those rare courses that could span all tracks. Its aims would seem highflown, its worth would be hard to assess, but we should insist on its inclusion if we believe thought is anything the public schools should have something to do with.

I am not saying, in my growing regret about the omission of philosophy, that thought is entirely neglected in the public schools. Mathematics and the laboratory sciences certainly require the exactitude, the ability to perceive patterns and follow them, and the sensitivity to relate and judge that distinguish thought. Language study may maintain some connection with formal logic. The social sciences and the behavioral sciences probably do some of what I have been asking for in a philosophy course. Of these, psychology and history deserve some examination.

The inclusion of philosophy in the public schools might come by way of psychology or with its help. Psychology is a very popular college subject, offering a great variety of opportunities for either theoretical or practical study. In our psychologically oriented age, the interest in psychology surely precedes the college years. Basic acquaintance with the subject should take advantage of that interest. Equally important, the large number of clinical jobs associated with hospitals, with social service agencies, and even with public schools could be prepared for at an earlier age than we envision now. However, these practical reasons for studying psychology early are somewhat aside from my main point: to use the subject to bring philosophy into the public school. The important connection is the intimate relation of philosophy and psychology at the point of how we learn and how we think. Knowing something about how we learn and think has consequences for the choices we make. The choices we make would be the focus of the work in philosophy that I would introduce into the secondary school.

Of history, and those many studies that are linked with history or that submit to a historical approach, I will say more in a later chapter. Here, I merely wish to use history as an example of a course that, in the secondary schools, gets transmitted from teacher to student without much disturbance of the mind. It should not be so, but it often is. Certainly we should know the facts of history (or know where to find them), but more important, we should acquire some few facts and think hard about them in order to acquire an ability to ask the questions that might lead to a sense of history. I suspect few secondary teachers of history have either the training or the confidence to ask such questions, much less to induce their students to ask questions themselves.

Instead we have an unhistorical confrontation of the most obvious social questions that can be tied to current headlines. Or we have—and this is probably superior to the first—the acquaintance with people and places in the past through a collection of facts about them. The sense of history, it seems to me, is very late in developing. It takes comparatively longer to break out of one's shell of self-concern than it does to be permitted to explore within. I am not here opposing the ease of acquiring insight into oneself with the difficulty of acquiring historical insight. I am simply guessing that the former is closer to a high school student's interest than the latter. Furthermore, it seems to me that history belongs with the humanistic studies, achievement in which only comes from a great deal of exposure to life, past and present. One must acquire a good many historical facts before one can see relationships, pose the larger questions of history. In practice, history has bent to the need to give the student a little basic history (meaning facts or near-facts) in what is presumed to be of most importance to the student, hence the requirements in state history and in American history. Since a little world history, ancient and modern, and perhaps some European history, and now Asian history, are also presumed to be important, secondary school history teachers are mainly concerned with spreading out facts. There is no time left to consider the implications of history, implications that would aptly extend to the philosophy course I've been asking for. Why have men and nations acted as they have? What choices have they made? What have the consequences been? Do men make events or events make men? Can ideals prove superior to expediency? Such attention to history might teach fewer facts, but might teach more in the way of thoughtfully considering the facts that are at one's command.

Facts are what our society has been incredibly good at supplying. What to do with them remains as troublesome as ever. But even that statement misses the essential problem for the educated man. There are never enough facts on hand for any decision on any question. More important, the habit of imagining what we cannot know in a factual sense is much a part of the thinking process and much involved in the decisions we make. For while a human being must bring into his mind the stuff of experience through his sensory apparatus, he is more than a creature of sensations, just as he is more than a thinking organism. The interplay of immediate sensory experience with what is already in the marvelous mechanism we call mind, of newly acquired concepts or images with those already in the mind, is what, it seems to me, distinguishes human thought. The task of a perfect education, in this particular, is to create the sensing individual whose heightened receptivity to the world outside creates the kind of continuing exposure that stirs the mind into an active involvement with fact and idea and sensation.

Knowing, in the sense of simple acquisition of fact, seems the easier accomplishment for education. "How much did you learn today?" we ask, as if the mind were a receptacle (as it probably is in part) and education's goal were to fill it. Yet that is only a part of the story, and maybe not the most important part. Certainly knowing is retention, a storing up for possible recall, an ability to say that Shakespeare was born in 1564 or that 1492 was when Columbus discovered America. Yet that is a particularly useless knowledge unless meanings cluster around Shakespeare or Columbus or America. That the one was a great writer and the other a great explorer and that America had to be discovered are the beginning knowledge one learns—learns, that is, if such knowledge has value in one's immediate cultural surroundings of home and school or in the larger cultural atmosphere of a city or a nation. Knowledge of this sort is, at least, a beginning and justification enough for a kind of fact-filled air in the lower schools.

It strikes me that almost all knowing, in the sense that we ask, "Who discovered America?" and answer, "Columbus," is of this kind. Knowing, in this sense, has a definiteness about it, a concreteness even in dealing with what are, after all, abstractions. There is a more important point to make about this kind of knowing. When we say, "I know when Columbus discovered America," we think we are saying something similar to saying, "I know how to pound a nail." But we prove the former by an abstract answer that tallies with what, in a sense, a culture agrees upon. (Columbus may have discovered America in 1492, but that is more a matter of agreement than anything else—however Columbus' contemporaries may have verified the fact, it remained largely unverified for them, wholly unverified for us.) We prove the latter, however, not only by an act that satisfies a sensory concrete judgment anyone can verify but also by the utility that now has joined one board with another.

The point is that this first kind of knowing does not have either the concrete, sensory proving or the utility of the second, and as such it is as incomplete, as useless, as inert as it is commonly regarded as being. Yet it is what too much of education consists of, and certainly too much of what learning, even intelligence are measured by all through the process of education.

I would not have its importance minimized, for the ability to take in countless impressions, both sensory ones and the abstract ones of word or number, and hold them for use is, I think, basic to learning. Such an ability is a tremendous resource, to be compared perhaps with having millions of dollars close at hand as a means of making more millions. Still, if I may push the analogy further, a man ends up with mere money until some kind of organizing and judging principle guides the transfer of money into goods that bring himself and the world about him some satisfactions.

So it is with the kind of knowing I am talking about here. As long as nothing is done with it, it is nothing, not even a source of the mild amusement that the displaying of any stray scrap of information may produce. We may envy the quiz champion, cultivate our own ability to retain odd bits of information, feel continuing

shocks of self-pleasure as we identify Faye Wray or date the composition of Mozart's symphonies or name the high school Jack
Armstrong attended, but these are simply small energy sensations,
like stimulating oneself with a pocket battery.

For all that, the ability to retain fact, number, idea is basic
for the larger act of the mind, which, except for immediate response to sharp sensory stimuli, probably seldom acts as a single
response to a single isolated sensation, fact, idea, or image. We
take our finger from the stove. We jump (though not necessarily
in the right direction) when someone shouts, "Look out!" We
step back at an authoritative command or gesture. Yet even such
simple acts as, for example, the boy crouched to begin a friendly
race jumping off at the word "Go," are surrounded by contexts.
The physical context is that of muscles tensing, breath becoming
more sharp, body pushing forward. The mental context includes
thoughts of winning, images of the racetrack ahead, recalled impressions of races in the past, imagined impressions of oneself in
victory or defeat mixed with visions of four-minute milers gained
from newsreels and the backs of cereal boxes. These contexts give
meaning—knowing—to an act of mind that could be regarded
merely as recognizing that the utterance "Go" means one can begin to run. The knowing of factual stuff can be looked at in a
similar way. The physical and mental contexts just mentioned—
and one might add sensory contexts—have much to do with the
outcome of the race, with the energy and skill the racer puts
forth. So has the large context of knowing—in this simple sense of
retained fact—much to do with the outcome of any education. To
make full use of the analogy, obviously such contexts can be both
useful and harmful. The racer may be physically bound up by too
much awareness of his own physical processes, or be so affected by
the other runners in his mind's eye that he runs a poor race, or, at
an extreme, be so much engrossed in the context that he misses the
exact moment of jumping off and so ruins at the start his chances
to win. The thinker may be similarly handicapped by knowing too
much, by being too driven to find another fact, too indiscrimi-
nately in possession of facts of the same order and value to make
something of them, too aware of the appalling vastness of facts he
doesn't have to make the most of those he has.

Clearly, however, we must side with the retention of fact, as
knowing that has a basic importance to all other knowing, even as
we recognize how it may delude us into thinking it is of worth in

itself and how it may encumber the mind in its attempts to arrive at a higher order of knowing. We cannot, it seems to me, side entirely with the advocates of the passional unconscious, or the instinctive creativitors, or even with the students and parents who downgrade factual knowledge because of the real difficulty of acquiring even that kind of knowing. A retentive mind may be far short of demonstrating the highest kind of learning, but, it seems to me, it cannot be poorly endowed, lazy, or unexposed. The prodigies of mathematical calculation among those otherwise classed as mentally deficient demonstrate an aberration of mental powers rather than a lack. Such minds are obviously highly retentive of certain kinds of factual information. The capable man with a head full of certain kinds of facts may appear both lazy and unexposed for having ranged no further either in depth or breadth, yet he must have been neither in terms of gaining what he does possess. Learning, in short, must have some mind to begin with and some stirring of the mind into activity to carry it on. Both are involved in the retention of fact. And, as inaccurate as our testing may be, depending so heavily upon measuring the retention of fact, it is both accurate enough and important enough in simply declaring that such abilities have a bearing upon a person's ability to know, however we define that term.

To put it another way, the ability to know, in the sense of acquiring and retaining facts, gives the person the great advantage of having the raw stuff of thought close at hand to work with. A man set down in a room full of colored yarn would have a better chance of weaving a blanket than one turned loose in the world to find his material. However we might prize the higher creativity of the second, we would find ourselves more quickly warmed by the first.

All my remarks imply a superior kind of knowing and in the context in which I am writing—secondary education—may suggest that I feel that a progression toward this superior knowing, a grappling with it, is or should be the aim of secondary schools. That is certainly my argument. The aim is not restrictively attached to secondary education but is rather a continuing aim toward which all formal education and the self-education that comes after are directed. Let me try to describe this kind of knowing. I think it is principally a matter of relationships, of placing the inert facts against other facts, perceiving their connections, and making something of them. It is the weaving of the blanket.

To return to the simplest of examples, such knowing is the

placing of 1564 against 1492 and being moved to ponder whether matters that close in time (and the feeling that they are close comes only after an exposure to a width of fact and the relating of many facts) have some connection. Centrally involved, of course, are the facts that for the knowing student cluster around Shakespeare and Columbus: the Elizabethan language and the world's geography in the fifteenth century, to use rudimentary examples. Such facts relate not only to isolated facts about either man, but the facts about one are related to the facts about the other. All this relating between retained fact and just-learned fact is knowledge of a second order of importance. Such knowing makes it possible, for example, to read a play with some sense of learning something, without really fully understanding or enjoying it. This kind of knowledge is, I fear, a necessary part of learning, a kind of hardship based upon taking much of the value and pleasure of learning on faith. It is the source of schoolboys' complaints and teachers' despair. Much of this knowing is the proper business of secondary education, just as rote learning is defensible as a part of elementary education—it seems to me the elementary school child can bear such learning, perhaps because there is a pleasure to be derived from knowing anything to which adults attach value when one is six or seven or eight.

This kind of knowing proceeds, to some degree, against the grain. Not, as in the elementary schools, only against the superior pleasure of play or the distraction of moving from infant to child, but also against the intensifying questions about the use of knowing, questions that become increasingly demanding throughout adolescence. At best, a school can only provide satisfying answers to such questions by developing certain skills and disseminating certain knowledge that may match a student's immediate need, such as giving a student sufficient knowledge of bookkeeping or typing to provide him with a part-time income or fostering an acquaintance with poetry sufficient to the necessities or desirabilities of adolescent courting. For the most part the teacher must try to develop the student's willingness to defer answers as one must defer the full development of physical skills that display themselves on the basketball court only after hours and days and years of practice. In many ways, secondary education is this kind of provisional knowing, not useful immediately and in itself but basing its value on the promise of a later purposeful and self-satisfying knowing.

Like the mere accumulation and retention of facts, this second order of knowing asks faith from the learner, and the learner's faith
needs all the support it can get from the surrounding culture.

Beyond that, and reachable in adolescence as in later life, is
knowing in the fullest sense—that is, not merely relating, placing
in context, but feeling the value of what is known, in terms of
what has been learned before, in terms of questings largely abstract
in character, and in terms of the sense of an organism satisfied, a
satisfaction of feelings as well as of mind. Thus when one finds
Shakespeare meaningful in terms of his or her actual response to
a line or a scene or an image, one may experience an awareness of
this kind of knowing. Such knowing endows the object of previous knowing with a value that comes almost entirely from self—
not only the instinctive self that some cultural primitives postulate
as alone capable of providing a "true" measure of art, but also
from the prepared, knowing self consciously aspiring to a higher
order of understanding. This knowing is, I think, akin to that
which distinguishes a primitive painter, akin to the response which
binds all men of good will into brotherhood, and even akin to that
superior feeling we get from perceptions we call intuitive, meaning
for the most part that there was no hard work or sense of hard
work expended in arriving at them.

However, such knowing is not confined to the kinds of artistic
or intuitive perceptions just mentioned. It may not necessarily arrive in a flash of light, but may slowly illuminate itself a long way
in advance. It can as easily grow out of one's facility with or
fascination with or even struggle with number into a kind of grasp
of the beauty that lies in mathematics, a beauty almost sensual in
character but at the same time conjoined with a sense of the power
that mathematics gives to one who "knows" mathematics. The feeling for a sense of place and time that underlies any really imaginative grasp of history is knowing in this highest sense and may well
develop (perhaps be developcd) out of a great deal of knowing of
a very rudimentary sort.

Such considerations take a leap considerably beyond what often
goes on in secondary education—beyond what could ordinarily be
expected to go on, considering what kind of school programs have
first priority for adolescents in the comprehensive high school.
Nevertheless, it seems to me to be possible for adolescents to move
toward the knowing that matches their own deepest and fullest

needs. The discovery that Shakespeare and Columbus are close in time may suggest a closeness in spirit that brings this incorporeal past into the range of their own questings for personal discovery, the one stimulating the other, both conjoining to bring them to some "knowledge" about the abstraction of adventure and to create in some particulars the sense of "knowing" what Shakespeare and Columbus are all about.

Obviously this kind of knowing embodies feeling as well as intellectualizing, makes use both of what has been retained and what has been previously related, and creates some kind of vital connection between this stuff of thought and the whole learning being. The necessity of moving adolescents toward such knowing is the necessity of endowing some aspect of their learning with sufficient power to push them on to further knowing, which becomes, ideally, the stuff of doing.

In a prosaic way—or in ways that should not be prosaic—we are talking about preparing a student for a vocation. We are saying what the vocational counselor says: What do you like doing, what can you draw upon of what you know to take your place in the world? The usual answer, except for those who have by accident or necessity—seldom by rational choice—developed one or two strong inclinations to the neglect of others, is: "I don't know." The usual procedure is to go on to college, to avoid both labor and the draft for a few years, and to let the pressures of accident and necessity force one into a vocation. The kind of knowing I'm talking about might direct a few into vocations that become more than mere work.

The drift of my argument is that the kind of knowing I am describing is close to doing, is that it leads to doing that has the full or almost full commitment of the individual. For high school students in America, knowing of this kind is likely to be unacademic. That is, what the students seem to know in this way has more to do with developing a skill in athletics or baton twirling or beauty contesting than with developing an understanding of any subject matter that promises to open out into a lifetime of doing. In many secondary schools removed from urban pressures these unacademic achievements—which are in reality the group achievements of communities starved for other identity—are still foremost. In urban high schools, the highest kind of knowingness may be explicitly academic, the kind that bypasses understanding,

often even commitment, except commitment to the desire to com-
pile the kind of academic record that will win a good scholarship
to a graduate school.

One gets the impression that for the majority of students in the
comprehensive high school such knowing never arrives or, when it
does, is undervalued. The many students who move on into college
and university do so with, on the one hand, a secure sense that the
storing up of facts that gained them high marks in high school will
get them safely through college and, on the other, a kind of vaguely
insecure sense that college will be rough but worth it, since it may
give them the employability that high school did not provide. The
colleges do not disappoint them greatly in either respect, although
the college student may find himself "knowing" more in the highest
sense and yet not able to convert such knowing into ready cash.
However, even that has its happy side, since graduate school is
there to provide for the vocational training passed over in secondary school and college. What is most regrettable in this progression is the disconnection between knowing and doing, most
often expressed as the opposition between vocationalism and liberal training. Such opposition seems to persist until professional
training—even in the liberal arts—becomes wholly vocational (and
often narrowly so), as in the preparation of college professors for
college teaching.

The need is certainly for more connection between knowing
and doing. Society, especially American business as a central part
of society, has insisted upon a high school diploma for most jobs
(and has failed to pay adequately for the training the public school
has provided for its millions of employees). Today, industry's insistence upon a college degree is almost as strong. Neither then
nor now has there been sufficient examination of *what* the student
knows or of the *kind of knowing* he possesses in relation to what
he is to *do*. There has been, of course, pressure upon the schools
both from the job seekers and from those who provide jobs to
add courses that would give specific vocational training. Yet neither
the employee nor the employer claims much for the actual (as
apart from the theoretical) applicability of such training. Since
the character of many specific jobs changes rapidly and many kinds
of jobs disappear and new ones arise with similar rapidity, specific
vocational training may provide little more than an entry into an
employing organization. Certainly the list is long, both after high

school and after college, of those jobs in which there is not much connection between what a man has learned, what he knows, and what he does. The *knowing* that is important is the knowing he acquires after he is on the job, precisely because it is related to his *doing*.

This is why I stress a higher kind of knowing that not only aims at establishing the maximum relationships between what is already known and what is being learned but also moves on to embrace the value of what one knows as related to what one does— what one *is* to extend it fully. Among other reasons for emphasizing this relation is that it might keep the work a man finds himself doing from becoming unworthy of his most "knowing" efforts. If secondary schools place emphasis upon this kind of knowing, then American business (since it is the largest employer of nonprofessional personnel) should attempt to find other ways to give value to the work that needs doing. Simply trying to give work a higher status by requiring a college degree rather than a high school diploma does nothing. There is still a quantity of work to be done that is the dirty work, the kind of work that education has always been used to avoid. (Being optimistic about it, one can see in automation a steady diminishing in the quantity of this work that has to be performed by human beings and can hope that the human effort still necessary to automation of such work will not be damned by calling it "mechanical.") What is at stake is the alliance between the world's work and education. The joint effort of those who employ and those who educate might be toward endowing work (and the leisure that increases as the clock-hours of work diminish) with value, helping one see not only the *utility* of the work one does but the *worth* of it.

Traditionally, theories about what secondary education should provide have been in terms of use. More awareness and competence in citizenship or more specific vocational aims characterize most of the reforms of the past. With the arrival of Sputnik I, reformers have emphasized the connection between American citizenship, vocations, and development of the mind and have forced a similar emphasis upon the academic. Perhaps we are at a point where there are very few vocational aims that a secondary school education alone can serve. I personally doubt it. There are many useful jobs needing to be done that do not require extended or specialized training. Arguments on the specific question can be set aside because—necessarily or not—the expectations of the culture force an extension of formal learning beyond high school. That higher learning may be specifically vocational, as in various technically oriented junior colleges, or specifically academic, as in the junior colleges that assume the lower-division functions of a college. In either case, secondary school is no longer considered terminal education, and the question of what vocational training secondary school should provide is therefore no longer so pressing.

It seems clear that the secondary school can afford to be less concerned with immediate vocational goals, just as it can be less concerned with intense and specific academic preparation. Thus freed, it might concern itself with the beginning development of the kind of knowing I'm talking about and furnish the sense of wider possibilities of *doing* that all learning has as its ultimate aim.

I have already suggested a good deal about how this might be done. Thinking, knowing, and doing should be moving together at this stage of a perfect education. The purpose of restoring to education a large measure of dialogue is not only that of keeping thought alive but that of allowing the personal confrontation of teacher and pupil to move the student to a higher level of *knowing* and so incline him toward a *doing* in which *thought* and *knowledge* may in time bring one close to *wisdom,* or at least enable one to recognize wisdom when one sees it. That seems to me to be the fundamental requirement: to provide teachers and teaching of a kind that permits the examination of what is being taught, the time for both teacher and student to turn the knowledge they are confronting around and around and see it from as many sides as possible. The best teacher is one who feels the worth both of the subject matter he is concerned with and of the social mission he is fulfilling, and who keeps alive in the classroom and out a sense that teaching and learning is *doing* as surely as is running the five-hundred-yard dash or clerking in a bank. That does not mean everyone will rush to become such a teacher, but it does mean that teaching can become something that is *to be done* rather than something that *can be done* when more attractive prospects fail.

CHAPTER VI

WHAT'S WORTH LEARNING

O F ALL THE THINGS that educators concern themselves with, none gets more attention than curriculum. Classical times furnished the trivium (grammar, logic, and rhetoric), and the quadrivium (arithmetic, geometry, astronomy and music), which became the basis for education through the Middle Ages on into the Renaissance. Today the trivium is barely discernible in language arts in the lower school, and the quadrivium has now expanded to include a large number of diverse studies that bear only slight relationship to the classical curriculum. As the trivium concentrated on the skills by which man voiced his humanity, so the quadrivium aimed basically at perceiving the order of the universe and stirring one into contemplation of it. Today's school curriculum scants both the development of man's powers of reason and expression and the consideration of a basic universal order. The emphasis is squarely upon man, upon the facts that record his existence and the questions which arise from his place in society.

American public school education is looked at very much in terms of what every citizen should know. There seems to be widest agreement that reading, writing, and arithmetic are skills that are to be developed in everyone. But even with such fundamental skills, the emphasis of the school curriculum is not upon the skills themselves but upon the simple utilitarian tasks than can be performed through acquiring such skills. Since my competence is in language rather than mathematics, I choose to examine reading and writing as something everyone should learn to do. I suspect even here, at the very cornerstone of the curriculum, one has to go beyond the question of what is worth learning and consider by whom and to what degree.

Reading, we can all agree, should be the aim of everyone.

Beyond the acquiring of basic skill in reading, literature in its broadest sense is a fundamental part of the curriculum. Reading, Bacon wrote, maketh the full man. It still remains the chief way of knowing, although its primacy is being challenged by the easier and more immediately effective devices of reproducing sounds and images. The peculiar virtue of reading as a means of access to the past as well as the present is that it requires a positive act of the mind, an expenditure of energy, that confers value on the knowledge gained and that puts the mind in a receptive condition for thought.

I have no professional competence in the teaching of reading in the lower schools, but I have had considerable with college students who read poorly. Such a basic deficiency, it seems to me, is not just the consequence of improper teaching methods, but much more the consequence of attitudes toward reading, toward books, toward learning. Undoubtedly it has some relation to the mental capacities and the psychological and physiological condition of the reader. The quarrel of "look-see" against "phonics," of one method against another, is a bogus quarrel, as far removed from either general truth or specific problems as the advertisements that cause adults to flock into speed-reading courses. For the most part, common sense furnishes as good advice as pedagogy. What a parent does in furnishing books, in encouraging the use of books, in providing the responses necessary to learning any skill, basically determines his child's ability to read.

In the secondary schools, nevertheless, there are now and will continue to be great numbers of students who do not read well. The skilled teacher can bring to bear a good deal of what has been learned about the teaching of reading. No special program in the schools is as important as this one. No overall attitude is more worthy of being fostered than one that brings students to reading. Such an attitude operates against the physical desires of the students, against much of the orientation of the culture, against the stereotypes associated with pedantry and bookishness. Still, there is as yet no substitute for reading as a means of access to a world that becomes increasingly abstract as one grows older.

One general aspect of reading that could be given attention in the secondary schools is the many different capacities a skilled reader develops. After a certain point, for example, speed in reading is more a matter of intention than of training. For people who depend upon reading in their lives or professions, speed in reading develops because of the simple necessity of keeping up. To train a general reader, the secondary school could consciously work from the premise that the speed of reading varies with the purpose of what is being read, almost according to the individual paragraph. No one can afford to read everything at the same rate or with the same degree of concentration. The average newspaper read by the average citizen should take no more than fifteen minutes, except on an extraordinary day. (The Sunday New York *Times* might take somewhat longer.) Some books should be read in an evening, some books take a lifetime. Books that can be read in less than an hour shouldn't be. Such observations are worth including, worth emphasizing, in the courses in the secondary school that still treat reading as a skill.

As important as reading is, a reading-skills course is probably not justified in itself. It should be part of a language and literature class, in which a wise and effective teacher naturally includes the *how* of the subject as well as the *what*. What to read in public school English courses is almost as thorny a problem as what to include in the curriculum. The questions are closely related, and what is said about selecting books for reading might well be applied to selecting courses in the general curriculum.

In the first place, schoolteachers are far too traditional, far too acceptant of what the authority of the past or the authority of state textbook selection committees or the authority of textbook publishers gives them as the best choices in reading. A typical high school English list is likely to include *Ivanhoe, The Merchant of Venice, David Copperfield, Silas Marner, A Tale of Two Cities, Adam Bede, Julius Caesar, Macbeth,* and *Hamlet.* With the exception of Shakespeare's plays, all these are nineteenth-century classics, heavy in costuming and morality, obtrusive in plot and action, and safely established as "good" books. Unfortunately, they are not very good books for encouraging and sustaining a love of reading in twentieth-century adolescents.

The anthologies should make the English teacher wonder about what an editor's judgment and a publisher's necessity have put together. An examination of high school literature texts suggests that more attention is being paid to four-color printing (certainly more money expended on it) than to the contents. Why is it necessary to print an *abridged* abridged dictionary at the back of an anthology? A dictionary is first among the books a reader needs. It is inexcusable to tuck a puny piece of it into a textbook, to excuse a student from acquiring a respect for words. Why is it necessary to reprint pieces of *David Copperfield* (*"Young" David Copperfield*) or *Silas Marner* as part of an anthology? Why, for that matter, is it necessary to make George Eliot (Mary Ann Evans) look like Maureen O'Hara? Why is it necessary for the editors to adopt that hopefully imperative tone to address student readers: "You may weep over the pathetic story of little Nell and her grandfather, but you *will* laugh uproariously at the misadventures of Dick Swiveller and the Marchioness." Why, if "Shakespeare, as everyone knows, was not of an age, but for all time" and the Pyramus and Thisbe story is "screamingly funny if acted," is it necessary to use three inches of footnotes for every column of text? Why, indeed, with the wealth of paperbacks, is it necessary to have literature anthologies at all?

What is important is getting books before the students in a substantial way and creating in them the feel for books and for reading as something that exists outside textbooks, anthologies, reading lists, and teachers' peculiar minds. Schools, it seems to me, deviated from virtue for the noblest of reasons when they began buying texts and renting or lending them to students. Thus they ensured that every student would have a book, but also that he would never mark it, never make it his own, and never regard it with real respect.

There is one caution, however, one should take. That is the tendency to assume that the more read the better. I have worked closely with the advanced placement courses in English—courses designed to give the superior high school student literature and composition at a college level—and greatly respect the work being done. The initial response of a high school English teacher to advanced placement courses is almost always to give the student too much. It takes no professional competence to judge that this proposed year's course, for example, is too much: "Utopian Unit— Emphasis on Controlled Research 3–5 days; Composition Unit— compiled from readings of Plato, More, Bacon, Bellamy and any other authors students wish to include. Semantics Unit—*Pride and Prejudice*—Culture Unit—one week each. Lectures showing music and art in parallel with literary periods. Novel Unit, Sonnet Unit, Unit in Satire, Essay Unit, Unit in Modern Literature, Bible

Literature Unit." All of this converging (inundating, it should be said) in: "Flow chart to be printed in permanent form—The Humanities Through the Ages—Coverage: Epic, tragedy, comedy, physical theater, music, philosophy, semantics." Such a plan would not produce a "reading" list but a "gorging" list. No wonder speed reading has been one of the most successful fakeries of our time. How much reading is not the point: The point is to get students close to reading that they can invest their full sympathies in, for only thus can they begin to realize how much reading can shape their lives.

Writing, Bacon wrote, maketh the exact man. It remains today as one of the chief academic ways of getting students to think and of examining those thoughts. For all its value in this respect, it is, in the way it is included in the curriculum and practiced in the classroom, a relatively unexamined subject. I have no question that writing is a skill worth learning, but I have a number of questions about the way we go about learning it and the uses to which we put it. Considering that the subject English, including composition, is so much a part of at least eight to ten years of public school education, why do we have so much trouble with freshman and subfreshman English in the colleges? And after the college student has finished freshman English and four years of study in which writing is supposedly a part of the training, why is it that the professional schools, the graduate schools, and the employers of college graduates still continue to deplore the inability of college graduates to write? Is it that they want a Holmes in every law office, a Bacon in every laboratory, a Shakespeare in every library? Though professional men and scholars—especially those capable of writing well—may tend to set standards according to their own hard-won facility, they claim to want merely clear, workmanlike prose with perhaps a touch of grace and effectiveness. Why can't they have that, at least from the highly educated men entering the professions, whose years of schooling and professional interests should have stimulated them often to express their thoughts in writing?

It seems to me that any answer must begin with full recognition that writing is hard work and that writing well is a very special accomplishment. The beginning of a common-sense answer is to be found in appreciating how many people glibly say, "I could write a book about that!" and how few well-written books get written. Or, to put it another way, it lies in the paradoxical effect that good writing creates: A book marked by lucidity of thought and grace of expression seems to arouse in the reader a distinct feeling that he himself could have written it. The more lucid the style, the more the reader is inclined to think of it as his own.

Surely it is this kind of attitude, a common enough one in a culture in which almost everyone can read and write, that creates the unexamined expectation that every educated person should be able to write well. Being able to read well is even more of an expectation, just as being able to think well is less. Perhaps that is because thinking is so intangible. More likely, it is because few people trouble to consider how difficult thinking is. At any rate, as eager as the public has been to damn the schools for not teaching Johnny to read, it has not precisely blamed them for not teaching him to think. As to writing, the expectation has not yet become a demand, although it is widely accepted as a necessary skill of the educated man. Since American education insists that everyone should receive twelve (and lately fourteen) years of formal schooling, it follows that all those who pass through such a process are assumed to be educated, which means there must be something wrong if they can't write. The dropouts and those who otherwise terminate their formal educations before graduating from high school are looked upon with suspicion. The dropouts are treated as social problems but it is not sufficiently recognized that the pressure of considering formal education to be a necessity for all *successful* folks, all *good* folks, may have helped make them social problems. The ones who succeed despite the absence of a high school diploma are regarded as exceptions that prove the rule that prolonged education is the only way to success and happiness. The feeling, then, that almost every educated person should write better than he does is part of the more inclusive myth that so many years of formal schooling make an educated citizen. In that respect too, we are constantly amazed that we are not better educated than we are.

To come to grips with the matter, it seems obvious to me that our expectations about writing are higher than they should be. The general result is that we spread inadequate training in writing for everyone throughout most of the years of formal education, never quite coming up with the general results we have in mind and probably doing less than we could for those who will find writing most necessary for themselves and for society. Writing is a skill that cannot be developed through mass instruction any more than dialectical reasoning can take place between one teacher and four hundred students. Whether a person learns to write well with the help of a patient, knowing, and available teacher, or merely by himself being patient, knowing, and available, he learns by expending great quantities of energy and time on it. Learning to write cannot be done cheaply, either by the student or by the teacher trying to help him. Individuals, of course, vary tremendously in their ability to acquire writing skill, probably as they vary in power of thought. But variance aside, no one ever learned to write well (or to think well) without much exercise of that skill either under his own discipline or someone else's. In schoolroom terms, that means that an attention to what the students write is mandatory. The English teacher cannot escape reading themes, although that is what gets neglected when the teacher is tired or lazy or pressed with too many other concerns. Apprentice teachers are faced with the same basic problem in the colleges. The assigning and reading of themes is pretty much the extent of our formal efforts to teach writing at all levels. Quality of teachers and students aside, writing is taught well in very few schools, because it quite simply takes too much time, effort, and money.

How do I know that writing is such hard work? Principally because even as I sat writing this page, I realized that twenty years of formal schooling and fifteen years of professional practice in writing had not made it much easier. I teach writing, I do it, I study it. In comparison with many of my colleagues, I write easily. Yet how laboriously all that is in this book came into words, sentences, and paragraphs.

So this is what makes me ask that we humble our expectations in looking at the teaching of writing. In a specific, practical way, it leads me to suggest that a perfect education would face the difficulties both of teaching writing and of developing the skill. It would recognize that with the incredible exposure to language common to children in this country, verbal facility probably develops faster than in the past. It would also recognize that by the age of thirteen or fourteen, a student in a public school might be expected to show whether further intensive training in writing is desirable. For students who show an aptitude and a responsiveness to instruction, the best possible instruction should be provided. This would mean that the teacher of writing (not necessarily of English) would do a great deal of personal, painstaking work. Such instruction would cost school districts money, although the total cost might be less than that of the present halfhearted efforts to provide instruction in writing for everyone. Ideally, there should be tutoring in *writing* (and in *thinking*) for almost all students, but if perfection must bow to practicality, then the only way our educational system can provide the kind of teaching that demands close individual attention is to discriminate radically between one student and another.

Even if we do intensify training in writing for some, this does not mean disaster for those not favored with such instruction. Not at all. Being able to read and to write should remain a requirement, but at a level basic to participation in society rather than one geared to either accomplishment or fulfillment in using the written language. For the sober truth, as regards our society, seems to be that even for those who supposedly learn to read well—the college graduates—reading occupies a very small part of their later activities, and writing, I would guess, even less. And although many of us devoted to defending a highly literate culture defend our ideals by pointing out how necessary writing is to advancement, we are not saying much more than, "Be smart enough and interested enough and work hard enough to learn to write, and you'll do all right, jobwise." But whether doing all right jobwise is to be attributed to writing more than to intelligence or zeal or hard work is hard to say. There are a great many ways in which people can be successful, well paid, and presumably happy without writing well, and, as I have said earlier, such ways are on the increase. My point is that maybe our loose concern with literacy measured by a high level of accomplishment in writing is a fussy one, and one that a perfect education for a large mass of people would eliminate.

In regard to what is worth learning, I am simply joining the many who argue for a flexible curriculum, being willing, even though I prize writing greatly, to argue that writing (not reading) should be treated with such flexibility. In addition, I am endorsing another commonplace, that whatever is in the curriculum is not as important as who is in the classroom.

Reading and writing and arithmetic are the basic "how-to" skills that almost everyone agrees should be acquired. Beyond that, public school education is much concerned with *what* every citizen should know. The attention to *what* is known, somewhat to the neglect of *how*, begins, I think, in the late primary grades, about the time the child begins, theoretically at least, to move from teacher to subject. The change is marked by the departure of the single-classroom teacher, who, by the pupils' standards, knew a lot about everything, and the arrival of separate-subject-matter teachers. The change is an important one for students, for it marks, in most schools, the lessening of the impact of the single teacher. When a group of teachers identified with their subject matter replace the single teacher, the personal experience of learning from a teacher becomes associated with the subjects in the curriculum, and the curriculum, in turn, takes on a semblance of personality. "English teacher" has, I suspect, connotations that "biology teacher" has not. (And the absence of "philosophy teacher" in the public schools suggests a personal kind of short-coming as well as an institutional one.)

Such personal involvement gives curriculum great force in American schools. School programs are built around a curriculum more than around teachers. A school's virtues are frequently measured by its having so much of this and this and this in the curriculum and having teachers officially certified to teach such approved subjects. Indeed, the supposition is always there that, given the right subjects, a student will be suitably educated. And although the lack of truth of that assumption—not its falsity—is immediately evident, we still must acknowledge that choices of subjects must be made.

It is no simple matter deciding *what* an educated man should know. Attempts to decide seem to get sillier the closer they get to deciding what *every* educated man should know. The Association for Supervision and Curriculum Development of the National Educational Association—certainly a body concerned professionally and knowingly with knowing—will illustrate the difficulties of dealing with the matter. The pamphlet *The High School We Need* confronts curriculum in this fashion. Under "Outcomes Sought," the authors, a selected group of individuals involved in public school education, advise:

Each youth should develop increased understanding of self and his responsibilities in society, commitment to democratic values, economic understanding, political acumen, and ability to think. These are qualities that will help him be an effective citizen. The extent to which a particular subject or experience fosters these qualities should aid in deciding whether it should be included in the school program.

I wonder if there is any truth here at all, or even any good advice. How does one measure "commitment to democratic values" and "political acumen"? And if these are difficult to measure in themselves, how much more difficult to measure the extent of any one subject's contribution to them. I do not think we get much real guidance here. Let us go on further in the document.

"No longer," the authors say in the next section, "can it be assumed that all youth can profit by the same program of mathematics, foreign languages, science, social studies and English. If the capacities of all youth are to be developed, the offerings of the secondary school should be as comprehensive as are the educational needs of the society which supports it." This brings a man up short. How willing public school educators are to make all knowledge their province, and how willing to have the secondary school offer all the knowledge that society needs to possess! And knowledge, as everyone knows, is but one concern among many in the comprehensive high school. Outside of the required courses, the "high school we need" should offer a variety of other courses and the students should be permitted some choice among them. The total number of the courses to be offered as well as their variety is staggering, if one accepts what is written seriously. And even if one makes necessary allowance for the curriculum planners' enthusiasm, there remains a blueprint of a high school curriculum that encourages the inclusion of a good deal more than a public institution seriously concerned with education needs to offer.

Going further, we read that "The program for each individual must contain general education." General education includes:

... a knowledge of democratic values and skill in implementing them, an understanding of our governmental and social institutions, an insight into our economic organization, a grasp of our national and international relations, and an ability to contribute to the functioning and improvement of our human life. The required courses and activities, general education, should be those which are directly focused on promoting these qualities. . . . Only those courses that are essential for competent citizenship should be required of all. These will be continuing experiences throughout the secondary school with English and communications as well as with fundamental aspects of our cultural heritage and our contemporary society.

Only when the document turns to elective education does it place some limits upon the knowledge a secondary school should offer. "Not all the possible courses that some individual might wish can be made available. Each community, within the limitations of its ability to provide financial support and its conception of what constitutes desirable education, should make available to students a range of elective courses."

I have quoted from this pamphlet at some length only to suggest the great difficulties of deciding what is worth learning. At the same time, the set of guiding principles the authors put forth are widely accepted by those most involved in the direction and conduct of American public school education. One can hardly blame a group of men for dealing in the generalities to be found here. The idea of education for responsible citizenship, which dominates their philosophy, is a cherished one in American education. But one does draw back from their confidence that they can prescribe a curriculum to achieve such an end. Despite the general acceptance of breadth and variety as an aim of the curriculum, the specific suggestions seem to be aimed at a much more narrow end. Although it is strongly suggested that mathematics, foreign languages, science, social studies, and English afford inadequate acquaintance with or training for the modern world, the essential courses are vaguely described as "continuing experiences . . . with English and communications as well as with fundamental aspects of our cultural heritage and our contemporary society." This last phrase is in keeping with the heavy stress placed upon developing political acumen and economic understanding, but suggests no more than is already heavily stressed by the presence of the social sciences in the public schools. More than that, the phrase places emphasis upon knowing things that are somewhat expected to relate precisely to vague aims. As long as we believe we mean something when we say "democracy" and "citizenship" and "political acumen," we can incorporate them in the curriculum of the modern school. The trouble is, we will never know what the level of American citizenship would be like with a different kind of public education, although we can fairly assume it would be worse were there none.

And yet, it seems to me, citizenship grows tangentially, not out of direct exhortation to patriotism, not certainly out of forced patriotism, not probably out of any set of school subjects. It rises most, I would guess, out of creating—creating a self or a nation—in which one can take pride. Thus a school suffers most when it begins to be looked down upon by those who are in it and who will become its alumni when they depart. And although we give it all knowledge to work with, we denigrate its value, nullify its effectiveness, when we do not urge its specialness as much as we might. If it is the community's chief social service agency, it is also more than that. For knowledge at almost every point of individual awareness defies school boundary lines, community needs, and curriculum developers who might wish to make it more parochial. Knowledge in this timeless and subjectless dimension is foreign to the thoughts and plans of the writers of this pamphlet. They would probably argue, as practical men, a concern for less lofty goals, all the while postulating the most visionary of schemes: an education that would not only bring about the great society but ensure every citizen's proper participation in it as well. I think I would be content with aiming at the development of the individual self.

If I seem skeptical of a curriculum that specifically aims at vague goals, it is not because I think the curriculum unimportant. Knowledge in its vastness, its diversity, and its valuelessness must be faced, and one must try to determine what, of all that can be known, is most worth knowing, or, more modestly, what knowledge of the knowledge that lies close at hand is more important than other knowledge, and how and when should it be incorporated into the school curriculum.

What indeed should a person know? Primarily, he should know ways of knowing, fundamentally based on an ability to read and to write and to figure. Thus, in literature and mathematics in the secondary schools, the student strives to develop his skills while becoming acquainted with the things these skills make accessible. Properly understood, reading and writing and arithmetic are not acquirements. They are terminal skills only in a limited sense.

One may learn to write well by his middle years if he works hard at it. Skill in reading may be almost as late in coming. And mathematical skills, early as they often manifest themselves, continue to be acquired throughout one's life. More important, for the person who will be neither a writer nor a mathematician, is the establishment of the worth of reading and figuring, a sense of their usefulness and the pleasure to be derived from them. For without some pleasurable response in the manifesting of a skill, the joys of literature, as of mathematics, are forever sealed off. Throughout the course of studies in the secondary schools, the majority of which are verbal or mathematical in character, the excitement, the discipline, the pleasure in exercising a skill should not be divorced from the informational content, which can too easily become the teacher's sole concern.

Similarly, one might say that studies in specific science subjects in the secondary school likewise need this linking of how one proceeds with what one learns. As a student's ability to work within a discipline in the sciences grows, so does his fund of knowledge increase. The promptings of curiosity, which devised means of finding out in the lower schools, develop into controlled scientific inquiry, which sets as much store by how one arrives at an answer as by the answer itself. The interest aroused and sustained by the study of nature grows naturally into the specialized studies in the biological sciences, and the interest in machines grows into elementary mechanics and theoretical physics. A secondary education in which an attention to technology was part of the concern of the curriculum could strengthen the understanding of scientific method while dealing with subject matter leading to careers in engineering, applied and pure science, and a variety of technological occupations.

Secondary education also seems to me to be the place to get at the scientific illiteracy many humanists and scientists alike deplore. I will not repeat the argument that knowing the second law of thermodynamics is as important as knowing something of Shakespeare. I think such arguments specious, true only in a negative way. That is, if knowing consists of that kind of informational acumen, then one might well argue that one is as important as the other. The far more important point is whether knowing causes any change in one's outlook toward the world or oneself. We give respect to the scientific fact as to any fact. As long as either remains mere fact, it might as well be paper clips. It is what is done with fact, in the context of a focused inquiry in a specific discipline, or in the context of man's position in the universe, that counts. Similarly, in acquainting a student with the methods of science as such methods can be described and applied outside the laboratory, the subject matters little. What matters is the exemplification of how one proceeds from the particular to the general, how one selects and groups, how one checks and verifies, how one applies the generalization to the particular case, and how one yields, often grudgingly, to the evidence his investigation produces. And beyond these considerations, applying to the position of both scientific fact and scientific method in the secondary school curriculum, is the necessity of somehow imparting the value of scientific pursuits to the student. Such can best be done within a humanistic context, seeing science as one of man's ways of knowing, its discoveries part of what gives a person's life its color, excitement, worth. Failing to see that, the student will remain a scientific illiterate however many facts he may know. Failing to impart that, the scientist can fairly be regarded as Robert Jastrow of NASA's Goddard Institute of Space Studies fears high school students now regard him: "gray, colorless and unaware of what's going on around him." Despite the increased activities and expenditures in science education in the past ten years, the appeal of scientific careers to high school students has declined. It may not be so vital in the secondary school for everyone to get a taste of "science" as for the scientific method to disclose itself in the curriculum at large and for the scientific subjects to be thoroughly invested with a sense of their humanistic worth.

Certainly history should be a central part of what is known—the end to be gained not historical facts but an historical attitude. That attitude should be one that holds before the individual the value of seeing one's life, one's time, in a larger context. The study of history should be the study not of facts, but of relationships, for which history provides not only vertical comparisons—times past and times present—but horizontal ones, between technological developments, say, and artistic manifestations. The study of history, then, is not only a school subject but part of one's developing attitude toward all school subjects. The early school years may expose the student to the fabric of the society immediately surrounding him. The secondary years should broaden that exposure in terms of discovering the past and should provoke thought, should make the student try to see how the past bears upon the present. Such studies should give the student a sense of himself in time and space, a sense of the unity that education seeks.

The fanning out of such studies into the separate disciplines of sociology, political science, and economics is a logical progress for secondary education. Despite my skepticism about the effectiveness of such studies as a means of creating the proper citizen of a democracy, I am not skeptical about their specific worth. I hasten to add, however, that I regard the fear of producing political or economic illiterates in the same light as the fear of producing scientific ones. No one wants high school graduates to be positively ignorant of science or of economics, but required courses giving the basic facts of one or the other have little to do with dispelling ignorance. Badly taught, they encourage disdain.

That is one reason for having these studies tied to history: to keep them from being mere "purpose" courses, an assembling of very few principles and some basic facts loosely related to particular ends. More than that, the relationship between man in time and man in society is basic to any full and satisfying comprehension of human endeavor. But that is very high-flown language to use in discussing courses in the comprehensive high school. The abstractions of economic theory as well as the actualities of political involvement are not likely to be vital subjects of study to students who neither vote nor earn a living. The claim for history is that the student can meet the subject on an agreed-upon ground: Everything has a history. From there, the imaginative teacher may be able to help the student gain a personal involvement in the social studies that moves beyond mere exposure to a thoughtful engagement with the subject, which builds a basis for future formal study or for man's activity as a producing citizen.

The study of history is too often presentational. History might gain from the actual and immediate dialectic of contending economic and political systems, while remaining concerned with enlarging the past as well as vivifying the present. A historically based course in which economics and politics, like art and music and playing games, are seen as part of the living context of an individual's life should be the aim.

I have already discussed the importance of the arts in the lower schools. There is no reason why the arts should not be as important a part of secondary school studies as the sciences. Certainly they should be more than an "activity" tacked onto the last period of the day. For the kind of knowing one perceives in art is other than the kind of knowing I have been discussing. It is experiencing on the one hand, and training of the senses on the other. Although the facts connected with the creation of art—the names and dates and careers of artists, for example—can be an ornamental knowledge, and although art history is a legitimate subject, neither is concerned with the kind of knowing that an artist must possess.

I am talking here about the knowingness that causes a painter to put one color here and another color there. It is not intuitive choice necessarily, for the choice is ultimately made because one's senses are attuned to the many possibilities of color. Such attuning undoubtedly comes from experience with color, although it may seem to proceed immediately from some inner color sense denied the ordinary mortal. Furthermore, it seems to me that the kind of artistic insight that appears to consist of an immediate grasp of relationships of space, movement, and color, in the visual arts and the corresponding qualities in music or poetry, is a kind of knowing to which all secondary students should be exposed.

One basic condition of art, the arousing of a powerful emotion by what is an essential manipulation of the stuff of the physical universe, has implications for the general student as for the potential artist. It is not only aimed at the useful development of an aesthetic sense, but also at the development of the feelings themselves, at making the most of experiences in which artifice engages both the intellect and the emotions. Art is, indeed, one of the ways one sees the world feelingly.

Beyond developing the individual student's sensibilities, a proper attention to art in the secondary schools might lead to a happier relationship between art and society. Our culture, like most others, has seen the artist as too much of a magician, too much the creature of agonized devotion, which makes one wonder if art is worth the price. No one can do much to lessen that anguish, to decrease the demands art at the highest level of performance makes. Yet one could postulate the possibility of developing a knowingness that prizes imperfect creation and flawed perfection as well as the completely realized and flawless entertainment which defines art for the majority of the public. How loosely we use the word "artist" to describe every performer of prodigies. And how we fall to our knees before any narrow zealot's development of a skill, however peculiar, however limited. Thus we push art further toward the wax museum or the sideshow and keep it from being the enlarging experience it should be. Thus narrowed, art never brings the participant to the point where what is felt enhances and is enhanced by what is thought, where one grows in two kinds of knowing.

The vexing problem of foreign language is the last I'll treat in these conjectures about what is worth knowing. The interest in foreign language study in America seems to go up and down in almost exact correspondence with America's position in the world. A recent study shows pretty much what one might expect: Interest in foreign language study picked up greatly during and shortly after World War II, declined sharply by the beginning of the fifties, then gained renewed attention with the Korean War and the cold war. What this shows is basic to a consideration of language study: Necessity is by far the greatest taskmaster in learning a foreign language, the United States does not provide the ever-present necessity that fosters the acquiring of a second language, and, other factors aside, learning a second language, however one goes about it, is probably wasteful of human energies—that is, one world language would save everyone time.

As basic as these considerations are, they can and probably should be set aside. Foreign language study, it must be acknowledged, will always proceed with difficulty in the United States, and we do not possess a one-language world, nor are we likely to arrive at one. A case for foreign language study might be made outside the argument for use, which dominates all other arguments. I choose to suggest that case here, because I am not convinced that a second language for the general student is a very sound investment. I also think the utilitarian argument tends to obscure the interest and merit that language study has in its own right. The sense of order that a study of language can help develop has already been mentioned. The sense of another culture that study of a foreign language helps develop is also a sound argument.

Principally, I would add that language study, like history, can be fruitful in enlarging the context in which an adolescent finds himself. Begun early, when the oral acquaintance with a language seems to proceed with maximum ease, the developing study of language might get beyond the deadliness of grammar into the access to a country's written records that knowledge of a language affords. Much of this, it must be admitted, can be gained through translation. But it seems to me that in translation, the connection between what is learned and the person learning it is very tenuous. The wrestling with a language is a physical act of reading that must engage the mind in a way that translated facts cannot. This is not to be construed as an advocacy of difficulty for the sake of difficulty, but rather advocacy of a kind of study that enlarges the student's awareness of ways of knowing and heightens his sense of knowing something personally, feelingly, at first hand.

Obviously I am idealizing here and, in doing so, passing over the vast frustration that is bound to attend general language study. For we must remember that the United States is geographically isolated, which makes it difficult in most parts of the country to put language into the real context of another country's usage and custom. Not having that, we must temper our ideals with recognition of the difficulties of acquiring teachers of foreign languages, of arousing interest, even of providing useful employment of a second language once learned. No studies really help us here. We must support language study or not as our analysis of need and pleasure and utility gives us reason. For myself, it seems a thing worth knowing, but not worth forcing upon a reluctant or inept learner.

Ways of knowing, it seems to me, are in one sense more important than knowledge itself, although obviously a great reader not reading, a writer not writing, or a thinker not thinking may have no importance at all. Equally obvious, although often overlooked, is that the continuing development of such skills as facility in one's own language is closely related to the sense of worth the subjects create in the learner. This is at the center of the argument in favor of the classics in literature: that they make the physical act of reading worth the effort. It also happens to be the argument for tolerating the cheapest kind of book if the young reader takes a passionate interest in it. If such a book develops in the reader a strong desire to read, it justifies its worth more than the "classic" that discourages the act of reading.

Exciting, easy-to-read books should not have to be the choice in the secondary schools. By that time, the student's skill and desire should attract him to a great variety of books. Beyond that, the literature chosen should illuminate a powerful civilization in which the fullest development of the individual could take place. That

can be by Greek literature, to a lesser degree Latin, English literature certainly, and French, German, Spanish as well—but we need
not run down the names of nations with impressive national litera-
tures. I am merely affirming that one of the traditional aims of
literary study still holds true: an acquaintance with the past as a
civilization and with the individuals in it. Such an acquaintance
may be gained with one's own language alone. It might be gained
with a second language if one develops sufficient mastery in it.

Any consideration of foreign language as necessary learning
makes one consider whether it is worth as much as something else.
But that, of course, is what we must consider with all subjects we
would give high priorities to. Without arraying the various subjects
one against the other, I would suggest that there is a good deal that
need not be known, that should not be known in any sense of
immediate and exact recall. In fact, the whole attitude of schooling
as a training toward a maximum of diversified remembering tends
to slight knowledge as related to both thought and action. The
schools could probably demand less of actual knowing than they
do. A perfect knowing would include *not* knowing that which can
be easily looked up, filed away, carried around, that which has little
in the way of relationship or is stored away without such relationships established, that which needs to be forgotten, put away, for
the acquiring of other knowledge, and that which puts an end to
inquiry.

CHAPTER VII

PATTERNS

I DO NOT KNOW how much attention professional educators pay to two chapters in Alfred North Whitehead's *The Aims of Education,* "The Rhythm of Education" and "The Rhythmic Claims of Freedom and Discipline." The essays go back to the early 1920's, a time of relative naïveté in the study of child development. Yet I find it hard to see how the basic contentions these chapters make could be improved upon. More, even though they might be proven inexact in their assigning of the three stages of romance, precision, and generalization to certain times in the development of youth, they could hardly be disproven in their basic argument that some such stages exist and that recognition of such stages is vital to designing a pattern for education.

Whitehead himself voiced the necessary cautions: "I do not believe that there is any abstract formula which will give information applicable to all subjects, to all types of pupils, or to each individual pupil; except indeed the formula of rhythmic sway which I have been insisting on, namely, that in the earlier stage the progress requires that the emphasis be laid on freedom, and that in the later middle stage the emphasis be laid on the definite acquirement of allotted tasks." It is not the simplicity alone, nor the rightness of utterance, that attracts one to Whitehead's organizing principles for formal study. It is that, however one examines them, as a student studying, a teacher teaching, a person learning, they square with what one observes and feels about the way human beings learn. They are the commonplaces of a good teacher's educational theory. Interest is necessary to learning. An imprecise and undisciplined enthusiasm is characteristic of the first response to a subject in which one takes an interest. A grudging but necessary submission to close and exacting study is a condition for further learning whatever the interest and however great the enthusiasm. And once acquired, the precise facts, the conscious techniques, give way to a broad purposeful comprehension of the subject and mastery of the skill. It was put in even simpler terms by Whitehead himself: "My main position is that the dominant note of education at its beginning and at its end is freedom, but that there is an intermediate stage of discipline with freedom in subordination: Furthermore, that there is not one unique threefold cycle of freedom, discipline, and freedom, but that all mental development is composed of such cycles, and of cycles of such cycles."

Every teacher observes the presence of such cyclic development every day. But wish as one might, a teacher cannot just stimulate, guide, discipline, and free again. He must coax and wheedle and entertain, and, at times, stand on his head. And having gained attention, even interest, and despite the ridiculousness of his position, he must speak convincingly on some part of what he knows toward a general comprehension that neither he nor his students can precisely define. That, of course, is not all. Often, by some trick of sustaining a student's momentum or by promising a bright prospect ahead or by establishing a faith in having come thus far or by ropes or cudgels or prods, he must bring the student across forbidding ground that offers little satisfaction other than that of leaving it behind. And more and finally, in school and out, he must renew his faith in himself as being capable of these tasks and in these tasks as being worthwhile.

The skill a teacher requires is not far different from that required of a skilled symphony conductor: the sensitivity to the human instruments he deals with, the need to draw them out, whip them up, hold them back, bring out this voice and hush another, the rare ability to hear all the parts and yet retain a grasp of the larger whole toward which all are striving. And if the individual teacher faces an immense task, consider the difficulties in trying to fashion a system of education. Whitehead is, as always, both wise and helpful here. Two observations stand out, the first a positive one:

Education should consist in a continual repetition of such cycles. Each lesson in its minor way should form an eddy cycle issuing in its own subordinate process. Longer periods should issue in definite attainments, which then form the starting-grounds for fresh cycles. We should banish the idea of a mythical, far-off end of education. The pupils must be continually enjoying some fruition and starting afresh—if the teacher is stimulating in exact proportion to his success in satisfying the rhythmic cravings of his pupils.

The second is a negative observation that challenges two of the assumptions by which instruction is commonly organized: that easier subjects should precede the harder, and that subjects should be taken up in terms of their necessary antecedents. The uncritical application of the latter, Whitehead wrote, "in the hands of dull people with a turn for organization, produced in education the dryness of the Sahara."

These are my points of departure for discussing patterns of education, with particular emphasis upon the secondary schools. The claims of freedom and discipline are relevant to all stages of education, but secondary education seems to face the maximum of chaos in the student with the maximum of organization of the kind Whitehead deplored. Coming, as it does, between the excitement of beginning learning and the commitment to learning essential to a vocation, secondary education calls most desperately for the "definite attainments," the "starting grounds for fresh cycles," that Whitehead proposed. Coming after the acquisition of basic skills and before the extension and application of specific knowledge, its organization is conditioned by fixed beliefs in subjects that should have been prepared for before or that should be more extensively prepared for after. I have already pointed out Whitehead's refusal to accept such beliefs. Yet the doctrine is maintained despite the superior truth of the contrary principle, that no teacher can safely assume that any pupil has learned anything previously about any subject. Perhaps such a truth easily escapes the attention of the elementary or secondary school teachers who see few of their pupils beyond a single grade. Conversely, it is a truth painfully evident to a college teacher, who often finds himself once again facing students who should have learned, must have learned, could not have avoided learning, vital truths that he himself had taught.

But yielding to such a principle is no great cause for woe. It is, rather, an invitation to abandon the idea of learning anything once and for all and then proceeding contentedly on to the next fixed lesson. Only naïve teachers bewail what the wisdom of an experienced teacher freely accepts: Any large amount of learning that has supposedly taken place does not remain to be drawn upon at a later time. Learning is, once again, far other than money stored in a vault, hay in a loft. It is more like ice stored in a tub under canvas on a summer afternoon. Before long it will slip away, leaving a mere fraction of its bulk floating in the rising waters. So our learning leaves us, the greater portion of it quickly losing its form, part of it remaining but not in the same form in which it was gathered or for the same purposes. But, as we can refreeze ice, so can we bring back into a solid form much of the learning that has slipped away. We can best do so by purposely forgetting that anything has been learned and going over the old lessons again.

Life is essentially repetitious. If it were not so, surely we could not find our way. From the routines of eating, sleeping, and sex to the performance of monthly and yearly duties, little that we do is new. A great deal of what seems new—most, certainly—belongs to the early years, so that we think of learning too exclusively as learning anew and treat repetition as less of a virtue that it is. Too often the public school pupil is not only encouraged to develop his abilities and inclinations to learn but is encouraged to think of learning as a thing he should "have," something he can have and then always possess. School becomes isolated as the time for learning and is expected to provide the stored-up fat upon which one lives for the rest of one's life.

That seems too weighty an obligation for secondary schools to carry and serves to slight the later years as a time for learning. We might consider learning less in bulk in the secondary years, think more about what we are learning, and make a maximum number of relationships between the various aspects of learning and the life surrounding them. We might leave more out to be encompassed later, might implant ways and habits of learning that would not only carry on into further formal study but into life beyond those years. The pattern that might emerge from an application of such principles would be highly repetitive, but it would be repetition of the kind one finds in music, where a theme returns clearly recognizable but with sufficient elaboration or modification to make it seem new.

A high school student might gain a more coherent picture of where he stands and how he got there if he were to have a historically centered humanistic education deliberately and wisely repetitive rather than strictly sequential. Beginning at the beginning and working to the end of anything implies that there is an entity to be grasped, which heightens the possibility that a second exposure will begin at a level advanced over the first. Thus one might imagine, in the grossest form, a literary education that began with the broadest of surveys, repeated with increased focus, repeated again from perhaps a different direction, repeated again with the focus sharper still, the direction still different, on into the pursuit of a graduate degree.

On the first run-through, one might learn to pronounce a name, find a book, compare a date here with one learned elsewhere. And, of course, one would be exposed to a good deal of literature of a varied sort and of indubitable worth (possibly even of high interest). It could be tightly bound to history, but be another way of seeing a world develop.

The second time the same material was approached, language might be the center of attention, the scope of the total course. The time would be spent in closer reading, an accumulation on the bare bones encountered before.

A third time might concentrate on forms. The scope of the course would be more focused but still broad enough to enable the student to see again the beginnings, developments, and achievements set forth in the previous courses.

Each of these returns to a basic subject would be one of the cycles designed to answer the student's general need for a sense of attainment, a fresh beginning. It would be exciting in its exploration, yet would not force the student into entirely unfamiliar territory. In loose ways, such patterns prevail now—in the English curriculum, for example. The broad survey of English literature takes up one year in many high schools, the American literature survey another. In college the sophomore survey is somewhat out of fashion but still often to be found. In advanced work, students meet the survey again, albeit in a more specialized form. But this rather haphazard repetition is not what I have in mind. It often creates an attitude of belligerency in the students' response to college instruction: They insist that they've *had* English literature, or Shakespeare, or Transcendentalism. The fact is, of course, they've not *had* any of these at all, and the school does them a disservice in encouraging them to treat learning as something they have had. For that reason alone, a cyclic pattern that encourages the acceptance of repetition as essential to learning seems preferable to a linear one.

The cyclic pattern also provides more places for meaningful stopping—consolidation for the successful student, termination for the markedly unsuccessful. The general student, good or bad, could be served to the point of diminishing returns, in terms of his interest and in terms of where he is headed. Rather than four years of required English, one might settle for one year for some, two for others, a full four for many (since such a large percentage goes on into college or university). What this means is an education with a backbone of literature and history, both conceived broadly, and neither forced upon a student whose intellectual or vocational development inclines him to other paths. It is one that has some chance of bringing a student back to such learning without the complete disorientation that adversely affects adults plunged into a subject common to lower school study that comes upon them as completely new. Above all, it is the filling out of a form that has been seen, can be shown, if only in crudest outline, and that can give the student the pleasure of creating for himself a piece of sculpture, however imperfect. For, it seems to me, secondary education must provide such chances for students whose selves are exploding in many directions to gain various places from which to stand and survey themselves. Much the better if they have a part in constructing the vantage points.

Finally, one is brought to a recognition, even a retention, of matters of primary importance, rather than exposed to matters that are of widely varying importance and are easily forgotten. The sense of a large design is directly and increasingly placed against the details out of which a portion of the whole, the whole itself, ultimately grows. Sensitivity to the way literature works—the current emphasis upon analytical study of the work itself—is kept connected with why it works as it does and how its method is affected by its attempts to see and present life during widely differing historical periods. I have already argued the case for a literary education. Here I am suggesting an overall pattern that might serve an education that can both break off at almost any point and go on into advanced formal study and beyond.

I do not think this kind of circling in varying and generally narrowing circles is necessarily dull, but any method that involves repetition risks becoming dull. As I have suggested, without particularizing or exemplifying, exact repetition is, of course, not what the student needs, nor what he should get, even with the same teacher. A student gets diversity in the mere fact of going over old ground at a different time of day or in company with a different group or for a quite different purpose.

But whatever one does to enliven repeated lessons, one may succumb to dullness, and education should not be dull—exasperating, unsettling, demanding, but not dull. Let us consider essential ways of countering the possibility that the pattern proposed here will become dull. The first is selectivity. "A certain ruthless definiteness," Whitehead wrote, "is essential in education." In terms of a student's mastery of a skill, that ruthless definiteness is much a part of a skillful teacher's ability to select from all that might be known the things that the student must know precisely to reach defined objectives at a stage of a subject's development. Such skill is most engagingly displayed by the superior teacher of a foreign language. The mediocre teacher, having no resources beyond a text in grammar, a supply of drill exercises, and a smattering of cultural facts about the country, covers everything equally, spreading out discussion and drill into every minute of class time, treating each point with equally exacting thoroughness—in effect, spreading out the dullest of covers on the smoothest of beds. The superior teacher leaves the contours in, the sheets rumpled, the covers tossed, and makes the most of excitement aroused by such shapes as fancy enlarges upon. Yet such a teacher must have the most orderly of minds, must know precisely what is of first and second and third importance. Knowing that, he may, in any one class period, concentrate a relatively small amount of time upon matters of first importance: matters that must be learned, and no nonsense about it and no wasting of the teacher's time in doing it. The rest of the time can be spent in creating the interest in the subject that will ensure that the student does come down hard on the essentials and is ready for the next lesson the next day. It is a painless kind of learning of what can be the dullest of subjects, but it takes a power of selection only given to those who have a full grasp of the language and a corresponding largeness of mind. Such a teacher can drive the most satisfactory of bargains between the discipline necessary to master selected pieces of information and the eventual pleasures to be derived from exercising a general skill about which the particulars have been forgotten.

Selectivity is a matter not only of what must be known but of what has maximum chance of arousing the student's interest. Here the skill exercised by the superior teacher is somewhat the reverse of that power of relevant selection just discussed. The trick—and teaching is full of tricks—is not to extract from the subject the essential points to be learned by disciplined study and to reduce the amount of time expended on them, but to extract from the student's frame of reference specific interests that will give the broad dimensions of the subject sufficient relevance to make it worth the student's disciplined application.

Subjects that appear to be basically informational in character —history, for example—require this kind of selectivity. At its weakest, drawing upon the student's frame of reference might consist of such practical exercises as conducting parliamentary discussions about revising the senior class constitution. At its most ambitious, it might consist of beginning with the commonplace observation that for most adolescents the questions of freedom and authority are pressing, immediate, and exposed in a wide variety of confrontations. To move from there to the many aspects of history in which such abstractions take concrete historical form would be one step. But to move there without making the student self-conscious about his actualities having a relationship to the imponderables of history would be another. To take those two steps and even to a small degree to create in the student sufficient excitement in the broad historical questions to get him to invest some energy in the particulars would be what this kind of selectivity aims for.

Variety is another way of countering the essential dullness of repeated patterns. There is a great deal of repetition already in the school program. English, aside from the study of literature, again and again goes over the same ground. One of the great advantages of the new approaches to grammar—structural linguistics and transformational grammar—is quite other than their merits in more accurately describing the language. It is quite simply that they give a new way of talking about old matters. The excitement generated by linguistic studies in college is surely in part traceable to that. For year after year, students who end up as English majors are exposed to grammar. When a study comes along that deals excitingly with what previously was repetitiously dull, no wonder students respond to it.

Variety is as essential to any satisfactory pattern of learning as repetition. The best teachers are often distinguished by their ability to show a many-sided nature, to be serious when seriousness is effec-

tive and joyous when joy is. The formal patterning of education unfortunately produces a formal patterning of a teacher's demeanor,
developed to its most unattractive extent in the officialness, the
good-fellowness, the sternness, and the fawningness sometimes
found as an identifying mark of principals and superintendents.
Such demeanor is not only unattractive in itself but unattractive in
what it reveals about the willingness to accept certain patterns of
official behavior that lack the essential variety one expects of un-
official human beings, teachers or not.

Pushed to its extreme, variety becomes surprise. And surprise
should be put down as a kind of subversive principle allowed to
operate freely within the deliberately unpatterned portion of a
school program. The best way to encourage surprise is probably
to give secondary teachers more freedom to indulge their human
moods and whims than they are commonly given. There is too
much of a tendency in the secondary schools to make proper behavior the end of schooling. There is so little tolerance of singular
behavior that group misbehavior goes on both inside and outside
the school and is often more destructive for being so rigidly
guarded against. I am not countenancing knife attacks or mass as-
saults—the kind of surprise that is a terrifying part of a teacher's life
in some schools. Rather I ask for the milder kinds of surprise that
interrupt routine when a wise teacher thinks it might be well to
let up at this point or when there might be something going on outside more worth looking at than whatever is within. This kind of
surprise is a kind of fire drill, incorporated into the program at
sporadic and unexpected times, not to save lives but to save students' minds from the drying up that accompanies uninterrupted
routine.

Education at all levels and in all times struggles with the formal patterns into which it falls. Philosophic considerations are
forced to compromise with the demands of space and time and
teachers and parents. The public schools, for a variety of reasons,
some of them good ones, pay great attention to the regulation of
education. In the colleges, educational administration probably
leads both business administration and public administration in
the time devoted to looking at itself. Although I am suspicious of
much that calls itself educational administration, I respect the
difficulties of administering a system of education as large and as

ambitious as this country's. The rest of this chapter will confront some of the specific matters with which educational administration is concerned.

Let me begin with the observation that almost any pattern is superior to no pattern—the pedant's insistence on getting the children indoors and drilling them day after day is better than merely letting learning come at random. Yet neither extreme is satisfactory, and neither can be sustained for very long. The first will sooner or later make the children revolt, and the second will inevitably fall into patterns of the children's own devising.

The current pattern of public school education depends upon the expectation created in the young and the patterns of work going on around them. The five-day school week in America seems to fit the pattern of current American life very well and is probably preferable to the six-day school week found in some other countries. Similarly, although the school day could be lengthened, its current span is convenient because the child's work world is less imprisoning than the adult's. Both children and parents—fathers at least—profit from that fact.

Neither the week nor the day is under much scrutiny in the current search to make more of the hours available to public schooling. It seems obvious that children need more free time than adults and that teachers need time to do essential work that cannot be done during class hours. Considering the after-hours work teaching requires, we do well to maintain a nine to twelve and one to four school day. Under the pressure of "enriching" the curriculum (a particularly mealy term, it strikes me), some high schools are beginning to tack on a good deal both before the regular school day and after. Much of this enrichment comes disguised as voluntary activity. As immediately praiseworthy as it seems to be, it may not seem so after further reflection. Very little that goes on under the aegis of the public schools is voluntary in any strict sense. Participation in athletics is one part the instinctive pleasure of physical movement and bodily contact and many parts personal, parental, and community pressure. The same can be said of strictly academic extra-hours activities. The placing of language study, for example, outside the school hours puts it in a dubious position as to the value the school places on it and dubious also as to what learning takes place.

Subjects worth learning are worth including in the regular day.

Ideally, if studies are to be continued in somewhat formal ways after school hours, they should go on because an in-school interest has pushed them on past the closing hour. Few after-hours study activities are of this kind. Even specifically extracurricular activities in the high school are often forced. Such activities do grow out of the student's need to identify with smaller groups than a school class, to satisfy certain physical and psychic promptings, to assert his own power of selection against what has been forced upon him. Clubs, gangs, fraternities, and sororities are as hard to put down as fads of dress and grooming. Few associations of this kind have much to do with the program of studies. Although in the past some academic societies had an avowed academic purpose, even then drinking seems to have brought more young men into extracurricular societies than scholarship.

In a way, current extracurricular activities are defensive gestures, protecting the individual's feelings from the discipline of the intellect and protecting the personal right to assemble from the society's growing insistence that it can and should impose group behavior. Yet from the individual student's and the individual teacher's perspective, extracurricular activities are often the most wearying part of the school's routine. The student who gets embroiled in them substitutes activity for thought, and the one who is left out substitutes thought for activity. The teachers, almost to a man and woman, deplore the required after-school-hours time that goes into such activities as taking tickets at ball games, supervising dances, and making appearances at school nights and assemblies. In a small-town high school (many of which have been consolidated into large regional high schools) such activities are traditionally the center of community interest. For all involved they furnish something to do. In a busy urban or suburban locality, that justification may prove to be more an irritation. A parent may be proud to watch his children (or someone else's) perform, be entertained, or entertain themselves, but he may be dubious about the worth of the activity itself.

Take, for example, the art of baton twirling. It seems a highly limited art, a highly artificial one. That is, it is not very likely that a child will see a broomstick lying around or break a branch off a tree and start twirling it. Baton twirling is, rather, the outgrowth of loneliness or boredom, as the cop on the beat, having no criminals to thump, turns to twirling his night stick. By comparison with such a spontaneous natural action as running a stick along a picket fence, baton twirling is a forced, artificial skill.

Artificiality is not grounds for condemnation, although it may be grounds for suspicion. Running, jumping, vaulting, throwing— all would be done outside formal patterns if no formal patterns existed. But baton twirling is an activity that makes one wonder whether the participant is being forced into the activity or whether the activity is truly at his or her pleasure. By now, of course, the child growing into baton-twirling has no choice. Its appeal is ir- resistible. Spangles and sexual strut having augmented its essential phallic appeal, it has become the chief aim of countless girls from five to (I would guess) twenty-five. Like most other manufactured products, it has a built-in obsolescence. I suspect that few pro- fessional football clubs have retirement plans for twirlers beyond their prime. Considering the great numbers of young girls fiercely engaged in acquiring a professional skill and the small number of enterprises that call for baton twirling, the activity has an appall- ing narrowness of opportunity. A church tenor's future seems secure by comparison.

There is really only one thing to do with a baton after one's twirling days are over, and that should not have been put off so long. Schools, in their collective wisdom, should have seen baton twirling as something other even than pole vaulting, soccer, social dancing, or work on the yearbook. Instead, they did what Ameri- can schools are constantly doing: Against what can be defended as overwhelming pressures because they did overwhelm, they cre- ated a dubious art by making baton twirling part of sponsored extracurricular activities. In this instance, the schools had much more than a passive role. There was a positive furtherance of the activity in incorporating it into music and athletics, making all three public spectacles representing the struggle of the body against the mind, of outer display against inner development, of the community against the school it finds in its midst.

My point in mentioning baton twirling is that it fosters the overdevelopment of a crude kind of manual dexterity while ren- dering sex flashily attractive but sterile. Such forces are perversely anti-learning, anti-education. Yet the school takes them on, as it has taken on many similar community activities. And though I began by agreeing that a school's basic pattern probably does well in being compatible with the society's patterns, I think it should prove superior to such patterns whenever it can, and superior too to the society's loosely examined ideas of what it wants. The school's chief obligation is to inform and shape students' tasks in terms of what best serves their fundamental concern—learning—rather than to be merely responsive to what the community would have it do.

I have no quarrel with the basic pattern of learning as custom has developed it. Yet within that pattern, some things might be done to make more of what goes on within school hours as well as what goes on after school hours. At one extreme from the American pattern of schoolgoing is that of Rabelais' Abbey of Thélème, conceived of as Utopian in a time when learning (at least in the way of historical generalizations we make) was never more exciting. The Renaissance was probably a time much like our own in the excitement that learning could engender, the worlds it was opening up. Under such a system, the students engaged in educational activity more rigorous than that of any of our private and public schools. The day began at four in the morning. The lessons went on while the student dressed, ate, and performed his bodily functions. By reading, writing, discussion, recitation, repetition, and review, the subject matter was drummed into the pupil's consciousness. Although the daily program of formal studies was relieved by free sports and attention to practical arts and crafts, the main relief from "this violent bodily and mental tension" came from the free days once a month, spent in the nearby villages and countryside. "There they spent the whole day enjoying themselves to their heart's content, sporting and merrymaking, drinking toast for proffered toast, playing, singing, dancing, tumbling about or loafing in some fair meadow, turning sparrows out of their nests, bagging quail and fishing for frogs and crayfish." Something of this pattern has found favor often in the course of history and still prevails in some schools—those where mingling of the sexes is regarded as detrimental to education and those that are still rigidly governed by religious discipline.

At the other extreme is the kind of seemingly informal education associated with the Socratic teachings. Wherever young men were desirous of learning, they sought out a master and gained his teachings pretty much as he lived, in the marketplace and in quiet spots and in gatherings in late afternoon or evening. As I have mentioned, such a personal confrontation was not necessarily unstructured, was not lacking in a very demanding kind of mental discipline. Yet it was strongly dependent on individual inclination and must frequently have lost out to other attractions. Alcibiades, for all his admiration of Socrates, must have been a desultory pupil, far too involved in too many activities and far too much at the mercy of his own brilliance to have been an exemplar of what the Socratic method could accomplish.

We could characterize these extremes by saying that one follows a pattern imposed by the institution, the other moves in a pattern largely maintained by the person. American education, I think it is fair to say, is institutionalized much more than it is personal. Yet, probably because personal development has such a high place in American ideals, the institutionalization in the schools tends to minimize the rigid discipline that might run counter to personal desire and seldom permits the full freedom that might be extended as a relief from rigor. No American school is so rigorous that a day off provides an overwhelming sense of refreshment. The extra-curricular activities, the social emphasis in the school, and the comparatively mild day-by-day discipline may dull both work and play. But on the other hand our schools are certainly regulated. It is quite impossible for a teacher to act very Socratic in the administrative setting most schools provide.

Without arguing for one or the other as the ideal, one might draw from both to suggest innovations that are, in fact, being put into practice with increasing frequency. A pattern for a perfect education would follow some patterns strictly yet be flexible when it was wise to be so, and it would rely heavily on repetition and orderly development and yet take advantage of surprise. It would keep in mind the large patterns of life, both to use them and to show how to enhance them. As to formal patterns, the schools could seek more interesting patterns than those imposed by class hour, class day, and school term. For example, the presentational aspect of a literary or historical subject might be done as one sees movies—once or twice a week to a large audience of students from many grades. The classroom teachers could well use such time, assuming they had previously been exposed to the presentation. The absence of such free time for teachers is a conspicuous shortcoming of most school programs. Immediately after the presentation, the classroom teacher would engage students in a discussion, with the intent of encouraging observation to become thought and for as long a time as interest could be sustained. This might be followed by a period of free time, during which the student would be given a chance to write down his thoughts, perhaps to be fashioned into a polished essay at a later time. Such an easily imagined scheme would play hob with half a day's schedule, and yet would move in the direction of getting students to think and write about a subject at the maximum points of stimulation. In an inflexible sequence of hourly classes, too much learning is fragmented, and the class hours do more to shape the subject than the content itself. Some subjects should be allowed to grow, as, for example, in the science laboratory, where flexibility within the general schedule might mean pushing on for longer periods of time, temporarily slighting other subjects but ultimately enhancing learning.

Some subjects, like foreign languages, mathematics, grammar and usage, and others involving the development of habit-formed skills, require daily exposure and practice. But surely we are approaching an age when various mechanical devices will do much of the work of drill—asking simple questions, requiring answers, and correcting on the spot. One might envision all of this kind of work tucked into small portions of the individual student's time— time that might be taken from the larger blocks reserved for subject-matter studies, as the student felt he could do it. Again, with the variety of recording devices at our disposal, the individual has a much greater chance to be left free to pursue a subject that occupies his whole attention and still be able to keep pace with the general progress of the class.

An imaginative secondary school program might be made up of definite goals to be achieved within roughly defined periods of time stretching from a number of weeks to a year or more. Such goals might include the writing of a historical essay demonstrating the power to find material and relate it and put it down, or the mastery of a certain level of concepts in mathematics, or the achievement of certain technical competencies in music or art, or the understanding and applying of a fundamental thesis of economics.

The school program would define these various goals in terms of overall aims, but would not have to insist on a uniform level of accomplishment in all of them for all students. Many of its goals would be briefer than a semester's length, and the variety and kind of work required would give more students a chance for genuine though partial accomplishments. The goals that involved work in one subject or related subjects for even longer periods than a single course would give students a chance for consolidation of formal studies or for accomplishments that created the sense of personal rather than academic direction. Both short-range and long-range goals could serve to increase the chances of a student's being moved along by his own interest, of his and his teacher's finding time to think, of his moving somewhat at his own pace and the urgings of his enthusiasms, and of his developing his own bent to ultimately useful ends.

A useful adjunct to such a plan, a necessary addition to many existing school programs, would be increased use of the summer. This is not to put the teacher on a twelve-month year, although a twenty-five-percent increase in salary would make the teacher's career more attractive than it is now. Rather the teacher might find herself or himself getting his own thoughts stimulated by using his students in an imaginative way to arrive at learning that the more orderly pattern of the regular year precludes. Summer could be a great time to push on with enthusiasm fired earlier in the year or to catch up with subjects that had to be neglected while pursuits of the first magnitude of interest were being pursued. And if we were thinking of goals achieved rather than of units presented, then the less rigidly patterned and voluntary summer program might prove more valuable for some students than the regular year.

And that is the point for American education, which without sacrificing high general aims attempts to embrace all students. Facing the diversity of the students who come to it, its first gesture is either to force that collection of individuals into a pattern that begins by breaking down individuality or to diversify itself and loosely and inadequately accommodate the wide range of interests. The pattern of American education is shaped by the necessity of dealing with so many students for a set number of hours, days, and weeks and of accommodating both the general aims and the individual interests.

The highest kind of educational administrative achievement is one that keeps the enterprise operating despite its rules. Rather than just watching over rules and regulations, the wise administrator should constantly be pushing his people to operate to the limits of such rules and even beyond. One might think of a perfect

educational design as a marvelous machine that must create with
its own components the most splendid and varied and exciting
kind of activity. Such a machine would have many eccentrics,
would have built-in random motions beginning at odd points in a
cycle and going to other odd points. It would have its large cycles
and its smaller ones, its whirlings and jerkings and vibratings,
creating a fear that chaos is upon us, but never quite arriving
there. It would, of course, have many buttons and levers and cir-
cuits controlled by human hands. Only those daring enough to
try them without fully comprehending the results could bring out
the glory of the machine. Once begun, it could not be shut down
completely, although it could be kept in motion only by the positive efforts of the administrator. He could be busy or passive, as
he chose, but since the glory would be in proportion to his movements, much would depend upon his guesses and his knowing,
some on his theory, most on his observations of things set in motion here that might have relationship to things there. That, I
think, is what a school should be, and the community could
hardly resist flocking around to gaze in awe.

PART THREE

TOWARD A LIFE
OF ONE'S OWN

CHAPTER VIII

A MIND, HEART, AND LIFE
OF ONE'S OWN

DESPITE EFFORTS to bring college and university education
and public school education closer together—pridefully
called "articulation" by professional educators—the two
still remain apart. That is as it should be. For going to college
affords the student another chance to feel the excitement of learning that he felt the first day he entered a schoolroom. The danger
is not in causing some the painful difficulties of adjustment, but
in allowing the many to feel neither pain nor excitement. Of
course beginning college work can be confusing, frustrating, even
defeating, but where it is most so, the fault is not in the nature
of college learning but in the nature of the institutions supposedly
concerned with it. Any entry into a life of one's own has its false
starts, rebuffs, loneliness, boredom. Compared with striking out
immediately after high school into useful work in a strange city,
going to college is a slow and easy entry into adult life. When
colleges and universities fail, it is not in orientation, but in what
the student is supposed to be oriented to. The difficulties of registration that continue to confound students and administrators
at most universities are symbolic of too much of what the modern
college represents to the entering student: jostling for a place near
the feast of learning and getting more exercise of feet and neck
and elbow than of the mind.

By now, after twenty years of increasing demand for college
education, many colleges and universities are engaged in a large
and wasteful enterprise of post-high-school, pre-dropout education.
The fact that for large numbers, and with increasing expenditures
of public funds, such education is being moved off established
campuses to new ones called junior colleges does not change its

basic character. Neither the major universities who do not really want freshmen and sophomores of the kind and number they get, nor the public schools, which anxiously hope two more years will accomplish what they apparently could not, have worked out a philosophy or a program for the junior college. There seems widest agreement that the junior college should not be strictly college preparatory and that it should not be strictly vocational. The acceptable compromise is the "comprehensive" junior college, defensible in theory, possible in practice, and fairly shabby as an intellectual enterprise when looked at closely.

Where the colleges and universities still take care of grades thirteen and fourteen, test batteries, section instructors, and special programs for deficients all conspire to put each student in the midst of a peer group as undistinguished as himself. Without really considering why these students are enrolled in college, the registration machinery puts them where they can get a maximum of diversified and traditional college work at a minimum of cost. A little history, a little English, a little mathematics, a little science, a little art answers for post-high-school learning, plus, in most schools, an extensive acquaintance with closed-circuit television. The only heartening aspect of the conditions that mark the beginning of post-high-school education is to be found in the high schools themselves, where various programs for superior students have begun to take over many of the customary studies of freshman year, many of the texts, and some of the approach and vigor formerly associated with beginning college work. The first years of college have been left higher and drier than ever—not very high, as a matter of fact, but certainly dry. It is as if a finance company had repossessed most of the furniture on the lower floor, while everyone was too busy upstairs to notice it was gone. Some of the old faithful employees still wander around. Some new secretaries and file clerks hover over the file cabinets that have not yet been carted off. The students come in, are given forms to fill out, and are left to mill around until such time as they may be called upstairs. That, as I see it, is about the position of freshman and sophomore work in many of our large universities.

Getting back the furniture and some semblance of a staff with authority, responsibility, and imagination is one of the major problems now facing higher education. Nevitt Sanford, in that formidable description of the college scene *The American College,* writes:

Typically, freshmen arrive on the campus filled with enthusiasm, with eager anticipation of the intellectual experiences they are about to have. By the end of the year, not a few have dropped out and a large proportion of the remainder are ready for what in the eastern colleges is known as "the sophomore slump."

The point is sometimes made that existing arrangements serve well to "weed out" inferior students. At some state universities, indeed, there is weeding out with a bulldozer. But nobody knows how many potential learners go out along with the unable and the indifferent; nor do we know to what extent remaining in college is a matter of gamesmanship or capacity to adapt oneself to conventional pressures.

Existing programs are easy to criticize. What are we to do? I would suggest that, where our foremost concern is with the development of the personality, the major aim of the freshman year should be to *win* the student to the intellectual enterprise.

Surely that must be the aim of a university in introducing itself to its students. With the current imbalance in higher education— the major effort being expended on upper-division and graduate students—it is the task that is most neglected. It is a grievous waste, not of a faculty's time and energy, but more of the student's mind and body at a time when the excitement of starting out, beginning again, might be caught and used to animate years of learning.

That is what I most fear about the junior college movement. The junior college, partly because higher education in its current temper does not want to deal with it and partly because the community very much wants to have it in its midst, invariably moves into the public school's orbit. Without criticizing the aims and attainments of the public school, one can say that it is organized toward the community, toward the life one has had, toward the stable world as it is. Such an orientation is precisely what higher education should not have, cannot afford to have. And although one may argue that twenty is as good an age as eighteen in which to begin thinking about a life of one's own, it strikes me that the lessons of mind and heart to be learned the hard way, the only satisfactory way—on one's own—are too valuable to be put off. And put off they will be if the junior college years, like the freshman-sophomore years in a university, are simply a prolonging of education for all. It is better, as I will argue later, that students get some years of acquaintance with the real world and then return to a higher education worth the name than that they stay on in formal education not markedly different from what has gone before.

As Sanford has defined the college's initial task as that of winning the student to the intellectual enterprise, I would define its overall task as helping the student develop a mind, heart, and life of his own. Throughout its long course, a perfect education would strive to see the world feelingly. At no time is this more important than in the years when one becomes conscious that what one does now bears upon all that follows, when the ardors of feeling are not yet curbed and the mind not yet turned into an instrument, when the world *can* be changed if one feels deeply enough and finds the means to do it—when, in short, one is acutely aware of a self being created and has some hand in the process.

By these rough measures we might judge a college. To the degree that it wins the student to the intellectual enterprise it has begun well and as it conspicuously contributes to each student's development of a mind, heart, and life of his own, it succeeds. The first phrase, though general, is clear enough, and I will turn to the subject again in a later chapter. But what, you ask, do I mean by the latter? Any mind, any heart, any life, so long as it is one's own?

Obviously I don't mean that, although I might argue that one has to make any part of his education his own before it becomes valuable either to oneself or to others. For developing a self or even a sense of self is no easy task, particularly in a culture nominally Christian that tends to support the restraint of conscience, the measure of otherness, against an assertive and aggressive selfishness. The college and university, were it not obsessed with busyness, might provide the opportunity for and respect for contemplation that is necessary for the development of both self and selflessness. For although the university is greatly preoccupied with things, getting and having and spending, it still provides its temporary residents some chance to be free from the harassment of things, and some freedom from things is a necessary condition for the search for self.

To be sure, American college campuses are glutted with cars and many American students run frantically back and forth from work to school, but even at worst the student is not quite under the same pressures to consume as he will be later, if only because his temporary status works against accumulation. And although student life is still characterized by chronic financial crisis, yet even that is not of the order of what is to come, beginning in paying for the education one has had and ending in paying for the education one's children will need. The poor student is still a possibility, relieved from his want by scholarships, part-time work, and deferred-interest loans. The casual dress on American campuses is more than fad. It is a manifestation of the acceptance of economic stringencies. Canvas shoes, khaki pants, cotton shirts, skirts and sweaters, and jeans are as cheap as workmen's denims and probably last longer. Although college students will become the preeminent consumers of the land, during their college years at least they can and do exist less ridden by things than they will probably ever be again.

That this seems to be still a characteristic of American academic life is greatly to our credit. Although college students represent an upper-level group (even now the ten students one finds in grade school become fewer than four entering college, fewer than two earning a degree), and although money is still a barrier to too many students, a large part of academic life takes place somewhat free of the grinding sense of material possessions and desires that affects all other American life. Freed from that, however temporarily and artificially, the student has a chance of seeing his or her developing self as something other than the provider or manager or procurer or begetter or accumulator he will so obsessively become. Given a chance to form a conception of self larger than what necessity will force on him, he may escape something of the devastating irony that accompanies one's realization that he carries his ton of goods only to the grave.

Another condition useful to the development of a sense of self is the diversity that colleges provide amidst a general equality. In a large sense, colleges do not foster a populist or socialist kind of equality. College students are sensitive to differences in economic and social standing within a college and from one college to another. And yet college values are sufficiently diversified, sufficiently held by the whole group, sufficiently scattered among the group, to give more of an appearance of equality within the college than prevails outside. This is particularly true in large colleges and universities, where this equality resides in anonymity, in the large mass to which the large university seems constrained to direct its efforts. So, although that large middle can be depressing to the teacher (and to the student caught in it if he becomes sufficiently awakened by his college experience to look at himself) it does provide a flat background against which a perceptive student may create a distinctive self.

The student finds himself—as long as he avoids the post office and doesn't run completely out of money—freed from his place in a stable world in which differences are pronounced. Rich and poor alike voluntarily and with a sense of relief give up the identity that community and family have placed on them. Part of this phenomenon, the most indestructible part perhaps, has to do with the time at which one goes to college, with the physical and psychic separation of the late adolescent from his family. But part too has to do with the kind of achievements colleges respect and with the fact that these achievements are connected to a real world coming into being rather than to a past world of someone else's making. There is plenty of family consciousness among college students, whether at the most expensive schools, where someone always turns out to be wealthier than someone else, or at state universities, where sorority and fraternity systems still seem to operate heavily in favor of existing family status. But, as a relatively poor boy like Scott Fitzgerald could enjoy a familiarity with Harvey Firestone at Princeton before World War I, so thousands of poor boys and a good many rich ones mingle in a temporary anonymity in colleges and universities today. Present Princeton undergraduates are probably aware that although the library is Harvey Firestone's, one of its great attractions is the Fitzgerald collection in the Rare Book Room.

A student's official family and community position is set aside when he enters college. His fixed position in adolescent society, his place in the high school stratification, is no longer relevant. The immediate result is a need to establish an identity. Often this causes adjustment problems. Far more often it forces the student to begin to create a fresh sense of self, one that lies outside the one given to him, forced upon him, by the world that has surrounded him since birth.

All this is of increased importance in our time, when college is becoming the most marked single way of breaking from the home and striking out alone. For boys, at least, and even for girls, it is an exciting time, fraught with peril as all exposure is, but a time when the human being, like some partially opened flower, begins to feel the sun pouring in upon him. By the time the student comes to take his freedom for granted, he may be on the way to recognizing that he has some years to create for himself the kind of person his adolescence began to acquaint him with. The earlier dreaming, wishing, self-heroics, give way, if the college is what it should be, to real possibilities and ways to bring them about. If the college is not what it should be, then the student's momentary glimpse of self may cease to interest him and he may take on any one of a number of selves that college life, like any institutionalized life, is more than eager to provide. The student needs to fight against such an easy acceptance, the college needs to fight against its tendency to stamp its impress upon him. The impress of a good college should be of another kind. The distinguishable selves formed by students led to fashion such selves begin to define the college. The impress is back on the college fully as much as forward on the student.

Finally, the colleges provide varied examples of lives worth living at a time when the effort can be made, may be made, to live them. The most depressing fact of public school education is that it provides but one compelling image: the sports hero. There is nothing else that so gains the total school's commitment, that offers immediate rewards of status and achievement, that takes some natural skill and develops it to fulfillment. It might not be possible for any high school to avoid such an image, considering the strong interest in the physical in adolescence. But the fault is not the presence of the sports hero, but the absence of other compelling models. When a boy is captured by the image of the sports hero, four years vital to his development are expended toward ambitions that even the flourishing of professional sports does not much satisfy. For a very small number, this is the beginning of a career as a professional athlete. For a large number it is the first push toward becoming public school coaches. For the majority, it is the focus of school life, the thing that engages their feelings and commitment fully. Although one makes generous allowances for the character building, the leadership training, and the sportsmanship in life that derive from team sports, such activities in the public school are, at best, narrowly vocational for a few, a release of necessary energies for some, and a lengthy preoccupation with an interest that has a small rate of return, either vocationally or educationally, over the span of life. The participants enjoy the maximum benefits (and some marked deleterious effects as well) from public school athletics, but they are a small fraction of the number affected by having a single ideal for development and emulation.

The nonparticipant has no corresponding activity to which he can give himself. Pep squads, marching bands, and drill teams, which develop in proportion to the magnitude of the athletic teams, are efforts to broaden the opportunities for a publicly recognized exposure of self. The difficulty is always that inner development cannot be seen, cannot often be displayed, cannot really provide entertainment for spectators, who were put into that role by the school's marked ability to develop the nonparticipant. The young boy in an American high school lives in a shadow, defers commitments, puts off satisfactions that he might gain from zealously pursuing passions other than making the team. The girls are easily drawn into pep clubs and baton-twirling organizations, which are the feminine auxiliaries of the team, and thus project their own desires into supporting the team—more specifically, seeking romantic attachments leading to marriage solely in terms of the school's athletic heroes. If not that, they may settle early for the image of schoolteacher (feminine), which is prominently before them, is open to them as it is not for boys, and suits them for the passive role they have already half accepted.

All this is regrettable as regards formal education. All the school really need provide is the gathering place where young men and women can form into teams to work off youth's excess energies. That early training and intense commitment is useful to professional sports is undeniable, but even then one could argue that a very high level of professional baseball has been maintained for half a century without the overpowering attention given to it that is given to football and basketball in the public schools. One might add, his prejudices toward one sport or another aside, that baseball has developed figures more satisfactorily within the range of probable human development than football or basketball, whose prodigies become more freakish by the year. That is the main point here, that the schools have not provided at the point of greatest possibility of self-development any large range of images for the student to emulate.

Although there was a danger that colleges would move in the direction of high schools, they appear not to have done so. For this, college educators can claim little or no credit. It has been largely a matter of the great increase in size and the rise of science, the support of research, and the powerful impact of the most visible scientific achievements. By virtue of their great size, for example, the Big Ten universities have diminished the relative prominence of athletics and its impact on the student body without decreasing the actual outlay for athletics. Economically, the pursuit of grants, the recruiting of grant pursuers, and the gate receipts of successful research programs have tended to diminish the prominence of athletic programs as sources of revenue and publicity. Scholastically, the possibilities that have exposed themselves in numerous ways in graduate work have provided a cluster of ideals that are more satisfying (and more attainable for a large number of students) than being an all-conference halfback.

The professionalizing and necessary specialization that go with creating a major college team have had an interesting and un-anticipated effect on college athletics: They have made them more acceptable by moving them into one rather definitely segregated corner of college life. The talk within this enclave is still lathered with manly piety and hypocrisy but, like the talk of professors and students of literary criticism, it is a patois that has only a small effect on language and habits outside. The number directly hurt by participation in college athletics is probably no greater than the number directly benefited by being led into careers that they might otherwise have had difficulty finding.

But the main point of this digression is to emphasize that the college or university today does furnish a wider variety of desirable choices than ever before. Within its walls are men of sufficient stature—scientists, writers, artists, economists, physicists—to inspire direct imitation. Within its laboratories and libraries are to be found the marks of even greater men and achievements. A university justifies itself in the names carved in stone around a central building—Socrates, Dante, Galileo, Shakespeare, Montaigne, Faraday. It justifies itself, whatever else it may stand for, in its standing for a kind of gathering place for fully developed selves from as far back as history gives us acquaintance with them. And it is precisely here that the college student does have a chance to assist in his own development into a broader, more generous, more fully realized self.

For it is only by the development of self and by an ability to have a sense of self that one has a chance of a life of one's own. Otherwise, life is lived either by the past and the someone-elseness that goes with the past or by an equal someone-elseness of the future. One's father pushes or one's children lead along. The past may be preserved, the present stabilized, the future methodically unfolded by such a natural response, but achievements go begging.

It is very difficult to separate the development of self from selfishness, as difficult as to argue that selflessness is as bad as selfishness. Perhaps there is no escaping the conflict, even as the glorification of the self during the Renaissance was followed by a denigration of it during the Reformation. But short of judging by ultimate standards, one who believes in education must declare for the Renaissance, for Athens in the fifth century B.C., for the Enlightenment, and for the twentieth century as opposed to much of the nineteenth. For it could be said with some accuracy that education has only flourished against great odds at other times. If we declare for education, we declare for self-development. Declaring otherwise, we display the suspicion of knowledge that resides in the Genesis story. We decide in favor of learning even though we know that the acquisition of knowledge separates children from parents, husbands from wives, and whole generations from the generations that preceded them. "The mind is a cleaver," Thoreau wrote, not intending to emphasize the damage it can do but unavoidably calling attention to its power to cut and divide. And for all that, up to and including man's having won, through knowing, almost ultimate power, to his peril, we declare for more learning rather than for less.

A life of his own is what Thoreau described as his purpose in seeking Walden:

I wanted to live deep and suck out all the marrow of life, to live so sturdily and Spartan-like as to put to rout all that was not life, to cut a broad swath and shave close, to drive life into the corner, and reduce it to its lowest terms, and, if it proved mean, why then to get the whole and genuine meanness of it, and publish its meanness to the world; or if it were sublime, to know it by experience, and be able to give a true account of it in my next excursion.

His was a curious way of finding it—indeed, the detractor asserts, sucking marrow was about all one could do in Walden—but there are many Waldens if one has the need and the courage that force one to find them. None can be found or lived in except by a powerful assertion of self.

Few of the college-educated leave college with any comparable sense of trying to pin down the life they are leading or to set a bold course toward some dimly perceived but ideal life they might lead. What holds them back is the lack of a self in the making, a self that has a strong sense of its worth and of the worth of asserting itself. The individual accepts the self that his accumulating possessions and his rising station in life entitle him to. The magnitude of our material abundance is now so great, the reflection of the achievements of others so dazzling, that the educated man can scarcely be moved from the vantage point education has given him from which to watch life.

And yet the power of education is such that the educated man does move to a level of reflecting upon his condition even though he lacks the will or the energy or the compulsion to do anything about it. The result is a vague discontent with what one is doing, feeling, moving toward. The social philosophy around him would advise him to still his discontent by absorbing himself in the life of the community. But such a course too often sacrifices any ideals larger than those that fit the domestic circle or the business circle or the larger circle that encloses the hearth and home and hustling, the acquiring and consuming life.

A life of one's own is differentiated from that of others not by whether one's house is stone or cedar or brick, but by what goes on inside. And if something powerful goes on inside, it takes the form of ideals strong enough to induce action. In so doing, what began in self may reach far out into the world. The love ethic of the late Middle Ages made the courtier a vassal to his lady, but in order to be a vassal, he first had to be a knight. The Christian martyr, dying obscurely, mingled his blood with that of thousands and still did not come up to Christ, who had a self to lose before he could find it again. The unworldly of any kind—scientist, humanist, artist, teacher—are self-possessed, driven to acquire that which makes the sacrifice of self worth it.

If one considers the ferment on American campuses now, it seems chiefly, for the student, a matter of finding one's way amidst causes. And although there are, must be, some who originate causes, it is almost always someone else's cause the individual is being asked to join. I ask for the cause of one's developing self, the cause of one individual seeking a life of his own before he stumbles into a brotherhood. Brotherhood so joined is as isolating an experience as the academic detachment that lies at the other extreme. If we must speak against one, let us now speak against commitment, however good the cause, before one has made a commitment to self.

There is a justified impatience in youth that has put the relative vacancy of academic life against the vague but certain feeling that meaning must reside somewhere. The conviction that meaning does not reside in the courses of study offered seems to be one of the animating forces behind the student uprisings at Berkeley. It seems obvious that such a conviction is not the result of close scrutiny and may never lead to self-scrutiny. And if the colleges are at fault, it is because they do not foster development of self that grows within but only the development of self that is but a borrowing from the group surrounding the student.

The students seem more ready, more willing, than their professors to engage in the shaping of a genuine self. Every major movement in higher education seems to be away from the kind of confrontation, contemplation, and discipline necessary to help a student shape himself. The overriding concern of the university—to meet the numbers coming in and speed their departure through—is at almost every point opposed to development of an individual. The student's introduction to college life is not marked by the impact that great teachers can make, nor by informal after-class conversation between student and teacher, nor by the give and take of discussion in class, nor even by the sense of being among great men that should be found in quiet corners of a great university. The entering student does get an immediate confrontation with mass education, which may, regretfully, be the most realistic introduction to modern life that a college could provide. No wonder students in ferment turn to mass action and overlook the necessity of their own self-development, since the university has overlooked it to start with.

College students now as in the past are distinguished by the need for commitment. One of the university's main tasks is to make the student aware that commitment to finding a life of one's own is as worthy as a commitment that takes them to the barricades. Education must fill out the territory within, must give the choices out of which a life of one's own may be shaped. There is some kind of vacancy in American colleges and universities that contributes to the ferment of young minds stirred by the real events of real life. There is too little incitement to shaping a life that can be reconciled with much of what has been learned. What is gained from a college education? A good job, an ability to exercise some taste in a wide variety of cultural matters, and a permanent sense of guilt about not engaging in worthwhile activities. None of these is bad in itself, nor are they negligible achievements. Yet they leave much out and help account for student restlessness, student need for commitment.

Colleges have every right to spawn revolutions, create revolutionaries, but a revolution must be that of one committed individual to himself before it becomes more. One can never be sure when contemplation should stop and action begin, and one should never ask that the university be all contemplation and no commitment. And yet the man on the way to becoming educated is forced to choose, and the university through which he passes must incline toward direct and constant and passionate communion with the great spirits of the past in preference to a fevered saturation with the present. Only by so doing can it preserve its own life—a life so broad, so diverse, so full of possibilities, that half a dozen years are little enough to offer to the young as a time for moving toward a life of one's own.

Throughout this book, I have been arguing for a kind of learning that develops both thought and feeling, sharpens one's sensory awareness, and not only disciplines one's mind but makes it more receptive. Such developments cannot always proceed side by side. At one time the feelings have sway, at another the mind. And at all times, those engaged in teaching and learning must maintain an ideal in which thought and feeling are intensely engaged, whatever the task that lies before them.

The intellectual aim of the university should be to assist a student in developing a mind of his own. That means, of course, that the student should acquire a sturdy independence of thought—not a positive antagonism to all ideas outside his own frame of reference, but a positive unwillingness to ingest ideas that have not been touched by his own processes of thought. It means most of what one asks in the lower schools—a dialogue in which ideas are not merely packaged by someone else and conveyed to a storage bin for some conceivable use later on. Ideas should be run through a thinking apparatus increasingly able to discriminate, to refine, to relate, and, at least by this time, a person should be able to make something personal, individual, of the learning to which he is exposed. The higher learning may differ from the lower in asking that the learner make something of his learning. Ideally, the something should be real, or a portion of it should be real in comparison with the artificial exercises in writing, in responding to testing, in researching, which characterize the passive confrontation of knowledge in so much of college work.

Far too much energy is expended in turning out the merely college-educated, the man or woman with a degree who will earn more money, bear more social responsibility, and yet develop no more mind of his own than the most acquiescent product of military or religious indoctrination. Surely there is something that could be called the college-educated mind—an intelligence that knows Van Gogh as it knows Bach as it knows the Rh factor as it knows *The Reporter,* that can name a Nobel Prize writer or the winner of this year's movie prize at Cannes, that can handle some of the dialogue in a foreign film or discuss the delayed effects of excessive radiation exposure. These are not unpraiseworthy accomplishments, yet this kind of knowing is irritating, in its expectedness, in the way it creates an immense overarching latticework upon which one can step along without ever getting inside. And it surely is a lesser achievement, a kind of polishing and finishing in a mechanical way, than the handcrafted product that shows some of the vagaries of a shaping, creating hand.

Colleges and universities are not very concerned with creating a mind of one's own. They deal in large masses of received opinion and in methods that supposedly make the most of received opinion. They have certain large amorphous aims—the well-rounded boy or girl, the generally educated specialist—that even when achieved do not mark the graduate by the individuality of his possessions. They stand for certain institutional goods that students and alumni are pledged to accept—none more certain than the worth of college education itself. And yet if only in their stereotyped defense of academic freedom, they still do expose students to some minds of a cantankerous sort and so keep the possibility alive of a student's arriving at the end of a college career determined to have a mind of his own.

A mind of one's own is not the precise opposite of the mind

that has a wide receptivity, a genial tolerance toward everything that could be vaguely labeled intellectual. It is not necessarily querulous or narrowly focused on some personal conviction that diminishes the number of acceptable ideas. But it takes the large fund of general references and predispositions and brings them before its own bar of judgment.

We have evidences of such individual minds in the art galleries that actually do spring up in medium-sized cities and that have the impress of the likely-as-not college-educated art majors who establish them, support them, and create their wares. We have it in the private laboratories and clinics that keep alive the questing that may have begun in professional school, in the lawyers who become public defenders, in the business executives who not only preach the value of the humanities but continue to explore them.

But where the evidences of such minds are fewest, I fear, is in the university itself, where the mind might be described as not far different from the collective mind of the students except that longer institutionalization has greatly diminished its freshness of response. One of the largest lacks within the university is the absence of any university mind that has powers of scrutiny, judgment, and independence which can be turned on the university itself. University faculties contain many men whose minds are startlingly original and critical within their disciplines, but who operate within the university in the most conventional ways.

What is missing often is a heart of one's own, or any sense that the development of heart has anything to do with education. Let me make this last point by example. No field of study is more concerned than literature with feeling as it manifests itself in actual human behavior, in man's desirings and conflicts, and in man's restless struggle for inner calm, outer respectability. In literature— the novel, the short story, the drama, in much poetry—feeling is a part of the living being under scrutiny, not detached as in psychology or quantified as in sociology, but still, so to speak, a part of living tissue. Perhaps the fine arts—theater, music, painting— would argue that they have a greater, more direct concern with feeling, but my point is not to argue for literature's superiority, rather to emphasize that literature does make feeling its major concern.

For all that, the college and university study of literature is often as deliberately bloodless as any study could be. In large ways, one can say this is a result of a scientifically biased analytic faculty sweeping away the sobbing of the enthusiasts, the exclamations of mere appreciators, the solemnity of the moralists. In small ways, the condition shows itself in the zeal with which the objective attitude, the factual paper, the research exercise dominates writing, whether at the beginning of literary studies or in the graduate school. If one thing is most frowned upon in the study of literature, it is any manifestation of feeling toward the subject under study.

The results are curious. The further one goes in a literary education, the further away he gets from feeling, and the more intensely aesthetic one's studies, the less capable they become of arousing aesthetic response. It is as if there were no middle ground between intellectual vigor and emotional effusing, when, in fact, there are numerous discriminations to be made in order to get the best out of both. The literature teacher, intellectually overcome by the brilliant management of symbol and image by a modern poet, fails to realize that the demands he makes upon intellect can also be made upon feeling. One can ask of one's students precision, scope, and direction in matters of feeling as of intellect. One can ask for the deliberate development of a heart of one's own as of a mind.

The climate that a university provides should, then, encourage development toward a heart, a mind, a life of one's own. The values exposed inside a classroom cannot be at wide variance with those outside. If we want students not only to feel, but to enlarge their feelings and refine them, even discipline them, we do it not only by providing a setting (which American colleges do well), but by giving feeling a real value in what is being done inside classrooms in all disciplines where feeling has relevance. If we want students to think, then we create an outside atmosphere that is more than a smorgasbord to be picked at on the run. If we want them to move toward lives of their own, then we try to see that college is both a life itself and a chance to begin a pattern for a life that will justify the time spent in formal education.

CHAPTER IX

EXCITEMENT AND REPOSE

IDEALLY, college intellectual life should offer the student numerous opportunities for both excitement and repose. The excitement is of the kind that sometimes sustains a class into which the students have been fully drawn and in which the teacher is fully aroused. The students find themselves being led on by the discoveries they are making, and the teacher experiences both the sense of discovery and the pleasure that comes from having what he abstractly believes in suddenly take on great meaning before his eyes. Then it is that students and teacher are one. The atmosphere becomes so charged that the classroom loses only a part of its life when the class departs. At a certain high pitch of intensity, the pleasurable exhaustion that follows tells one how high a pitch was reached. As with all intensely pleasurable experiences, one can hardly bear to have them stop, can't wait to begin again. The class breaks up with reluctance and everyone waits impatiently for the next class to come.

Such experiences occur at all levels of learning. They occur probably more conspicuously in college, not because the instruction is better or the pupils are more receptive, but because teacher and student both recognize the difficulties of learning, are mindful of the necessary discipline always close at hand. Such classes are rewards for the drudgery, the painful slogging through the forest, as all stand in the clearing and feel the excitement of getting to a place where they at last can see the sky. The excitement of learning in the lower schools is of a slightly different kind, mostly delight and wonder at what is happening for the first time. The lower school's delight is often pure discovery, sometimes at the wonder of learning itself. As my seven-year-old son said one day after a long period of staring at a cereal box, "Once you learn to read, you just can't stop! You just see the letters and you're reading!"

That kind of unadorned perception, with little like it ever verbalized before and with the learning that lies ahead a mere undefined glow, is seldom to be found later. Instead, one has the awareness grow out of a formal context—usually a verbalizing context and usually a fairly placid or routine or dull context. The excitement comes with a conscious awareness of the excitement of learning itself, and may come as an afterthought rather than as a part of the immediate experience.

An education that functioned at a high level of excitement all the time would be unbearable, simply too exhausting to be sustained through any long period of study. How long it can be sustained may mark one of the differences between what we loosely call creativity and mere productivity. The former seems connected with the person's ability to sustain an excitement through the involved, often lengthy, and often hit-or-miss process of bringing something new into existence. The latter can take place, given discipline and mastery of routine skills, under all conditions and may take the form of only gathering and shaping. The former finds new relationships, brings into being something that was not there before. The latter may show superior powers of assembling, even organizing, but leaves the world unchanged. The former creates a momentum of its own that drives past obstacles, often leaps them, and arrives at some strongly if indefinitely perceived end that brings sufficient satisfaction for the person to feel a sense of completion even though the end may fall short of the full achievement the excited mind and senses are after. The latter proceeds at the prodding of outside forces, seldom acquiring any inner momentum, seldom drawing upon the full range of a person's talent and skill. The achievements of higher learning are more those of production than of creativity: A large number of students doggedly perform routine chores as a means of accumulating sufficient credits to get through college, and an immensity of published material in every discipline is produced, very little of which was generated in excitement or generates excitement. If one thinks of higher education at its best as that kind of learning in which knowledge and skills are extruded, so to speak, into forms of which not even the extruder is fully aware, the compelling agent in the process is excitation.

But if excitement is one necessity of higher education, repose is another. At the present time, one could safely say that there is hardly a college or university in the country that is not too busy. Wisely, and for so long that one feels the condition has always existed, higher education has provided comparatively few class hours for the total amount of work to be done. In residential colleges where the students have enough money, the theory may work out in practice. Elsewhere, neither faculty nor students show sufficient respect for free time. For the faculty, it is not the need for repose that reduces teaching loads and sweeps the office clear of students, but the pressure to bang away at the typewriter, knock out another article or write up a proposal or just give notes the permanent form that may make them last a lifetime. For the student, work replaces repose. Working one's way through college shows more strength of character than of mind. Certainly it is the only way for many students, and, within reason, it causes no great harm. And yet, how necessary to true learning are the free hours, not only for preparation of lessons, but for contemplation, for periodically taking stock, for simply learning how to spend a quiet evening with oneself.

American universities do not have a contemplative atmosphere. If the student is not working at a paying job, he can fall prey to dozens of nonpaying jobs, with which campus life abounds. It is amusing, until one considers the lost opportunities for contemplative thought, to observe how students ape the activities of their mentors. Student committees and conclaves, for example, are as numerous and as time-consuming and as shattering to calm as those of the faculty. Long before he has much to say, the student can become thoroughly familiar with the proper settings for saying it. And although student energies on many campuses are directed toward bringing academic activities into extracurricular life, this is often done with the kind of haste and bustle that allows little time for savoring the experience. Before it can work down into the vital centers of thought and feeling, the student is pulled on into another cultural happening.

There is too much of almost everything on an American campus but the opportunity and the encouragement to sit down alone and think. There are too many books, too many courses, too many lectures, too much culture, too much of all that is worthwhile of all kinds. The student who wants to find a quiet place for a quiet hour is not distracted by frivolous pleasures competing for his interest but by serious interests competing for his time. The multiplicity of urban life sets the style for today's universities, and in neither setting is there much provision for repose.

The problem is how to bring an air of contemplation to a campus overrun with cars, students, and culture. Reducing all three might help for those who remain, but American education would simply and rather quickly rise to former levels. Barring cars from the campus is usually an act of desperation committed when the administration realizes that parking space can never accommodate the number of cars. Similarly, when large universities resort to limiting the size of entering classes, it only comes after years of mounting difficulty in making the number of faculty adequate to the increasing number of students. As for culture, this at least has been a positive pursuit motivated by the defensible notion that a campus should be culturally rich, but it has also been motivated by the indefensible notion that the more culture the better. No one has really challenged this last premise, perhaps because the academic program might have to prove superior to the general cultural one and no faculty member wants to enter such a competition. There are attempts to reduce purposeless movements on American campuses, to lower the level of noise, but they appear to be negative if necessary gestures. Repose, contemplation, must be recognized as academic values and deliberately sought and defended. Otherwise quiet will seem to be only the accidental result of such desperate administrative measures as abridging the students cherished freedom to move anywhere by automobile.

Lest I seem to be attacking everything that lies outside the classroom and library, let me emphasize the great importance I attach to the total campus climate. Nothing, not the course offerings, the professors, the library, the laboratories, has more importance in winning the student to the intellectual enterprise. Yet, although the campus climate includes everything that goes on within the campus confines and some of what goes on outside, the creation of a favorable climate is not given adequate attention. The climate results from disparate activities, some of which do get careful scrutiny. What body of overseers is there to look at the high and low pressure systems that create campus weather? Recent national studies have given us measuring instruments by which campus climate can be described, but few campuses have tried to modify the existing climate in ways that seem most favorable to academic life. Faculties, I suspect, would argue that they are in the position of meteorologists facing the weather—that against the magnitude of forces, some known, many not, their efforts can effect small changes at best. Yet meteorologists have not been daunted by even larger tasks, and numerous examples exist to show that man-made climates can be created to enhance other work and play—building missiles and playing baseball, for example—that society places a great premium upon.

One of the piecemeal efforts to create a favorable campus climate, physical construction, is currently having greater impact than changes in the academic structure. One can only praise the attention being given to campus architecture, to peripheral parking, to maintenance of open space and landscape often against intense demands for building. If buildings seem to continue to get more attention than anything else, they at least seem to be being built with an awareness of the function for which they are intended. A handful of well-designed buildings can have great impact—not primarily on the campuses on which they are found, for the forces must have been already present to bring them into existence there, but on campuses where neither the buildings nor the ideas they embody are in existence.

Architects, now that the overriding passion for glassy exposure seems to have abated, do appear to have a respect for both excitement and repose, perhaps because architecture confronts form in large enough detail to see the importance of these two basic properties. Our own time is fortunate in this respect. Although "form and function" and "structural integrity" are architectural cant, modern architects do construct buildings in which the fundamental structure is not hidden by excrescences.

Such architecture, like campus planning, can help create the physical conditions conducive to maintaining an air of excitement and repose on the campus. In respect to the latter, nothing could be more helpful than the incorporation into buildings of small, enclosed spaces that the student can come upon by surprise, that offer havens close at hand for quiet reading, writing, and reflection. Few buildings afford enough such spaces, and those that do probably face considerable pressure to turn them into classrooms and offices. They defy systematic use-studies, being often devoid of occupants at hours when a survey may be taken, being immensely wasteful at all hours unless space utilization studies recognize repose as immensely useful to learning. They do create problems for security guards and deans of women because they furnish sanctuaries for lovers as well as scholars. Yet even that is not an uneducational function and at times invites the student to a contemplation of beauty rarely to be found in the classroom.

I am praising campus architecture for what it can be, not for

what it often is—modernistically showy buildings remarkable for
the fundamental economies in their construction and demonstrating imagination to the extent of having not only square and rec-
tangular classrooms, small and large ones, but even round ones.
Such a building is constructed around a central core of lavatories
that in elegance, utility, and permanence confer the measure of
immortality for which the architect has striven. If I choose to
emphasize the achievements and pass over the mediocre and the
unsatisfactory, it is not because I believe that a satisfactory campus
architecture prevails. It is rather that the current rate of building
and the formidable size of many individual buildings do have an
effect upon the campus climate. A survey of campuses from one
end of the country to the other would certainly turn up some exemplary buildings, and such buildings are likely to have an impact
on campus buildings throughout the country.

My main reason for calling attention to buildings is that elsewhere on the campus—and nowhere more noticeably than in the
academic program—laudable models are hardly anywhere in evidence. There is the rather impressive spread of honors programs,
more impressive from a distance than close at hand. There are
some new, experimental colleges and some cooperative ventures
that one hopes will make more impact than they have yet made.
There is a good deal of underground murmuring and recently
aboveground protesting of students. But these do not alter the
basic fact that the undergraduate program is for the most part im-
poverished in idea and in execution. Nowhere is it more lacking
than in its ability to create in beginning students the twin pulls
of excitement and repose that I offer as essential conditions for
higher learning.

The first two years of college have suffered most from the impact of numbers, from the feeling that bigness has engendered: that
the educational enterprise is at the mercy of bureaucratic forces
too diffuse to have a center, too large and complex to permit the
thoroughgoing overhaul that the academic program needs.

To speak directly, general education, the prevailing pattern for
a student's entry into college, a pattern to be traced as far back as
Columbia's program in the 1920's and strongly influenced by Harvard's report of 1945, is bankrupt where it is applied to very large
numbers. In the large universities, and to a degree even in the
best of our colleges, forces outside any one university's control have

brought changes in faculty and students that have weakened the entire undergraduate academic program. Daniel Bell's recent study, *The Reforming of General Education,* is almost the first sign that undergraduate education is about to get the critical attention it needs in every American college and university.

Two main forces are now influencing undergraduate education, particularly in the freshman-sophomore years, so greatly that neither excitement nor repose is to be found there. The first is the steady withdrawal of the college and university faculty from teaching, particularly undergraduate teaching. The second is the magnitude of college education, which the writers of the Harvard report could and did imagine but which did not press upon them with the immediacy that now presses upon every campus. The two are closely related, for if it were not for the magnitude of higher education, there would probably not be the large research program that is the main lure away from undergraduate teaching. It is magnitude, again, that has created a scarcity of college teachers and that has made it possible to choose the kind of university career that comes closest to a faculty member's personal desires. It is magnitude, finally, that creates among students a feeling of being a mere IBM number, a feeling any program, any faculty will have difficulty in dispelling. Yet the American commitment is to this magnitude. However one may be distressed by it—and there is, it seems to me, much to be distressed by—it must be regarded as something other than a transient phenomenon to be met by expediencies until a previous condition reappears. It is a permanent condition with which the entire academic community must deal.

The problems created are acute ones, the most important the university faces. There is a short supply of college and university personnel of all kinds—college presidents, administrators, and research workers as well as faculty—and there seems no end to the chronic shortage of money and physical facilities. All this of course, is related to the expansion of knowledge, which is not only being madly pursued but is being increased madly in the very pursuit of it.

But despite the seriousness of the problem, it seems clear that few if any students showing up for college will go untaught, for in gross, instinctive ways, colleges and universities are immensely adaptive. The basic response to a shortage of teachers has always been to increase the size of the classes and to lower the requirements for teachers. Neither of these reflex actions has, I think, fully reached the college teacher, but I think administrations are well aware of them. The professor basking in the actuality of fewer classes and the prospective professor bargaining for even fewer may not notice that as his teaching load goes down, the number of his students goes up. And even the undergraduate teacher who is aware that classes are getting larger is at least teaching classes he wants to teach. Even if they are not precisely in his specialty, he is not teaching the kind of introductory basic courses that his Ph.D. has ill-suited him for. By lowering the requirements for teachers and assuming that part-time apprentices can do the job of full-time professors, the lowest of lower-division subjects still are taught. College composition, for example, an English department's confrontation with the raw masses, has passed, like the vast unarable lands of the West, into the hands of a subjugated people—temporary instructors, graduate assistants, faculty wives, and others—and has done so without having to resort to whiskey, firearms, or killing off the buffalo.

The fully qualified college faculty member is in an enviable position today as compared with any period since the 1930's. His personal fortunes are booming, just as higher education is booming. Still, it seems to me, he cannot be comfortable when the pressures are so great upon him. The fact that he cannot stretch himself to cover all that his conscience might demand of him is the personal embodiment of the difficulty facing all higher education. The elementary educational and economic necessity operating in the midst of this shortage of faculty members is that the available faculty gets employed at the higher levels of instruction. If the professor is saved for the lower undergraduate division, it can only be as a lecturer to the multitudes or as an image on closed-circuit TV.

It is hard to argue with necessity, and, numbers aside, this college teacher, who has hopes of operating on the frontiers of discovery and the training to do it, has difficulty relinquishing his specialized study for the humbler tasks of dealing with beginning undergraduates whose abilities, backgrounds, and interests vary greatly. Graduate study has become more specialized in all areas. The nature of research grants, the expansion of knowledge, and the increasing sophistication of machines and techniques in the sciences have all pushed in that direction. In the humanities and social sciences, the large number of graduate students and the magnitude of research since World War II have led to a focusing on smaller, more specialized topics. In almost all fields, the prospective teacher knows that the best positions go to the specialist and that scholarly eminence in a specialized area is the best way to professional advancement. Consequently, he specializes to a high degree in graduate school, continues to do so as a teacher filling a spot within a department, and trains his own students in a similar manner. All these forces tend to magnify the attraction of graduate teaching over undergraduate teaching—an unfortunate magnification, since graduate work, by mere virtue of being higher, possesses greater prestige already.

Closely related to the attractiveness of graduate over undergraduate classes is the attractiveness of research over teaching. Clearly the opportunities for research have never been so abundant, and the prestige has never been so high. Even the professor with a great love of teaching finds it difficult to resist doing something else that he also enjoys and that has a higher likelihood of giving him greater professional standing. For many a professor, the problem in its present form is not even whether research and teaching are compatible, for clearly, in terms of his presence in the classroom, they are not. With the large sums being invested in research, the question for an individual professor is not how to combine research and teaching but more bluntly how soon he should leave teaching and for how long. Psychologically, that may be good for the college teacher. At least he is not under the daily strain of feeling that classroom teaching is taking time away from his research or—a less common feeling, I think—that his research is causing him to neglect his teaching.

Yet, I suspect the emphasis upon research and the way all areas have aped the sciences in research does not diminish many professors' feelings of being caught in the middle. For, except for a very few, the genuine contribution to knowledge is no more likely to come out of faculty research than out of doctoral dissertations. The contributions that are made by most professors engaged in research are likely to be small, special, and isolated, so much so that when the researcher looks up from the task at hand he is likely to get the feeling of having climbed a small hummock in the midst of an awesome range of mountains. And such a look, glancing to right and left to see the great numbers of undergraduate students who have yet to reach the foothills, may even lead to anguish.

Had I any confidence that it might be possible, I would suggest that in many areas we draw back from probing the mountains and concentrate on making the most of our civilization on the plain. Academic research has a way of piling up, the new causing the old to sink out of sight. The same tasks can be performed again and again, giving an air of industry that stands in the way of doing something with all the knowledge and insight research has supposedly gained. But human beings, scholarly human beings among them, are not likely to draw back either as individuals or in a group. So the university teacher, attracted by the challenges to be found on the frontiers of knowledge and by the material advantages enjoyed by those working there, is likely to be pulled away from teaching the beginning students who are arriving in such numbers.

One of the great dangers to higher education is not being forced to countenance really bad teaching but rather increasing the already large tolerance for teaching of a middling sort. A college faculty's tolerance of mediocre teaching explains why it always seems so easy to stretch faculty, to get classes taught, to find someone to man the classroom in times of crisis such as these. It also explains why the teaching part of a college professor's responsibilities has such low status. Although the professor has many reasons to be satisfied with his current comfortable, comparatively affluent condition, I think he cannot escape discomfort. Some is the common discomfort a man experiences when faced with conflicting desires and responsibilities. But also a man of conscience must be disturbed by how infinitely extendable teaching seems to be, by the eagerness with which a teacher seems to give up teaching, and by the narrowness of the range of teaching a teacher seems eager to do.

My own anguish and my more specific concern grow out of my distrust of the adaptability of institutions of higher learning. The response most institutions have made to increasing enrollments and the shortage of faculty has been so primitive one cannot help but think that reflection and intelligence might have done better. And it is hard to shake the idea that there is a connection between undergraduate ferment and the conditions and practices of college teaching.

Fewer professors lecturing to more students at lower levels and more professors teaching fewer students at upper levels does not strike me as serving the highest aims of higher education. And yet, that is what the majority of large colleges and universities have to one degree or another committed themselves to in making the simplest adaptation to increasing numbers. It seems to me that large lecture classes should be fairly few for an undergraduate's work and more numerous in many areas of graduate study—and in both cases carefully considered in terms of subject matter and teacher. The great number of apprentice teachers at the lowest level of instruction seems to reflect a simple kind of common sense and yet is almost as topsy-turvy. Where college teaching should be strongest, most exciting, it is probably weakest, most passive. It is cheapest, too, at the lower levels—but maybe not so cheap in terms of what might have been accomplished in the first two years of college.

Colleges have not actually been forced into the practices that now prevail. It is more, I think, the pressure to give higher education to all, the immediate problems created by that effort and constantly pulling men away from reflective planning, which keeps any wiser action from being taken. It may be too that without really recognizing the fact, certainly not admitting it, administrators, professors, trustees, state legislators, and even the parents of many of the students have reached an unvoiced agreement that trying to give college education to everyone is a hopeless task and that the show of doing so might as well be done as cheaply as possible. I hope that this last is not true, or if it is true, that it is not totally determining. For there are alternatives that any group of college educators willing to invest their energies in the problem and able to find the time for reflective thought about it should be able to come upon.

I would propose that any large college or university (for the situation is not so acute in the smaller schools) look at its teaching not from the professor's end, the department's end, but from the student's. What kind of teaching is a student likely to get over a four-year program, and what kind of pattern does it have? These are basic questions, and the answers should be compared with the institution's ideal as to the kind of teaching a student might most profit from. As much effort as is customarily expended on curriculum should be expended on bringing up to the ideal the way the student is actually taught—lecture, discussion, tutorial, large and small and medium-sized classes—and by whom and at what place in the student's progress toward a degree. Such an ideal should offer variety: some small-class work with the best minds the university has to offer as well as exposure to eminent men in a large lecture hall, some of such exposure at the beginning of one's work as well as at the end, some opportunity for discussion classes, lectures, seminars with a variety of teachers, some independent study, guided reading or research, and tutorials as well as formal classes. It should offer discipline: closely supervised work in laboratories or by sections under the eyes of the most disciplined of professors instead of the least disciplined as is now the rule. It should offer excitement and the arousing of the imagination—a task perhaps for a group of professors or one which breaks away from conventional patterns of instruction. Finally, it should offer the students many chances to identify with the college teacher at his very best.

These are ideals, of course, that colleges have long professed, but I have not observed them very often of late in practice. More than that, I suspect such ideals have not even in the past risen to the visibility of recognizable objectives. Our energies have been directed toward the formalization of subject matter and the granting of credit, toward providing the curriculum that would produce the well-rounded man without reflecting that however rounded he becomes he is as much the result of the teachers as he is of what is taught. I am not criticizing the attention given to curriculum, or to the granting of credit, or to debating general versus special education. I am asking that similar attention be given to finding ways of providing the student with an exposure to college teaching that will most enhance his learning. It strikes me that the failure to give much specific consideration to the actual patterns of teaching, the exposure to the teaching process, may be one reason for the low status of teaching today. It is a strange omission, too, since that aspect of a student's program could be looked at and planned for as clearly as the curriculum.

Having considered some desirable objectives in terms of the student's actual classroom experience, I would propose that the faculty of a university as it now exists be as carefully considered. What kind of teachers characterize the faculty? What kind of teaching do they do best? What kind of pressures do they feel they are under? What way of dealing with such pressures would enhance teaching? Such considerations might be a good beginning toward revitalizing the undergraduate program, particularly in the first two years. The reason that general education has lost its vitality lies not with an outmoded curriculum or even with the viability of the general-education philosophy, but with the fact that an adequate supply of the kind of college teachers that once gave the program life no longer exists. Despite the gravitation of faculty members to teaching fewer courses and more specialized upper-division and graduate courses, I think much could be done to attract the faculty back to the undergraduates. It is not impossible, I think, to place the most eminent faculty member in an introductory course if it does not come labeled "Introduction to Such-and-such," and is not pressed into a rigid institutional pattern. It is not too expensive to have seminars for freshmen and for seniors too, if one plans large lectures at appropriate places elsewhere in the program to offset the cost. It does not take a great stretching of the imagination to envision some graduate assistants doing varied teaching and tasks of other kinds rather than merely taking over the teaching of the freshman year. It is not, in short, impossible to do a great deal more than has been done to give the student rewarding teaching experiences, even during a time when colleges have too many students and too few faculty.

As much as I deplore a teacher leaving the classroom, even for a good reason, I would argue that assembling the pick of a college faculty to face this task of restoring teaching and a program to the undergraduate years would be a justification for their temporary absence. They might consider old-fashioned homeopathic remedies, for we are dealing with an infection harmful to the total health of the university, however it appears to have improved the health of a part. Giving to the undergraduate program in small doses some of the sources of that infection might help to check its spread and nullify its harmful effects. Such doses would include small classes and specialized ones, special freedoms in conducting such classes, leaves of absence to improve teaching, opportunities for travel, substantial grants for superior teaching, and institutional awards for refraining from publication and for continuing teaching. A commitment to teaching in today's academic climate does involve some expenditure of will, some sacrifice of opportunities, some putting aside of other strong desires. Colleges and universities and the profession as a whole need to give concrete indications that it's worth it.

Exciting teachers, thoughtful teachers, are not easy to come by, regardless of the efforts the academic world makes to honor them. There is something about teaching that defies all efforts to make the teacher stick only to his tasks. And the better the teacher, the more likely he is to be willing to range into other activities and to be asked to do so. He would probably be a worse teacher otherwise, would certainly be a bad teacher if he never thought to take himself beyond his classroom walls. For there is not necessarily an inverse relationship between a man's ability as a teacher and his eminence in the world outside. It may be and often is quite the opposite. His teaching profits from his other experiences, and his students profit too when and if his physical presence can be captured for the classroom.

I would guess that the more the teacher possesses in mind, in sensitivity, in personality, in creativity, the more he may be led away. Perhaps this is because a person with a strong and interesting mind (such as a good teacher must have) may be reluctant to commit himself without stint to the minds of others. Perhaps it is because a creative mind tends to follow out its impulses in defiance of the necessities of teaching. Perhaps it is simply that even the light routine of teaching comes to weigh heavily on those who became teachers in the past to escape a more deadly routine. Perhaps the exposure teaching gives to many other possibilities creates a desire to explore them. And perhaps, as regards the truly great teacher, it is the almost accidental capturing of him as a teacher that is to be wondered at rather than his flights away from it into more passionate pursuits. We should be thankful for the loneliness outside that cannot always be borne.

Scholarship—teaching and research, *learning,* in its broadest sense—is the ultimate strength of the university. Today's campus is an exciting place and almost everyone seems caught up in it. And yet much of that excitement is generated by the magnitude of the enterprise, the busyness of it that keeps it operating. Looking closely at the college or university as a place for learning, one feels dissatisfied with the educational ideal implied by the title "multiversity." For, as I have argued previously, education is essentially personal and the multiversities we have do not seem to foster the relationship between the single student and the single teacher (whether he is actually alone with him is not precisely relevant) that is important beyond all others. Customarily, the idea of a university is best seen within a college—a body of men united by common purposes and working toward common goals. How large such a body can be, how precisely it must define its purposes, is nowhere precisely set down. However, tradition seems to make them the units of which a university is composed, and they are therefore smaller than a university. Tradition also seems to favor a size that creates an actual sense of relationship between one member and another. Obviously, colleges in many universities are no more than names for very large academic divisions. Within such large entities, the growth of departments and subdepartments (areas of emphasis, programs, institutes, etc.) attests to the inevitable need of the academic organism to break itself into units within which there can be closer identification. Finally, to become evaluative for a moment, such actual units, such as the college of medicine or the football coaching staff and the squad, both of which are kept small in number and give intensive individual training, seem to produce the greatest measurable effect from formal instruction.

As elementary as these observations are, they have had little effect on the growth of universities in the past twenty years. What breaking down into smaller groups has been done has seldom been the result of planning that considered the overall institutional goals, much less the effects upon individual students. There are, in the sense of what actually happens within a university, no universities of the amazing size—30,000 to 40,000—that statistics describe. It is arguable that such a large institution might well shelter departments in which actual learning takes place, learning of a more personal, intimate kind than at many smaller institutions. What cannot be argued is that institutions of such great size have much total coherence. Rather, groups will break off the way excess accumulations of any kind break off from parent bodies. The large institution must look to its parts, the relationships of its parts, and the impact of both parts and whole upon student if it is to defend, not its size, but its educational effectiveness.

I hope to have dispelled any notion that I am arguing against bigness as in itself bad. Bigness, as a matter of fact, is likely to create the excitement that seems so necessary a part of real learning. That excitement is one reason that there is a higher level of creativity on a large campus, as in a large city. It may be sheer force of number, the fact that among so many people a certain number are going to be creative. Or it may be that the need for identity within the large mass forces more individuals into creative activity.

It is also probably true that the bigger a campus becomes, the more busyness seems to be a part of it. Thus the modern university seems to have reached a size that generates excitement, and now it might seek to create groups in which a sense of intellectual identity and common purpose might offer the repose necessary to contemplative thought.

It would be possible, of course, by strict regulation of all activities, to reduce the busyness on campus. The official way, preferred by both faculty and students, would be to set up a committee to explore the possibilities. The best way might be for a professor and some students to leave the campus for a week or a month, taking an adequate supply of food and drink and the handful of books that interested them most, and hole up in a place as far removed from culture as possible—an old mining camp, a summer hotel in midwinter, or a cheap suite of rooms in some nondescript office building. At worst, it would provide a kind of sea-lab experience, useful to space exploration if to nothing else. At best, it might force some continuity of thought, provide some sense of personally confronting higher learning, and give some idea of the real attractions and repulsions of the life of the mind.

The trouble with such a proposal is that it runs counter to institutional necessity and perhaps counter to human nature itself. The fifty-minute hour, the scattergun curriculum, are necessary to the efficient functioning of a higher education that embraces the widest of aims for the greatest number of individuals. And American students, perhaps all students, do not have very strong motivations to independent study. Perhaps only those who are denied institutional advantages but have a strong need to develop a skill or increase their knowledge are capable of independent study. The acceptance of institutional patterns is for the most persuasive of human reasons: It is easier. Few men can maintain the discipline of learning by themselves or can be certain of their progress without having an outside standard. An educational institution provides intimations, signs, and rewards for recognized, countable, almost physically ascertainable progress. So our observations here come back to the beginnings of this chapter: The climate for learning must be such that it provides the excitement that will commit a man to learning and lead eventually to the repose that marks a man deeply engaged in thought.

CHAPTER X

A TIME FOR LEARNING
AND A PLACE

W HEN IS THE RIGHT TIME for learning? Life furnishes many examples of misspent youth, much of it misspent in lower or higher education. The colleges and universities are full of students who not only learn some things too late but don't learn many things for being too early. A certain number of these leave college to pursue more pressing lessons elsewhere. Some come back later and do very well. Others get a better education for staying away. Except for that somewhat scary group whose progress is an uninterrupted march from kindergarten to the highest earned degree, most students pass through periods when formal learning is unbearable. Measured by the attractiveness of higher education to those who missed out on it in their youth, there must often be times in adult life when formal learning is irresistible.

Higher learning is a little like romantic love. Both come when a person is too young to enjoy the experience fully. Much is wasted for the participant's lack of understanding or want of appreciation. How much more one seems to get out of love and learning later in life when he knows something of what he is about. And how much more precious are both when one has had sufficient rubbing against the world to heighten the experience by contrast with many less satisfactory human experiences.

At the usual college age there is fierce competition for the student's attention, from sex, from physical activity, from rebellions and attachments to childhood and family, from vague but persistent intimations of the future, from the whole sensory being reaching out for the many attractions a college provides. In many ways, it is a bad age for learning of a formal sort—the physical selves held to classroom and library by one kind of restraint or another, the mental selves chasing off in all directions. Yet the chances are never greater that the self will be open to an excitement in learning just as it is open to the intensity of its own conflicts. That is the greatest argument for a beginning college education that involves much active participation, the antithesis of the packed lecture class in which too many students spend too much of their time.

The requirements made on higher education are great, since the public school finishes with its pupils at seventeen or eighteen and the public's expectation is that almost everyone will continue with formal learning. Although colleges and universities could encourage high school graduates to defer college education until other experience had better prepared them for it, they seldom do. Rather, they seem to say, college education is for kids, and they confront the students with an array of forms, requirements, and procedures that only cowed or callow youths could long countenance. I have already discussed the shortcomings of freshman-sophomore programs. The lack is the more painful because youth demands a great deal. If college is to confront its students at the commonly accepted time, it must face the fact that learning must in large measure come up to the life that a majority of the students are finding out about on their own for the first time.

That fact may explain why so many scholarly professors gravitate to teaching advanced students. It is not only that their interests are more specialized than the general interest one can hope for from the beginning student. It is that at the higher level they feel less need for arguing the worth of their subject, for disclosing what they know in colors that will attract the eye. For it takes a good deal of learning before ideas catch and hold a student's attention merely by virtue of the plain truth they reveal. Until that time, the teacher is, indeed, a teller of tall tales, a bargainer for attention, a candy butcher whose customers buy his wares for the large general truths they hope to find in each and every box.

College is the time for creating the grandest of speculations out of the scantiest of substance, for the most heated defense of principles backed by the flimsiest of arguments. Such abilities, as highly developed in sophomores as in seniors, are not to be sneered at. More learning often takes place in defense of a shaky premise than of a sound one, just as more imagination goes into creating something from nothing than in rearranging what already exists. Erecting some shelters in a new territory is more important than worrying about how long they will last.

To accept students as they are, one must acknowledge their penchant for plunging at once into the deepest of waters and rising on the airiest of enthusiasms. That is precisely the opportunity and task of undergraduate teaching: to bring out the particulars of the general truths students are so eager to declare, to destroy some simplicities and introduce them to others, and at the same time to keep them at the various tasks of acquiring competences. This last may have to be accomplished by the kind of bribery that distinguishes one kind of teaching excellence: the promise of soul-warming, mouth-filling verities if the student will patiently pursue the less sweeping tasks at hand.

What I have said about excitement and repose in the previous chapter is based on the premise that college age is chiefly the period between eighteen and twenty-two. Such a narrow age range does not, of course, accurately describe the college population. Many older people who missed out on the college education their sons and daughters expect as a matter of course now form an older group on campus. Another group are those who dropped out short of a degree and return after a few years' absence. The success of both groups suggests that colleges might advise the deferring of college education for many students.

A number of widely accepted studies have followed the progress of those who drop out of college and later return. The rather alarming attrition of a class as it moves from freshman year to graduation—upward of 50 percent—seems less alarming when one finds out that a good many of those who leave do return and do graduate, albeit years after their former classmates. While some kinds of intervening experience—travel, other schooling, for example—seem more valuable than other kinds, the fact of being away seems most important.

Statistics hide the many reasons both for dropping out and for coming back. The adolescent who can't control his passions, the athlete not up to the first team but unwilling to be hamburger, the unfortunate victim of family disaster, the ill equipped, the unprepared, the don't-give-a-damn—the range of possibilities is almost endless. Nevertheless, whatever the reason for leaving school and whatever the reason for returning, a period of life outside the halls of learning seems to have beneficial effects.

Though I do not often draw upon my own education as pattern or parallel, it is particularly relevant here. Had it not been for the war, I might never have entered college, for I had neither the money nor the purpose to get me there immediately after high school. Nor was I, in the days before World War II, under the same pressure to go on to college as today's high school students are. I spent almost two years working before the war pulled me into military service, and my entry into college after basic training was by a circuitous route. Basic training is uncompromising in the discomfort it causes to nonbelligerents like myself, and when after a spring and summer of basic training I was selected for the Army Specialized Training Program it was a deliverance out of Egypt (actually out of Texas). And still, the Army had a final twist before letting me and my fellow soldiers arrive at various universities throughout the land. We were brought to a staging area—an abandoned POW camp with the fences still intact. There we stayed for a week or so, waiting behind barbed wire for each new shipment of the lucky ones being sent off to college and gibbering at them in impossible German and worse Japanese. The symbolism was exactly right, and never has college been a more freeing experience than it was for us.

Without arguing that my own experience is conclusive, I do think that the delay in going to college and the difficulty of getting there were beneficial. It seems to me worthwhile to consider ways in which college could be deferred until some confrontation with the world enhances its value. The draft or other military service is one way. Although one cannot use the conditions of World War II and the GI Bill as an exact parallel, the achievement of the many who came back to college after the war is a strong argument in favor of the greater sense of purpose that experience and maturity bring. With our present affluence, federal scholarships for peacetime military service would not be an impossibility. Such scholarships could eliminate a good deal of artful dodging that now goes on between the college student and his military obligations and would remove some of the economic barriers that cause inequality of educational opportunity. If conditions permitted some changes in the concept of basic and advanced military training, ROTC might be removed from the campus, its academic components taken over by academic departments and its military components returned to the armed forces, where they belong.

The war in Viet Nam will cause many thousands of students to defer college. The passage of a new GI Bill will provide opportunity for college work for many who return. But the tie between military service and college education should not be the only means by which the nation gains the services of the young in return for providing for their higher education later. Voluntary service in performing some of society's unskilled and uninspiring dirty work might be another means. Almost any work can be borne if it promises to come to an end. Even now, college students earning money for the academic year perform a good many useful but dead-end jobs. There are still many such jobs: janitorial work, work involving the handling and moving and storing of goods, seasonal work and piecework, maintenance work—work that requires little skill, some physical strength or manual dexterity, and perhaps most of all a high tolerance for repetitive tasks that have no end in themselves and offer no opportunity for moving on to more rewarding occupations. Right now, many of these tasks are done badly (or left undone). The job corps is already a movement toward getting some of this work and other useful work done and at the same time providing untrained youth a chance to find a vocation. What if the concept was extended to include those who might already have sufficient preparation for college and who were willing to do a number of years of useful work as a means of "earning" a college career? Certainly this country needs a very extensive system of federal scholarships for higher education. The GI Bill furnishes an excellent model for scholarships to be awarded to those capable of profiting from higher education and in accordance with length of time served in a domestic job corps.

The arguments for these proposals are basically economic. The general investment in widening educational opportunities is certainly sound. A scholarship program which made its investments in individuals when they were sufficiently experienced to get the maximum return would be still more sound. Federal scholarships that would be available only to those without college training who were past the age of nineteen or twenty might be awarded without regard for military or job corps service. Colleges and private enterprise, too, might set aside some scholarships with such an age provision. Scholarship programs which encouraged the deferring of college education could have tremendous consequences for higher education. That simple step might not only put a more highly motivated student body into the first years, but would provide a far cheaper way of sifting those who should go to college from those who shouldn't, and would be simpler than admitting everyone to college and losing such great numbers in the first years.

There are some other matters relating to the proper time for learning that I'd like to consider as a kind of campus miscellany: hours of instruction, the academic calendar, the length of time for attaining a degree, and the extension of a time for learning past that ordinarily given to formal education.

What should be said of the fifty-minute hour? Is it a product of custom, convenience, or some mysterious inner rhythm of the individual and the universe? Certainly it does have something to do with the attention span, as it has to do with the ratio of the time taken to arrive somewhere for a meeting and the time spent there. An hour is a convenient unit, enabling large numbers of people to keep track of when to be at one place and another. Psychiatrists observe a fifty-minute hour too.

These justifications for the prevailing class hour are probably as good as can be easily brought forth. But although the fifty-minute hour may be convenient for both institution and student and may be physiologically and psychologically natural, it loses justification the more inflexible it becomes. Almost everything important about the process of learning has been insufficiently studied, whereas the forms that define learning have been studied to excess. Thus, college self-study groups periodically inspect the packages in which learning presents itself from department to department, complain about labels and sometimes about content, but rarely question the whole matter of packaging. More, they seldom have considered the effects of quantifying learning, although they show much alarm about the proliferation of courses that quantification tends to encourage.

Almost everything a human being does, almost everything nature does, is worthy of study, as is everything that has been done, as are the possibilities that may arise in the future. That alone sets the basic dimensions of the university, elastic dimensions that push outward as does the expanding universe. If the way we attempt to encompass this continually expanding knowledge is to put pieces of it into courses and the courses into the fifty-minute hour, the result is more and more pieces and more and more hours. On the other hand, the time given to any one human being has only in small ways increased. The life span has stretched out. The speed of physical movement, the rapidity of communication, the extension of human efforts by nonhuman means have also given us more time. Yet, against the sum of knowledge, how small our expansion. "We must take it as an unavoidable fact," Whitehead wrote, "that God has so made the world that there are more topics desirable for knowledge than any one person can possibly acquire." What should a university do to reconcile its own expansion of the dimensions of knowledge with the limitations of those who come to the university to learn?

The most obvious answer (admitting that any satisfactory answer is impossible) is to make more of the time the student gives to higher education. No large formal educational system does that very well. Once in motion and running efficiently, it forces the individual to accommodate sufficiently to keep the system moving, though not necessarily to keep himself working at peak capacity. It does not make the most of its parts, but lets them operate as they will within permissible tolerances. In American institutions, the tolerances are fairly large. Time lost in class can be made up by extra hours spent outside, and efforts routinely called for in fulfilling daily assignments, term projects, and final exams are sometimes allowed to be expended on one particular enthusiasm. The system has its flexibilities within as well as its rigidities overall.

Still, it seems to me, the course system could be more flexible than it is, and, far short of getting every professor and book and student at the maximum point of response every hour of the day, much could be done to make the fifty-minute hour less the determining force in both the packaging of knowledge and the dispensing of it. In the heart of many academic men is some image of a grove in which schooling is leisure, where faculty gather not at the tick of the clock and students arrive not at the ring of a buzzer. Whatever *needs* to be known is to be found elsewhere. Here, free learning takes place by a process of excited exchange within a structure that has no previous design but grows out of an inner ordering of parts to a final harmony that all recognize. Such, of course, is myth, as seemingly possible and actually elusive as the refining process by which the right woman brings the right man to fulfillment of both his higher and lower selves. Yet it is a myth worth holding out for, worth violating the fifty-minute hour for, worth turning the students outdoors for on a fair day and worth keeping them at the bench for long hours at other times.

The academic calendar is a larger ordering of time. It probably has more consequence for learning than is commonly thought. The university calendar is a result of custom, climate, holidays, public school practices, and other forces. The weight of all these probably accounts for the large amount of tinkering with the calendar that goes on and the small amount of change. Currently, there is much talk of the year-round academic operation, of the trimester system, of the merits of the quarter as against the semester plan. Most of these are discussed in terms of cutting down the total time it takes to get a college degree. Except for some vague notion that we must speed up to catch up with knowledge, the reasons for shortening the time are not very clear. The lengthening of life, the increase in wealth, and the shortening of the work day and work week might argue as forcefully in the other direction—that we should get students at a later time and be in no great hurry to certify them as educated.

Before tackling the academic calendar, one might try working on the regular calendar. It leaves much to be desired. January, to begin with, in most northern states at least, should simply be crossed off, its cold dirty gray swept out with the Christmas bills. Surely the year should begin as nature does, with May, or move it back a month to April, to give some brief anticipation of spring to come and to have winter end with March, as vexing a month as January if not quite as dull. Such a beginning would make fall more central than it now is, keep it from being pushed off into winter prematurely. One would have three full months to sink into winter rather than being deceived by the present calendar into believing that by December the worst is over.

As to holidays, we could do with more. That embarrassing central holiday season from December 25 through January 1, that trough into which all neuroses run, would be done away with, to be replaced by frequent holidays through the winter months to get us to spring. There, at the actual end of winter, the old year would be dispatched quickly and the new year would be begun in warm rain and spring green. An extended May holiday could restore some pagan abandon to a calendar in which deaths are more celebrated than life. June, too, should have its holiday, a minor one to balance Memorial Day but not to detract from the Fourth of

July, whose presence at midyear in the present calendar does much
to redeem an otherwise faulty instrument. In the new calendar
Columbus Day would fall at midyear, making us for once put
first things first and place political beginnings second to geographical ones, exploitation second to discovery. Thanksgiving and
Christmas would remain, but encouraged as hibernal festivals to
get us through the worst of winter. With the end of the year has-
tening on, February's short span would seem shorter still. The
birthdays of our greatest national figures would bring us to the
new year reflecting on our own accomplishments of the past.

Thus one might envision the regular calendar's reform and
use it as a model for looking at the academic calendar. No one
can quarrel with the academic year's beginning in the fall, although one wonders why it must begin so late. For whatever date
it begins in the fall, its end is dictated by the Christmas holidays.
The quarter system accommodates by beginning late and cramming
in its course work and awarding grades as holiday blessings. The
semester lets its tail sprawl over, few colleges or universities having
the sense to use the lame-duck weeks as a reading or meditating
period. For reasons hard to fathom, the four-month semester, one
on each side of Christmas holidays, is scarcely to be found, despite
the fact that public schools invariably begin very near the beginning of September.

The public schools do, in fact, account for some peculiarities
of the college calendar. Summer school cannot apparently begin
until public school teachers are released in late May or early June.
Even so, it has been possible to accommodate public school teachers
under the trimester system, which may have a third term beginning
in May and ending in August. And if the trimester seems to com-
plicate such matters, a full month of independent study in May,
looking back at the whole year's work, might be as useful as any
division of the calendar. The calendar could be managed to serve
a variety of ways in which learning can take place—not managed
as it is at present, chiefly in terms of administrative functioning.

How long a college term should be is as unanswerable a question as how long the class period. There is much complaint about
both the quarter system and the semester system, and the trimester
system, which seemed to promise so much, does not seem to be
any better. Which system is adopted by a college depends, as do
most considerations involving the time and place for learning,

upon economics or administrative ease or accommodation to out‑ side interests. For certain kinds of academic work, for example work that involves large amounts of reading, ten- to twelve-week units seem very short. For some studies, such as mastery of certain basic concepts in mathematics or in laboratory procedure or the acquiring of factual knowledge divisible into almost any size blocks, the semester may be too long. The quarter system does work against unity, does fragment knowledge more than the semester, is harder to manage in terms of yearlong courses or even longer periods of concentration. And although institutions seem to feel pushed to choose one or the other (or go all out for the trimester), why need they choose? An academic year with a short term before Christmas and a long one after would not make scheduling im‑ possible, and it would aid studies that gain from a prolonged period of time and still effect the economies of consigning some courses to short terms. It would, of course, mean that someone might have to consider what the aims of every course were and what aims courses should have. It might mean that one sort of noneducational force (the difficulty of scheduling) acting upon an‑ other (the number of classes) would result in an educational gain (the reduction in number of classes).

The continuing but seldom very consequential discussion of the academic calendar is currently linked with the movement of col‑ leges to full-year schedules. Many universities are announcing to trustees and state legislators that the plant is operating around the year—some are almost able to say around the clock. And although there is some willingness to treat the summer term as a fourth quarter, most schools still operate summer schools as somewhat separate entities. Summer schools are still somewhat the creations of colleges of education, designed to provide additional work for public school teachers and to keep faculty members in the college of education from reflective thought through the entire year. End‑ ing summer school as a separate entity would aid the effort to make teacher education a respected discipline. It is not that summer schools should not have a special character. But the special charac‑ ter should not be that of simply providing for the inclusion of courses that cannot justify their existence in the regular year. Teachers would probably be better served were the summer term treated, in fact, as one more term of the regular year.

I doubt that it harms many students—and the numbers already

doing this are large—to attend college for eleven months a year. And yet, summers for college students, as for teachers in the public schools, can be as profitably spent outside the academic life as in. The generally favorable results with students admitted early to college under the Ford program seem to show that students can master higher education at a younger age. Great numbers of students shorten the time to a degree by going straight through every summer. It would be possible to increase the number of candidates for degrees of all kinds by merely speeding up the process. But for the broad area of learning called the humanities, for historical studies, for the many disciplines that draw the student on into advanced work (the extra years of which give point to beginning early), there is a necessary ripening along the way that argues for a more leisurely pace. The end of education is not, after all, to get through, although one watching the process as it goes on on the American campus would never guess it was anything else.

Where does learning end? For many, it is said, with the departure from public school or the awarding of a college degree. That, of course, is nonsense. The kind of learning and the ways of learning may change, but the need to learn, whether in the small ways that enhance one's life or in the momentous ways that put one on a new course or renew one's zest for the old, never seems to slacken. However, self-discipline in learning is difficult, and the majority of adults would probably prefer to rely on the discipline of formal instruction rather than provide their own. The college and university open their arms to such students coming back for one subject or another, but these students are put into an unfortunate competition with the larger number of students pursuing credit hours and degrees.

Although institutions can take steps to encourage lifelong learning, the most significant encouragement is personal—it somehow develops in the student a sense of learning as a development of self that has no end. A large part of whatever learning takes place in college must be not merely the acquisition of techniques and skills but a respect for techniques and skills worthy of being developed to a much higher degree than four years, or ten years, of college can accomplish. A large part must be not in the mastery of or exposure to a body of knowledge except as it provides a pattern and an incitement to master or explore other bodies of knowledge. A large part must be deliberately open-ended, must never let the student be wholly free of the large questions about what enhances life for himself and for others. And a large part must be learning that affords intellectual and sensory satisfactions that will be remembered along with the gut-pleasures of campus life.

Such emphases would not leave much for the merely vocational, the merely informational, the merely theoretical. As regards training for work, what higher education can best provide is the stamp of institutional approval, that student X has been inclined to such and such a vocation and that he may have a capacity and willingness to use his mind and passions in such work, provided it gives to him in the measure he gives to it. The institution can provide the labels that satisfy personnel departments, stamping its men and women graduates as being roughly competent or having an interest in teaching history or guiding investments or performing on the stage or collecting specimens.

In fact, this is what colleges do, even when they have larger pretensions. What teaching major is prepared to be a teacher at graduation? What writer ever learned to write in college? What broker ever mastered the intricacies of investment in a business school? I am talking here about undergraduate education. Advanced work has always been very specifically vocational. Increasingly, it seems to me, undergraduate education is less specifically vocational, regardless of how hard it tries to keep pace. It is in the undergraduate areas most inclined toward vocational training, such as engineering and business, that changes in technique, changes in demand, make obsolete by graduation time much of the specific job training that a curriculum contains. Certainly it is useful to the student to complete college training supposedly qualified in *some*thing rather than *no*thing or even *every*thing. And since it is too much to ask the world of work to practice what it often preaches— that a man or woman with brains and interest is a valuable addition to any enterprise—the colleges should properly provide labels. One could imagine every student taking a standard curriculum and getting a degree in whatever specific subject he expressed a vocational preference for at the time of graduation, and not see much of an adverse affect upon the vocational utility of the college degree. Specific, short-range training necessary to assigned work should be the employer's responsibility. Further formal learning would then be either specifically vocational in professional schools that honestly swear that the additional learning is necessary to the

vocation and that the vocation is worth spending additional learning upon, or it would be learning to enlarge the man's life, of
which his work is but a part.

A time and a place for learning. What would a person have if
he had his heart's desire?

First, I think, the time should not follow hard upon public
school education. The effects of twelve years of formal education
need to wear off somewhat. The continuity of learning in some
subjects, such as a foreign language or mathematics, should be
sacrificed for the gaining of wider experiences of other kinds. The
entrant should have had some battering against the world, partly
just to be exposed to less desirable alternatives than further learning, but also to contribute to the world's menial tasks—something
like a price of admission. Roughly speaking, he should have done
enough useful work to make it economically feasible for him to remain largely idle for a number of years. For many, such experience
in the world has usefully broken in upon the enclosed world that
may have defined their family experience. The world is a less expensive, if not more understanding, place than college to begin to
assume a life of one's own, and the college could benefit from not
having to cope with the effects of first separation from home and
family. The world would have confronted the student with the
need to know many things and the frustration of not being able
to find them out. It might even have aroused idealism sufficient to
encourage the youth to attempt something other than that which
is forced upon him by necessity, opportunity, or drift.

The school would be a residential college, in the sense that it
would provide a place of residence, not force a place of confine-
ment. It would not be monastic—it would invite both men and
women—and it would strive to assemble a portion of youth, of
culture, of physical setting, superior to a random sampling of what
the world affords, although not necessarily very different in kind. Its
isolation would be that of any enterprise that requires quiet, com-
muning, and freedom. Such isolation would not be such as to deny
easy access to the world. Ideally, it might be a bit of greenery and
space set down in some area other than the blighted area of a large
city. Or it could as easily be removed from the city, although then
it must create an excitement of its own or give ready access to
some great metropolitan area. Space and shelter would guide one

172 TOWARD A LIFE OF ONE'S OWN

aspect of its architectural design. As places of instruction and study, its buildings would give the distinct sense of being enclosed, being sheltered. They would provide places within that could be drawn around one's shoulders. Yet that cloistering should be so designed that, moving outside, one would feel the sense of space as providing freedom to move, to stretch, to let the eye roam and the mind expand. In their total order, they should not dominate the individual either by their magnitude or by their fastidiousness of arrangement. If the setting is urban, then nature has to be brought in, not with fake mountains or babbling brooks, but with honest courts of grass and trees and shrubbery, suited to its urban existence. If the setting is rural, then buildings should be placed with respect for geologic time and geographic place—wind and water, sun and rain.

The calendar would be regulated by the surrounding climate, by the seasons in the country and by the movement of life, which is only partly seasonal, in the city. And within the calendar, the work itself would seek to make the most of the long stretches of winter, the early twilights, the rainy seasons. There would be somewhat flexible schedules for certain tasks, with some allowances for human failings. There would be a close relationship between what was to be learned and the time and the kind of time necessary to such learning. There would be no regular march through evenly spaced hours, but fixed and regular times for studies that profit from such hours and varying times and places for those that need variable hours. Students would be guided in using the scraps of time that our rough schedule not only permits but countenances —the fifteen minutes to drill on a language, the ten-minute walk that shapes a composition, the before-dinner lull filled with discourse.

My university would be one you walk into. It would have some kind of wall around it, and lots of inviting green grass, and enough architecture of a traditional kind to conceal the fact that it was just built yesterday, and the gates would be open wide—not wide enough for automobiles, but sufficient for humans. Permitting the automobile has not only caused problems and increased noise, it has supported the idea of the service-station university where young men get pumped full of intellectual gas and get greased for a smooth passage through life.

So my university is a walk-in place. Having taken the effort to walk in, the student just might decide to stick around awhile. Once

there, the student certainly wouldn't begin, as American universities now have him do, with registration. What a dispiriting introduction to college life! The only useful function it serves is to
eliminate those who can't find their way through the process. My
university would begin with classes, if, after thinking it through,
we of the university—students and faculty—really felt classes were
necessary.

It might be quite feasible to begin with lectures. Professors
would certainly rather talk than issue class cards—they would
rather talk than do anything. The professor might announce that
at such and such an hour on such a day in such a place
he would begin talking on his favorite subject and continue as long
as he and his students wished to stay. Stamina varying among the
faculty and the threshold of boredom varying among students, this
might be enough to destroy the present pernicious structure that
has almost all learning presented in fifty-minute packages.

As to students, they would walk into these rooms, stay if interested, come back if excited, eventually start lecturing themselves
when they felt they had something to say and could prove it. Under
this system, some vexing problems might be met, if not solved. The
dull might be chastened, the glib might be detected, the university
might become more concerned with the drop-ins—the students who
keep coming back for more—than the dropouts. Without the obligation to live up to the idea that class cards and credit hours give,
the inept, the bored, and the impenetrable might abandon university life, and neither the sense of guilt in the student nor the sense
of frustration in the faculty would be aroused.

Very soon, I'd hope, the lectures would give way to the kind of
interchange that must be at the heart of a university. The best
professors would get tired of hearing only their own voices, the
most excited students—and that's the kind that would be sticking
around—wouldn't be able to keep their mouths shut, and pretty
soon there would be discourse, people learning from each other, a
condition that is the "unifying" principle of the "university."

At this point, administrators—and these might come from
among the professors whose lecture halls were by now empty (it
would give them gainful employment and in time would likely
develop in them a strong sense of doing worthwhile work)—would
probably begin by lot or color of eyes or by initial letter of last
name (as is now the prevailing practice) to arrange place and time
where small groups could, when the excitement occasioned it, con-

tinue discourse. In time, these might be called classes, but their growth would be slow and capable of being checked, so that their harmful effects would be minimized.

As to what is being taught, nothing, quite obviously, is. Some things are being learned. Under this system, a good many subjects wouldn't appear at all—those for example, that now infest college catalogues, about which Socrates himself could not be interested. The Administration of the Elementary School Lunch Program, for example, or An Introduction to Indo-European Phonology, or Managerial Functioning of the Home-Owned Retail Mercantile Establishment. How could even the people doing such things be interested? These are things human beings tolerate in order to do other things that do engage their interest. The university has no business being as dull as life.

The other large group of things that would not be taught are all the things that one should and can learn by himself or with the help of books or machines. The grammar of a language, for example, and the principles of sociology and most other such subjects. Much that involves counting might be so learned—not basic mathematics, which requires a teacher sensitive to the aesthetics of numbers and capable of communicating that sense, but the many other counting chores that involve putting things into columns and boxes and applying them to merchandise or machines or mankind. And much dear to the defenders of the liberal arts might be partially removed from the classroom: books, music, drama, art would be removed as objects of study in favor of their becoming objects of doing and love.

In my university we might have to sacrifice classes to preserve learning. If we did get rid of classes, we might not only develop the mind but preserve its sanity. A national magazine writes about how Tim, high school honor society president, didn't just walk into Yale and start learning, but was screened, registered, and matriculated in the manner of our best universities. His beginning French class was conducted entirely in French, and after a few days, he began to fear he might flunk out. The trouble was, quite obviously, classes. A halfway bright student might walk into a lecture in French and sit there wholly unable to understand what was going on. A very bright student might even sit there long enough to flunk. But the fault is that there is such a class. Of course one learns a language by exposure. A child, abandoned in France, should end up as a French-speaking adult. But a formal college class can only faintly copy such an experience and at the peril of driving the student away from language study altogether. In a proper university, the student would depart at once and come back to class, if he came back at all, when he'd mastered—with the aid of obliging electronic devices—enough French to understand and be excited by what was going on. Or better still, he would have a constant informal exposure to a foreign language which came much closer to duplicating experience abroad.

Not that the student in my university wouldn't work. However, I'd like to think that the student spent long hours because he was on to something he just couldn't let go of, and that the flexibility of the university would permit his doing so without interrupting him by vexing matters such as classes.

Our course of study would have a termination, but it would be even more arbitrary than the four-year degree program is now. It could be determined by one means as well as another—by the financial resources available (an extended period in good years, a shorter period in lean), or by determining when a student actually reached a level of accomplishment. It would necessarily be a matter of years, for a student needs to see how one year's studies carry over into the next and to experience the kinds of development that can take place only over a year or more. A course of study of a certain duration is necessary to convince the public that these students have had a long enough time to become the geographer, the copy-writer, the archivist, the statistician, the botanist that is stamped on each diploma.

At such a place of learning, alumni and deserving friends would come back frequently—not for reunions and alumni weekends, not for degrees or certificates, but to finish up projects that they had to abandon when they left the first time or to take up studies that years later seem to have great relevance to what they are doing or feeling or wanted to be about. Properly conducted, universities would be most exciting for those whose additional experience enhances their learning and the university's as well. These returning students would pay for the privilege, and their employers would provide the time. And when they left, as when they returned, they would be going as students just carrying their learning to another time and place.

CHAPTER XI

A SENSE OF STYLE

D EVELOPING A SENSE OF STYLE may seem to be too high-flown an aim for American higher education, may even seem precious to those who have never given style much thought. And yet, viewed either close at hand or from the philosopher's distance, style is one of the great ends at which education aims. American college students do acquire a style, although most often it is a superficial one. One might claim that both the undercurrent of discontent and the overt agitation on the campus are not so much over issues as over style. Barren as much of bohemianism is, it is a recognition that though style is partly dress and manner, it is also the way one lives. At its opposite is a similar, less fiercely held, but more acceptable conception of style, which is defined chiefly by position, income, associates, and the like. Perhaps what is missing is the sense of style as something more than either of these postures, as something the educated young man or woman might give some careful thought to.

Here, I think, the American college or university is lacking in affording no very clear sense of the worth of style. It permits the student to reject conventional patterns of behavior and politely encourages him to examine various responses to life. But this falls far short of actively encouraging students to value style. In some classes they are exposed to style as an artistic concept, and they may in other courses gain at second hand some idea of what style is in a larger sense. Even the most successful students—successful in an academic way, that is—do not acquire a sense of style. In fact, among the peculiar results of academic exposure is that college students develop an invulnerability to style and come to regard "no style" as among the greatest of virtues. It is almost as if college prepares its graduates to live without style and feel smug in doing so. Certainly it does not place the acquisition of style very high on its list of aims.

Yet style has always enjoyed the philosopher's favor. Whitehead called it the ultimate morality of the human mind, a phrase that requires some thought. Did he have in mind the unified sense of one's being that judges the rightness of one action as opposed to another, the fitness all actions should have to the center one's life seeks or should seek? Did he mean that the measure of a man's mind is not in what he thinks but in the characteristic way his thought proceeds, not in his fidelity to logic or even to imagination but in acquiring a sure sense of the workings of his own mind? The examples he gives are the administrator hating waste, the artisan preferring good work, the engineer economizing his materials. He might have offered examples of a writer's sensitivity to the sound and shape and feel of words, of a historian's insistence upon making the individual fact bear upon the large hypothesis, of an architect's concern for space, mass, and movement.

But what does style mean to the man who is neither artisan nor architect, writer nor engineer? Certainly the sense of style in one's profession or craft argues its worth, as Whitehead has it arguing, from its utility. As common as it is to think of style as mere fiddling and trifling, it is still style that immediately and powerfully communicates to a common audience. It is as evident in the superior physician as in the superior athlete. It has some dependence upon the audience's knowledge—a writer's style, as a carpenter's, is more apparent to one who has tried his hand at the same occupation—and yet, I think, it has more to do with the interest the audience takes in the act than with its intimate knowledge of it. The spectator sees not only skill, which practitioners can best judge, but what is beyond skill, the deployment of the full range of skills with the ease and grace that define style. Style comes from the whole self being fully involved in an act over which the person is so much the master as to show no sense of strain.

It is what Hemingway describes as "grace under pressure," Whitehead as an aesthetic sense, based on admiration for the direct attainment of a foreseen end, simply and without waste, and Gibbon as "the image of character."

Still, we have not begun to answer what it is in life, except that it is the man himself, as Buffon said, and evidently, then, the center and circumference of his being. Reasoning from what style is in terms of man's skills, we must require a similar definition for style in life. It must be the mastery over all one does, with simplicity, harmony, and grace. Obviously, attaining a style of life is

no easy accomplishment, nor is it likely, once mastered, to be always maintained. Like style in speech or in dress, it must develop
through an awareness of style itself and yet not betray that awareness as a self-conscious manner put on for the occasion. One can,
I think, deliberately develop a sense of style, in life as in writing.
Like poetry, as Marianne Moore writes, style will often strike us,
should strike us, as not being worth all that fiddle. A man loves to
slop around unshaven a part of the time, a woman to let the
muscles relax in the privacy of her bedroom. If style is a consuming
obsession, something that must always be maintained, then it becomes mannerism. A satisfactory style has some looseness, some
tolerance for imperfection even as it performs an act or lives a life
in ways that may seem to others to be quite beyond reach.

The sense of style grows out of an awareness of life's many
possibilities either to act against or in harmony with the physical
needs and the spiritual hungers without which a person is neither
alive nor human. I am not talking about a life lived without passion or a life lived under such control that physical needs and
spiritual hunger are never felt. Quite the opposite. That is like
expecting a tennis player to display style against an opponent who
never rises to his game. For life is a hard skill to master, and no
one ever masters it unless he extends himself against it. It is very
much a matter of who is master, life or ourselves, and how much
we can get through to its essentials to answer with essentials of our
own. Style establishes a harmony—temporary perhaps, but firm
nevertheless—between ourselves and life. Out of both the struggle
and the reconciliation come the words and acts that reveal style.
Not to live life meanly—that would define it. Nor to squander it—
that would define it at the other extreme.

More to the point, what could higher education contribute to
developing a sense of style? As I have argued previously for the
development of certain senses during the early years of education,
I will argue now for their being emphasized again as the college
student begins to shape a life of his own.

The senses of play, discovery, and order, fully developed and
not allowed to atrophy, give a beginning for acquiring a sense of
style. One cannot free himself enough from any of the demands of
life to show grace or to inspire imitation without the sense of
play. The best style is very much a possession that, however it is
acquired, has the look of being natural to the person. An indi-

vidual's nature is seldom attractive if it does not show some sense of play. An ability to let up, to squander time profitably, seems characteristic of those who have acquired style in living. Although one can speak of a grim style, the very terms are contradictory.

Americans, some critics say, work hard and play hard, desperately at both. But it is not the fervor with which a person enters into one or the other that prevents a satisfactory style of living. It is whether either one or the other is done insensibly. Work can be the most satisfactory kind of play if one brings to it imagination and zest and if one does not believe that work is all that matters in the world. There are times, of course, when work will be dull, will be unanimated by anything but the necessity of getting it done. And there are times when one's imagination and zest are such that a particular piece of work is all that matters in the world, although even then, this is a condition of the moment rather than a truth one should hold fast to. Play, on the other hand, can be very hard work, as demanding of one's physical and psychic energies, as the hardest, most frustrating workday. And certainly it is work if the player cannot convince himself that it is play. Something is lost if such an argument even has to be waged. Thus, when I talk about keeping alive a sense of play, I am not talking about an arbitrary division between work and play, or even about the games, the diversions, that men and women turn to in leisure hours. Rather I am talking about a spirit that runs through all our enterprises, a laughing spirit, a loosening spirit, a freeing spirit, a mocking spirit, which always has at hand a make-believe world that can be held against actuality to show its make-believe characteristics too.

Higher education could, I think, foster that, and probably it does not do so very well. Fun and games are all on one side of the fence, the life of the mind on the other. Lessons are pursued too systematically, and courses of study are too firmly mapped out. The cheerful hedonism that is still to be found in undergraduate life leaves the person with a lifetime of regret that he didn't make more out of it or gives him the opportunity for conversion to serious study in graduate school, where drink and reproduction are the chief reliefs.

The act of scholarship tends to enlarge that area of experience we deem serious, to make small things significant, and to diminish the sphere of joy. A bug when it is a bug often brings delight. When it becomes an insect it begins to take on significance. When it becomes a centipede it drags in both fear and Latin derivations. When it is truly and accurately and naturally known as any of a class (*Chilopoda*) of long flattened many-segmented predaceous arthropods it has lost most of its "bugginess" and is well on the way to becoming a life work, an object of "serious" scholarship. It is possible, of course, for entomologists, as for Anglo-Saxon teachers, to make their increasing knowledge of the seemingly small illuminate the larger world, adding to man's joy as well as to the sum of his knowledge. But that is rare, and even then, the joy is of a different kind than that commonly associated with the world. More often, I think, a scholar's specialization is inflated to give it more universal currency than it is worth, the scholar is encouraged toward pretentiousness and pedantry, and, worst of all, joy of any kind is squeezed out in the process.

The scholar is always in danger of defending his peculiar, often esoteric, pursuits, by automatically urging the seriousness of his endeavors instead of admitting, as he should, that he is temperamentally incapable of making his living any other way, that he is too fine an instrument to be employed in coarser pursuits, that he is having too much fun of his peculiar kind to bother to defend what he is doing. From urging its seriousness to asserting its superiority is an easy step, to the loss not only of joy but to the growth of some of the snobbishness of academic solemnity. In turn, the seriousness of the professor infects the student body, the graduate school grimness creeps down into the undergraduate years, and before long—unless the professor looks askance at his own absurdity or the students reject such joyless pedantry—education gives up joy and gains little in return. Worst of all, a sustained and deadly seriousness in the pursuit of knowledge is probably detrimental to the free play of mind whereby the great leaps in our understanding are often made.

The sense of discovery would also enhance a style of life. The greatest accomplishment of any college (and most colleges succeed in this respect to some degree) is the opening of doors the students were not previously aware of. The student may have to climb over the machinery, tolerate lackluster instruction, dutifully fill requirements, but given a group of young men and women doing as many things as the colleges provide, given a library of a size he has never seen before, given a faculty of some size and peculiarity (if not distinction), he cannot escape the sense of new ventures.

This openness to experience, to life, is much a part of the style higher education might help one acquire. I do not mean either mere receptivity or anxious restlessness, either bland tolerance or committed prejudice. Both are dangers that education exposes one to. For every peace-marcher, sit-inner, John Bircher among college-educated youth, there must be ten whose experience has rendered them too flabby to join any but social clubs, religious groups, or the organizations that adults are drawn into because of their children. For these, the championing of different points of view, the granting that all questions are more complex than they at first seem, may have resulted in a passive acceptance of almost everything that does not seriously threaten the life close around them. Such attitudes make neighborhoods tolerable to be lived in, at least up to the middle years, when many college men and women find the life they tolerated increasingly intolerable. Then it is that regrets begin to arise over lives that might have been lived if one had not so easily accepted everything and selected nothing. Nor is the kind of discovery I mean the restless chasing after culture that college-educated people are prone to. The discovery of a new painter, a new parlor game, a new bootery, a new hairdresser, a new restaurant is not as important as discoveries of another kind, such as how a child learns, how much an adult can still learn, how a life can remain open to discovery and yet not become unmoored.

If we are to have the sense of discovery as part of one's style, the universities could contribute greatly by keeping their doors open to their graduates, not merely to entertain them, but to welcome back the inquiring mind. In turn, one's life need not consist of abandoning dreams of one's youth, but of picking up dreams set aside and finding new ones. The university community does provide the graduate—one can find adult education courses in almost every large university in the land, and in the college town an informal educating process goes on simply because there is a college in its midst.

But as important as it is for the university to continue the graduate's education, it is more important that it help its students discover enough in themselves and in learning to make self-education a continuing process. For style is much a matter of self-discovery. The writer who possesses a style finds not only the characteristic manner of expression that is his, but enlarges his self, refines that self, almost every time he writes. If a person arrives at a style at all, he very likely arrives at a better self than he would otherwise have. The university's part is to make that discovery of the best self among the multitude each of us contain worth trying for.

The sense of order is the last of the senses I would have a perfect education develop. Without order, one's life has neither style nor contour. What style in writing or painting or sculpture most discloses is the way the stylist establishes order among the unruly elements of which his work is made. The sophistication of one's response to works of art is related to the kind of order, the complexities of order he can perceive. The "plain style," as defining certain English prose, is one in which order rules over all else, and yet not in a fastidious way but in a straightforward way that will have a man say what he has to say with the least fussing around. The baroque style in writing, as in other arts, is at an opposite extreme. It impresses us by its very ability to build toward a collapse into chaos and yet to achieve an ordered relationship between even the most distant parts. The two extremes pose some difficulties for those developing a sense of style. The one seems to have no style at all, and the other exhausts our patience in trying to follow its intricacies.

One might compare prose style with life. Thoreau may seem to be seeking the plain style of living, but the merest open-eyed attention to his writing suggests that such an easy assumption may be wrong. Rather he is seeking—burrowing is his favorite metaphor—some imagined bedrock, there to plant his feet. And yet the stability he seeks is a relative one only, a place to stand to assure himself that there is such a place, but having arrived at that assurance, a place to depart from. The simplicity he constantly seeks is, I think, a maximum response to the large orderings of human life. The seasons provide him both a literary design and a simple marking of the time he drifts through. And that is the point for Thoreau, for many men who seem to have achieved an exemplary plain style of living. The ordering is not an imposing of simple systems upon what should be a rich life. It is rather the finding of certain basic verities by which one can mark a passage, like noting as one walks through a woods a fallen tree or an outcropping of rock or a patch of lush green if one's intention is to return by the same path. It is also the enhancing of life within the plainness one decides to strive for as his life's fashion. Thoreau can be accused of provincial narrowness when he says that Concord is his Paris, and yet, if Concord lacked a good deal that Paris possessed, Thoreau's Concord was a good deal more for him than it was for others whose lives went on there.

The plain style demands a good deal, particularly in our time, when we have so much that is not plain to obscure the essential plainness, drabness, of an existence. How much of the abundance of consumer goods ministers to other than convenience and comfort? A tenth of what we buy that no home can be without? The average house of a highly educated, therefore highly consuming, American is choked with things that suggest a richness of life as deceiving as it is seemingly attractive. The refrigerator gleams, the soft water flows, the oven shuts off with the politest of clicks, the little fan turns to dispel the rising odors, the serving cart rolls along, and in the background soft music plays.

All of which says very little about the life that goes on. Certainly it fails to disclose the many lives ruled by petty anxieties, not only the anxiety of keeping pace as consumers, but the more deadly anxiety of keeping pace as people. The children are sent off here and there for the lessons, the therapy, the preventatives, the anticipatives, that will make life easy and make life rich. The mothers speed them along, bundling and unbundling, telephoning Jane and Alice and Lucile, and popping a frozen dinner into the stove in one or another passage through the kitchen. The fathers work away, staying late at the office and rising early to provide for all these needs. The fullness of such a home life may never afford any of its members a confrontation of the plain self. All the movement and all the machinery do not hide the fact that lives lived in an excess of doing or possessing may have no style at all.

Yet what goes on, particularly as one moves higher up in the college-educated income bracket, passes for a rich life. Nervously baroque, one might call it—not daring enough to be fantastic, not certain enough in its basic architecture to be deeply satisfying even in its excesses. It is, it strikes me, the most common life style college-going affords. It is an outwardly attractive one, a physically pleasing one, but it lacks soundness of design.

That, of course, cannot be blamed on the colleges alone, although higher education can take an increasingly large share of the praise and blame for middle-class and upper-middle-class culture. College does whet our appetite for the rich, full life, and whether it increases our need for possessions or not, it helps create the income-gaining power that brings possession. Young men and women do go to college so that they can have a nice car or two cars and a nice house with nice furnishings and nice children in nice surroundings. And if they are somewhat intelligent and pursue studies to which they give a measure of their attention and get a degree, they may have all these things. Perhaps that is all we can expect of human aspiration, all we can expect of colleges and universities.

Yet it seems not unreasonable to wonder whether anyone enters a college or university for the purpose of learning how to live. That must be what Thoreau found so lacking at Harvard a century ago. Failing to provide him with a means of earning a living, it also failed to tell him how to live. For that, he went to the woods. There are fewer woods today. The colleges and universities that do maintain some spots of green might reasonably be asked to consider whether their purpose is not that of shedding light on how to live, of suggesting that in life, as in man's separate skills, acquiring style is one of the highest achievements of learning.

In a concrete way, what might fairly be asked of higher learning in helping its students acquire a sense of style? First, in the pursuit of any subject, from the first undergraduate degree to the highest, there should be conscious attention to the style of practice, study, and formal research. Let me take literature as an example, partly because it is a very broad discipline, inclusive of much that is centrally humanistic, and partly because style in writing is probably the most studied, the most obvious use of the term "style."

In literature, I think it is fair to say, there is an inverse relationship between the attention to style and prolonged study within the discipline. Most college English majors come into English because they have been voracious readers or amateur writers, or often both. They may be attracted greatly to a certain writer not only because they respond to what the writer has to say but because they sense that his way of expressing it is somehow right for them. He has a style to which they respond even though they cannot describe it very well. Similarly, most of a beginning student's efforts at writing, if he pursues them with any seriousness at all, are attempts to set himself forth in terms of what he has experienced or what he feels and believes and in a language that seeks in itself to express that identity. That too is style. The formal study of literature at the present time, favoring as it does the close scrutiny of texts, could be expected to draw attention to style, but the subject is still neglected in literary studies. Critics do study a

writer's style, but they do it as they once might have studied his
theology, giving a kind of limited attention to language because
they think it may help with more important considerations of the
writer's worth. The analytic approach to literature is useful in examining the particulars of a writer's style (the computer can sort
out the analyzable factors), but it easily leads to the dissection of a
writer's work, which is far removed from considering the whole-
ness of a man to be found in his style. For, although style in
writing is certainly made up of many analyzable language factors,
an analysis of style can easily become so involved in describing all
the particulars that it loses the sensitive and full awareness of
style that motivates the analysis in the first place. One might even
argue that the horror with which modern analytic criticism re-
coils from the personal in writing is a recoil from style itself.

At the undergraduate level, the prevailing tendency of the study
of literature is to damn appreciation and overpraise analysis. The
result is that the literature major is not encouraged to develop any
style of his own and is made somewhat insensitive to style in the
literature he reads. It is disturbing that senior English majors have
so little sensitivity to the style of the authors they have been reading, and more disturbing that they see so little relationship between English prose style and their own writing.

The condition is worse in graduate work, if only because further literary study might be expected to bring a student to the development of a style of his own as a kind of culminating achievement. Anyone who has read one dissertation or a dozen in any
humanistic discipline will be struck by the foolishness of such an
expectation. In part, of course, one can blame this on the artificial
conditions that surround the writing of a thesis, from the central
fact of its beginning—that the subject is likely something neither
the writer nor the faculty sponsor has an intense interest in—to the
central fact of its end—that completion comes slowly over a long,
frequently interrupted period of time. The writing of a thesis is
seldom the quarrying of an object out of hard stone, but more often
the dribbling of blobs of researched fact into a standard mold.
The scholars who write dissertations and receive the highest earned
degree seldom finish with much sense of style, or even much respect for style, although they may develop both later on.

I cannot speak for the pursuit of scientific subjects from first-
hand knowledge, but considering the speed with which the degrees
are earned, the collaborative aspect of most research work, and

the small fraction of a discipline that becomes the object of study, I doubt that graduate students in science develop a sense of style in their research, except perhaps as it may rub off from close collaboration with an unusual scientist. One way of bringing the two cultures together might be the shared appreciation of the fact that style is as necessary to scientific pursuits as to humanistic. Scientists often urge that every educated man should have some generalized understanding of the ways of science. But what is more important is that students of a scientific bent acquire style in their work and students with other interests gain some appreciation of a great scientist's style. Not one-hundredth of the way a great musician or a historian or a scientist goes about his tasks gets across to the liberally educated college student. Science as a humanistic discipline having history and consequence has been neglected, but so has style, in the scientific disciplines as in the humanistic.

What I am getting at here is the style of a man, his total conduct in working at whatever has his highest commitment. It is, after all, the style of a teacher that does most to excite emulation, that exerts maximum influence on others to follow teaching as a career. In any discipline, such style is more than the generally accepted practices of the discipline—the accumulation of facts, the classifying of facts, the application of inductive and deductive logic, the painful comparing of results. It is as much the guess that leads one's labors in one direction rather than another, the hardheadedness that keeps on against repeated dead ends, and above all the willingness to assume that one's puny efforts can extract something from the universe, can add something to what is already known.

If higher learning shows respect for style, then at least for those whose training goes beyond an undergraduate degree a development of style within a discipline should become one of the expectations. We might be forced to begin by making less of the merely informational or analytic. All graduate studies are bedeviled by the absurdly quantitative phrase "contribution to knowledge." The criterion cannot be defined or measured and is largely responsible for the piling up of scholarship that buries wit, pleasure, and invention. Instead, if we must have some dignified utterance about general aims, it might be that the student should acquire a style in the practice of his discipline. That criterion might not only include teaching but *be* teaching, and the candidate whose major

activity is going to be that of a teacher would either be a practitioner with the rudiments of a style before he began his career
or would feel obliged to develop a style as a mark of competence
in his profession.

There is, of course, style in conducting investigations and re-
porting on their results, which can be encouraged if not actually
developed in university work. Such style discloses itself in the problem chosen and in the tools chosen to work at it, in both the commitment and detachment shown in pursuing its course, in the pride
and humility with which one faces the successes and defeats involved in any following out of one's curiosity, in the ability to
place what, after all, may be one's self-indulgence as well as one's
discharging of a debt to posterity in perspective with other learning and other living. There is much more to this kind of advanced
study than the ability to accept the requirements of a scholarly
discipline, to follow out recognized patterns of inquiry, and to get
results in a form acceptable to some organ of publication.

Finally, as regards the application of an academic style to life,
the college experience should encourage developing a style of life
more than it does. The uneasiness the undergraduate feels about
precepts and practice, about getting a job and getting an education, about specialization and general education, about ideals and
realities, makes of his experience an education in compromise.
And although that is, from one way of looking at it, what all experience affords, yet that is precisely what the development of a
style works against. College can be looked at as the exposure to
choices under a condition of suspended commitment. What one
chooses in college—to play the social game, to bend to the books,
to have a go at art—is not the last word on what will happen next,
or, particularly, what will happen in the more distant future. But
a college can go too far in making it possible to defer choices while
getting the most general of educations. When it does, or seems to,
there is always a call for more precise training, for more rigor, for
making the college more a part of the real world. That is not my
point at all. If I would ask for anything, it would be to let college be even more artificial, even more unlike the world, even more
evasive of realities, so that the habit of compromise that life can
alone enforce upon one will not be positively inculcated by higher
education. Let some other, cheaper agency, like marriage, teach
that lesson.

Among the freedoms I have been quietly espousing throughout this book is that of following out one's bent. Only by doing so, it seems to me, can one really acquire a style. Four years of college are enough to give it a try, for the institution to sanction the pushing out in positive directions with no guarantee, of course, that the student will arrive at where he vaguely would like to go. Yet he would have had, as few students do now, the sense of a whole life committed to some central interest, and the manners, the gestures, the satisfactions, the frustrations of that interest would be reflected in his entire life. To some degree, colleges do that now, but for the most part they offer only some vague institutionally approved manner of conduct that can easily be carried over into adult life. Toward such style, a minority properly feels disdainful, but such disdain easily becomes a mannerism that may permanently disfigure the intellectual's style.

Nor am I sure I am giving good advice, either for the institution or for the individual. What is to be gained if one's zeal flows into one of the various dead ends that await those whose bent is not up to the development either the individual or society demands of it? What is to be praised in the premature zealot? What is to be lost in letting the individual close out opportunities for himself before he is even aware of what he *really* is after? And how, pray tell, does one find his bent, and finding it, how can he be certain enough of it to give it as much attention as developing a style demands? Yet, short of drift or supremely one-sided endowments or great wealth or powerful family (and even these give no certainty), the individual faces such questions inside college or out. What I am challenging is the drift that college-going permits, the lulling that goes with a smilingly varied course of development leading to career choices somewhat in keeping with the social climate. It leads to a high level of outward comfort with a correspondingly low level of inner satisfaction. A style of life asks more than that. With style a man may live his life at ground level, turning up the riches at his feet. Or he may live on high, so intoxicated by the swiftness of his flight that he scarcely notices the ground at all. At either level or at any of the other levels men occupy, style is living in a way one can feel, in a way that shows the impress of a man on life, the mark of the stylus from which the word "style" originally came.

CHAPTER XII

A SENSE OF WORTH

No QUESTIONS arouse more general interest on a college campus than questions of morality. It has always been so. The age and interests of college students and their removal from their families make it almost certain that their desires and means of satisfying those desires will be at variance with society's established conventions. Today, students argue for a new sexual morality, and within the traditional moral province of theology discuss existentialism and neo-orthodoxy and God-is-dead and the consequences each formulation has for an individual's actions.

Since the parents are absent, college does give the student a large responsibility for his own conduct. It is understandable that colleges, like parents, seem to concentrate on sexual morality, since if left somewhat to themselves, college-age men and women are likely to put sexual activity first among their electives. But however intense the individual's pleasure, the colleges' view of morality as chiefly concerned with sexual conduct is too narrow. It is the broader definition of morality that should particularly concern the colleges. Any experience on their own may give the young the opportunity to let their natural desires lead them to a "new morality." But few experiences give them the chance to ponder on questions of worth, before marriage and work and family diminish the necessity of such ponderings. Questions of morality are often no more than questions of opportunity. But the educational experiences that stimulate the students to question almost every concept of worth are opportunities of another kind, which have never been as available to as many people.

Traditionally, the colleges did not have to worry very much about finding bedrock on which character should be built. Education was determinedly moral, and as higher education was higher, so it capped the construction of the Christian gentleman, which, it was generally assumed, was the builders' aim. That some tenets of Christianity seemed to be contradicted by advanced learning was regarded as no more dangerous than the higher criticism of the Bible. But this was dangerous, as subversive of religious college values as the higher criticism was of a literal reading of Scripture. The religious colleges have steadily lost ground to the secular universities, and the firm moral traditions on which parochial education rests are challenged even by students in large part selected because of previous piety and the promise of further obedience.

Even Whitehead's assertion that the essence of an education is that it be religious, and that it inculcate duty and reverence, seems to carry something of the past's assurance that duty and reverence were enough and less of our time's recognition of the conflict between duties, of our reluctance to show reverence, and of our willingness to settle for the less lofty qualities of tolerance, respect, and understanding.

I am not sure I would accept Whitehead's formulation—for I am, in fact, unsure of precisely what he means. Perhaps education has no definable essence, its very nature being to expose multiplicities, to increase one's awareness of life—always at the risk of obscuring the grand simplicity that holds the world and one's perception of it together. If we seek ultimates, we might find them in education's power to confer worth, to give value to existence. Yet as formal higher education proceeds from day to day or, more precisely, from subject to subject, it confers worth upon some important concerns even as it detracts from the worth of others. The intellect is a great creator of discontent, a great displacer of simple satisfactions. The high virtues of the contemplative life have always been advertised by those who gain satisfaction from contemplation. We hear much less from those on the other side—too busily content with bodily pleasures, perhaps, to find time to record their satisfactions.

The point is that education of itself tells us very little about matters of ultimate personal worth. It may induce us to ponder them, it may add to the store of things we value greatly, it may offer models and paradigms by which to judge. But more, perhaps, than any other institution, it gives us no unassailable values to which we can subscribe. If it has any demonstrable effect, it leaves us freer to choose than before and with more to choose from. If, as some believe, it is in the agony of choice that one confirms his humanity, then education serves ultimately to keep one aware of the human-ness of our condition, both to our pleasure and despair.

But this is a wrestling with ultimates, essences, and aims that is certainly not the preoccupying concern of American education. As much as values may seem to be the proper core curriculum of education in some Golden Age, most formal learning confronts questions of value at more mundane levels. The confronting of values is the comparing of this major with another, this means of having a pleasant upper-class existence with other equally attractive possibilities, this way of serving self and society with other ways. If we argue that the total college experience results in a clustering of such choices into recognizable value systems, we may suggest that essentially there is a choice between a life given over to comfort and culture and a life lived according to one's deepest passions and highest ideals. College, of course, may make a person passionate about comfort, may make the acquiring of culture the highest ideal. But I am speaking only of the college graduate's superior position with regard to both vocations and culture. Bluntly put, college graduates make more money. Similarly, college-going gives more acquaintance with culture, increases the possible satisfactions to be derived from music, art, books—all those liberalizing aspects of college education. On the other hand, this highly attractive version of the good life may seem lacking in comparison with the life that begins in college as a commitment to ideals beyond those of success and culture and that has more intensity, more of a center, and more possibility of growth. One's personal sense of worth can grow from one as from the other. Nor does one choice necessarily preclude the other. Those who live the life in the world often find themselves drawing upon the ideals to which they have been exposed without fear of being corrupted, and the life in the ideal is not necessarily incompatible with a high standard of living.

College life reflects both sets of values. The fraternity-sorority system in a general way identifies those who wish to move comfortably within the upper-class world they occupied before they came to college and will occupy when they depart. And yet, of course, such a generalization leaves out those within the system who find vocations in as sure a sense as those most opposed to the fraternal aspects of fraternity life. And many things are highly regarded in both camps: recognizable achievements, an easy familiarity with culture, exposure to great ideas, and a desire for interesting acquaintances doing interesting things. Whether the fraternity group's first allegiance to materialism is debilitating to the spirit is hard to tell from the outside. Inside college and out, the group shows a concern for the trappings of culture, which the university in a general way equates with man's spiritual development. What is regarded as of greatest worth for them was succinctly put by a university dean of my acquaintance: "The basic aim of the College of Business," he wrote, "is to help prepare young men and women for a full life in post-college years."

Although there appears to be a sharp division between this group and the group clearly identifiable as campus intellectuals, both groups are influenced by the promise of a full life. The individuals who can be included with the campus intellectuals are more varied in their origins, probably less varied in where they will go. Many will become college professors, and most will be associated with university-oriented enterprises for the rest of their lives. Perhaps that is because even in college they show greater affinity for the life of the mind, a greater respect for the higher ideals of learning. Among them, of course, on campus and after, are those with marked resistance to the formal aspects of higher education. They find the libraries and laboratories cramping to the organic development their beings demand. Still, when they *are* in a conventional posture of learning, their beingness is much more manifest than that of sorority girls clustered around the tables in the reserve reading room. Their values differ most from those of the first group in their disdain for vocationalism, their qualified respect for professional schools, their somewhat aggrieved air about how much more money they could make elsewhere, and the carelessness with which they regard culture.

I offer these as by no means inclusive of the values higher education holds. They do seem to be present inside and outside class-going, a part of the social as well as the intellectual life. And they afford the means of speculating about how a sense of worth might be developed by a perfect education.

Achievement ranks high with both groups, although both dispute the worth of various achievements. If we deplore the mass of students who seem never to lift their desires above the mere attaining of a degree, we should also consider that most of them would not have it that way. If they are made comfortable in mediocrity, it is a tribute to the humaneness of a system in which the emphasis upon achievement makes the underachiever secretly question his worth. Although the varied campus life offers compensations in providing for achievements of many kinds, such compensations never match human needs.

The public schools have sentimentalized unduly over human differences, and yet they have been mindful of the absolute necessity of giving a sense of achievement if learning is to be accomplished at all. Colleges have been only slightly more tough-minded, and not entirely devoid of sentimentality. There is no denying the attractiveness of college life, which freely opens its doors and displays its wares to the public. Any place set aside for the gathering of young men and women would be attractive. Add to that the opportunities for winning a well-paid job, for gaining respectability in the community, for acquiring access to a richer, brighter world, and the appeal is irresistible. Having been so seduced, the middling student has justification for settling into a drift that will do little to enhance his actual sense of worth but will give him a college graduate's place in society.

Perhaps no education can do more. Even self-education faces the individual with tasks beyond his mastery, with vistas he will never see, with the blunt rebuff of his own limitations, and with the reproach of private failure. And what would life be worth if it did not give us things to try for, some of which we may gain? How many undeniable accomplishments come into being because the individual has been exposed to the achievements of others? One could postulate that the level of creativity in Athens or Florence was so startlingly high because of the presence of high achievements at close hand by which young men and women could measure their own achievements, stirring them into attempting to surpass their peers and predecessors.

Still, achievement is not of unquestionable worth in education. Given a very high and small area that defines achievement and a very large number of would-be achievers, an emphasis upon achievement may work against learning. For example, the small number of National Merit Scholarships awarded and the large number of applicants casts some doubt upon the wisdom of the whole program. One also wonders about the competition for admission to the best colleges and the behavior of many first-rate students in the atmosphere thus created.

One may begin to make the most of an achievement if it is given genuine worth not only because it is a human yearning but because it is to some degree within the realm of possibility. The bane of much teaching, in humanities and out, is the preoccupation with great achievements that are obviously worth the student's emulation but are presented in a way that keeps them completely out of reach and denies their relevance to the student's personal development. One cannot be a Newton or a Shakespeare or a Hume, and yet one can be exposed to qualities in each that can be developed to the fullness that one's capabilities and zeal permit. Some college professors, after all, have pulled themselves up to within conversing distance of the immortals—they should not discourage students from listening to the conversation. The atmosphere of a perfect education would be such as not to diminish the worth of achievement but to make the most of that which is achievable in each. It goes without saying that most individuals can achieve more than they do, though not more than they dream of achieving.

What I propose is very difficult for an individual human being to accomplish, much more difficult for an institution of higher learning. A student is hardly a student without the yearning for achievement that accompanies learning. Nor can an education be regarded very highly if it fails to distinguish between kinds of achievement as well as degrees of achievement. Nor does it improve the educational climate to parade minor achievements as great ones or to create bogus achievements, both of which colleges frequently do. Finally, given even a small handful of students set to learning roughly the same things, rivalry inevitably sets in and ranking begins. Still, it seems to me, rivalry is preferable to the institutional grading and classifying that goes on incessantly within the American academic system. There is no escaping the predefined expected achievement, and the standards are always out to check how much one has achieved. Learning proceeds under the measuring stick, and the spirit of learning for its worth (not for the achievements of the learner) is not much advanced. The bitch goddess success, even dressed in blue jeans and a sweatshirt, is still much around.

Some learning in the years of higher education should, it seems to me, be free. The learner should be free to move at his own pace, his own interest, his own ability. Achievement should be discarded as the measure of highest worth. The learning is what is worth anything (so long as the subject is worthy of study), and although any exposure to a course that doesn't result in failure is loosely regarded as an achievement, the marks of high, measurable achievement could at least be removed so that the student does have the experience of learning for its own sake. This might have beneficial effects on the college program, and it is likely to do even more good for the individual after college. Then, perhaps, we would have an educated citizenry willing to learn without the quantifying that goes on in college and university, willing to dare some learning other than learning that almost certainly results in achievement, willing to be both more modest in reflecting upon what they've learned and more proud about having learned something, however short of notable achievement it may be.

If there is one value above all others on the American campus, it is probably what can loosely be called culture, the refinement of thought, manners, and taste characteristic of the cultured person. I have alluded to culture in a previous chapter, observing that it contributes to the excitement of college life but takes away some of the chance for repose. Here I will extend that discussion to consider its central position in creating the sense of worth that may arise out of higher education.

The "full life in post-college years" that a dean stated was the aim of his College of Business is certain to include large doses of culture. Considering the level and the impact of what passes for culture on television and radio and the movies—the means by which this country has a common culture—it is fortunate that a responsiveness to a higher culture exists in force somewhere. Yet the attention given to culture on the campus arouses suspicion, if only because its worth is as unquestioned today as Biblical truth was in various periods of the past. More than that, one is suspicious of the overwhelming way in which culture saturates higher education. Surfeit is surfeit, regardless of what.

That there is a surfeit of culture may be all the objection I have, all the objection that can be argued convincingly. The particulars of that central objection are easy to state. When so much that is cultural is constantly present, much has to be snatched at rather than savored, read on the run, worked in between a precultural tea and a postcultural discussion. A superficiality toward

the arts—to single them out here—seems inevitable, so that the
artist has an audience of sorts, but very little impact. The person
ends up as a collector who doesn't read his books or listen to his
music or even look very often at the reproductions of masterpieces
that adorn the walls. Better one book that reaches the center of a
person's being than a shelf of books that never suggest to him
that he has a center, better one composer whose work quietly or
stormily invades the listener's feelings than dozens whose sounds
merely wash over, better one painting that changes the viewer's
vision than hundreds that please his sense of being currently cultural. Admittedly, the colleges respond to the need for exposure,
and students who are given the widest possible sampling have a
lifetime to have their interests deepen. The single book, the single
song, is, of course, not the alternative. We could have a measure of
the richness of exposure to the arts and still imagine that love
could develop rather than an endless number of brief flirtations.

Such reservations about culture in the university are also reservations about creativity. The two are linked, and the value of one
is urged as unquestioningly as that of the other. For the potential
writer or artist or craftsman, the abundance of culture may have
the effect of making him an observer or commentator rather than
the creator he might have been. The university is inclined to encourage study and preparation as necessary to achievement, and
intimidating the potential artist further may influence him to
adopt a lifelong posture of keeping up with the arts rather than
to develop his own skill. One cannot blame the dominance of
criticism upon the universities' sponsorship of culture, and yet, if
there is a single villain, the universities could certainly be named.
The universities impress on their students that an ability "to talk
art" is a prerequisite for the cultured individual. And although
the universities are major sponsors of the arts, the kind of return
that grows out of the investment has not been carefully examined.
Once again, of course, creation of the earth itself would lose significance were the Creator to bring one into existence every day
of the week.

There is also a protected quality about the booming creativity
of the universities that makes one wonder if it, like other visible
aspects of American higher education, is more to be praised in
quantity than quality. Fiction and poetry might well disappear if
writers had no place to publish their work. Yet appearance in one

of the many literary quarterlies that have made up, to some extent, for the disappearance of poetry and fiction in national magazines is more interment than publication. I think that the great number of magazines publishing creative efforts and critical articles can have an adverse effect upon the writer. Although they leave him free from commercial taboos and the public's whims, they do not provide either the standards or the payment in hard coin and readership that can spur a man to his best efforts.

In short, creativity on the campus is like almost everything else there. It is encouraged and even sponsored and rewarded, but still as a somewhat hothouse growth. And although the first-rate does emerge along with much that is mediocre, the institutionalized passion for creativity is often greater than the actual creative efforts put forth. The truth may be that despite the university's dedication to creativity and the arts the university does not provide a very good training ground for the poet or painter or musician. That is, few universities are flexible enough to give the potential artist the freedom to fix upon his skill with anything like the singlemindedness necessary to fruitful apprenticeship or fully developed competence. If he stays within a discipline, as he is likely to do, he is further harassed by the scholarship (with its preoccupation with origins and influences and major and minor figures and its necessity for surveying broadly or examining in depth) that seems most often to stand against fresh creations. The poet who is to be a poet, the composer who is to be a composer, or the painter who is to be a painter would be well advised to get out of the university if he is serious in his interest, and even if he feels he must debate whether he is serious, the university may offer too many distractions to allow him to debate in earnest.

In this respect I would have a perfect education take one of two directions or find a way to take both. One direction is to regard creative work as one of the marks of the educated man. The amateur artist would not be regarded as a failed professional but would be given the respect due a person whose education has permitted him to develop such skill. The other direction is to separate the professional development of the artist from the general university program. The university would face directly the question of the worth of artistic creation as against university training. A man might elect either, rare individuals might attempt both, but the artist who appeared to have a real gift and who could summon the self-discipline that would convince the university of his worth might well, with full institutional approval and rewards, go his intense, even narrow-minded, way. It would take some doing for a university to accommodate either view. The passion for high specialized achievement stands in the way of recognizing the amateur in almost any discipline and especially in the arts. The other view requires some relaxation of the university's conviction that the only road to full development is through general education followed by a college major, both pursued amidst the richest possible culture.

A last objection I raise toward the high place culture, in the sense I have given it, occupies in university values is that it too easily substitutes for all other values. A tremendous sense of worthwhileness runs through the culture of a university. "Significance" becomes the banner around which everyone rallies. If a playwright cannot fashion a play rich in secondary layers of meaning, if a composer does not extend human or electronic capabilities, if a painter does not paint the throbbing something beneath the clothes, beneath the skin, beneath the bones, he had better be at something else. The reaction is so automatic that much of popular culture—comic strips, bad movies, television commercials—is swept into the currently significant. "Camp," one of the sillier cultural games some people play, is probably best explained as a kind of extension of culture to a maximum of objects that surround university people, or as a not quite hilarious spoof of the worthwhileness that marks the cultural preoccupations of a university-trained audience. Either way, it raises some doubts about the worth of culture not only as "art" but as an all-embracing "value" in higher education.

For there are a good many things of great worth with which higher education is concerned that fall outside of culture as I am defining it here. I will not name science and the scientific outlook, or the scientific vocation, because what I have said of culture is a condition created and fostered as much by the university scientist as by the aesthete. There is probably a tapering off of the culture epidemic as one reaches pharmacy and the manlier branches of engineering and the administrative areas of education (although I suspect few members of these groups would like being called uncultured). But there are scientific avocations—astronomy, collecting of all kinds, mathematics—that are of equal worth with culture and that might as usefully occupy a man. I would suppose that a number of seemingly practical matters, ranging from personal ethics to educating one's children, might be brought more squarely into a central place in a perfect education. And I would ask that a great number of purely private pleasures might be elevated in the scale of worth for the educated man. For what I fear most of all, I think, is that culture becomes what university athletics has become: public show in place of private development. Already, it has taken on some of the pompousness, vulgarity, and deceit that seems inseparable from college athletics.

One last value seems to have wide currency on American campuses. University-trained people set great store on "interest." People must be interesting, children must, houses must, shops must, supermarkets must, pets must. Life need not be joyful, satisfying, upright, or wholesome, but it must be interesting. Much the same could be said of twentieth-century art, with its craving for newness, for originality, and of the modern audience's demand for a new sensation every hour. To have some reservations about the incessant demand to be interesting is not to praise dullness—college professors fall too easily into that posture. Rather it is to ponder whether such attention does not suggest a certain nervousness, an aversion to sitting still, a resistance to the quiet, the traditional, the inconspicuous, that denies a range of satisfactions both in the years of higher education and after.

There is a seeming fear of being bored even within a setting that furnishes all manner of studies and diversions. It is a fear that probably increases after graduation and that the transplanting of the removable parts of college experience—social life, community service, cultural activities—is designed to quell. And yet, paradoxically, among those supposedly educated for the fullest lives, the search still goes on for interesting people and something really interesting to do. In part this may be an exhaustion of culture by the means I have just described—concentration on culture as the only worthwhile thing and superficial exposure to all that can be called cultural. It may be that education brings everyone to feel the weariness of study and the hopelessness of finding anything new.

There are no certain antidotes for such feelings and not many institutional safeguards. The insistent cry, "Interest me, interest me," is one no teacher can disregard, and yet it is a cry that may become a habit signifying the exhaustion of self rather than of the surroundings. A perfect education would not undervalue interest, but it might seek to foster some single skills, expose to some particular knowledge, to the degree that interest resides in the act or the thing itself rather than in the mere shifting from one diversion to another. The preoccupation with the interesting, the defining of worth by the degree of interest provoked, may result in obscuring questions of value. And that, it seems to me, is inimical to the development of a sense of worth, without which one is at best half-educated.

In being critical of the values of the American college and university, I reflect my suspicions that none of these values creates a strong sense of personal worth in the student passing through. They seem to argue so effectively for the general worth of college-going that the person accepts higher education as an unqualified good without seriously considering the specific worth it has for him. Secure in the worth of the training that a university-approved discipline provides, the student can study values as an elective if he has the time. But the attractiveness of idealistic service after graduation or as an interruption of undergraduate study seems to me to speak for the need many students feel to confront values and for the lack of confrontation they find on campus. The large issues of our time—civil rights, nuclear disarmament, the emergence of new nations—could not but help draw youth in, but the college youth's involvement is in part the need to feel a sense of worth in what he is doing, which is not provided by the general values university education stands for. I suspect that the search for personal worth sometimes runs counter to other values—may make culture seem inconsequential and measurable campus achievement seem inferior to service in the world. It may be simply a matter of interest to bright students whose private or public schooling has already exposed them to much of what they encounter in the first years of college. Certainly there is one thing to be praised in the unrest now evident on the campus: Whatever the driving force, however dubious the motives of the leaders of such movements, the strength in numbers comes from students who find that their university existence gives them an insufficient sense of worth and who strive to do something about it.

There is one other paradox to be uncovered. Although many, probably most, American colleges and universities are dedicated to service, such dedication has apparently not been sufficiently meaningful to students looking for something, someone, someplace, to serve. Although universities offer the student the isolation of highly specialized theoretical studies, they also offer him more than ample chance to serve himself, his fellow man, his country, and mammon, often in very attractive combinations. The fastest-growing undergraduate college is the college of business, which advertises its service to the economic well-being of the community as to that of the individual. Although I think it might be proved that it is not so much service-oriented students who are found in campus protest movements as students whose studies provide little sense of serving, preparing a student directly and specifically for a service vocation may not develop the sense of worth toward which higher education might draw its students.

If, then, neither the general culture of a campus nor its specific preparations for service develop a sense of worth, what will? The answers are as various as the individuals who must face the image in the glass and ask and answer the question as best they can. What guidance I offer is done humbly, gropingly, for I am neither sure of where I stand nor where I would take others.

Begin, I would say, in passion—in the teacher's enthusiasm, in the student's inspiration. How much of this is lost in the self-consciousness of our time, the unwillingness to expose oneself, the restraint that goes with objectivity, the caution that goes with patient, often erring, search. How easy to ignore the lesson that youth would always teach age if age would only listen: that passion confers worth. The notion is a romantic one, and a notion only. Yet if the passion of commitment conjoins with a high development of skill, the worthless may suddenly or slowly take on worth, become a poem or an idea or a perception. Without passion, a person waits for significance to fall upon him, for the world to drop before his startled eyes. To such placid natures, *worth* needs only the right kind of packaging to make it recognizable to everyone. The perfect education, respectful of reason as it is, preoccupied as it must be with mind, courts passion so that it may arouse passion in those who come to it constrained, keep passion alive even for those who show most need of constraint.

This is far from saying that passion alone defines worth, that powerful feelings justify murder and rape. It is not even sanctioning a "passional unconscious" that places our judgment in our bowels. It is rather arguing for a learning that partly answers the individual's questions about values by urging the need for passionately held beliefs, passionately felt responses to the experiences he has had, and passionate expectations for the worth of learning to come. The general lines of our endeavors are already put down—man's institutions, man's personal needs, man's place among other men. What remains is the awakened self moving among them, testing, judging, discriminating, but with the willingness to feel deeply, passionately, about what our learning has brought us. It is this kind of inquiry that arouses our deepest satisfactions, that draws from us our continuing commitment to learning.

My argument is against the kind of learning that would arrive at an equanimity of response, in which value is lost because in the unaided light of analysis and comparison all learned pursuits seem about the same. I ask no hierarchy based on some absolute standard of worth. I ask that one give to the learning he wishes to acquire all his heart and all his mind and all his self. "Does a firm persuasion that a thing is so, make it so?" Blake asks, and Isaiah answers, "All poets believe that it does and in ages of imagination this firm persuasion moved mountains; but many are not capable of a firm persuasion of anything."

I would ask, second, that passion bring expression, force out of one the smile, the gesture if that is all one has to offer, but at least that. More, of course, should be demanded, for learning is worth little if it does not provide means of expression—writing in which there is joy, music in which there is song, science in which there is the curious man poking into corners that may produce such wonders as we have not yet known. I do not think the schools have been deficient in working with the skills of communication, although they are more optimistic than I am about the possibility of large numbers of people developing such skills to a high degree. But more important is the necessity for dignifying utterance, not keeping it forever confined to an ordained size and shape and fashion, not keeping it held in for fear it weighs too little or reveals too much. There is a pathos in the way supposedly educated men seek out courses in communication, as if they could say anything while they remain ignorant, as if they would be wise when they learned how to communicate. The silent fool may conceal his foolishness, but how will he masquerade his silence? He remains the fool, however he may hide it from the world. Speaking out, he may convince the world of its own foolishness.

Again I argue against an education that has the effect of overpowering those it would educate. One hesitates to speak amidst the music of the spheres. The scholar conversing with antiquity may forget to speak to his time. The student cowed by his books and overawed by his mentors may forget to speak at all. Scratch on a rock, shuffle one's feet in the leaves, scrape out a monody on a fence wire—but find voice for what has been taken in. Passion compels utterance. Become, as Emerson advised, one who listens greatly, but do not fail in letting your voice be heard. For a man has difficulty in finding out just what it is he most values. By speaking out, if only to himself, he has a chance to raise questions about worth, to expose his prejudices, to confirm his judgments, to be moved by his passions.

CHAPTER XIII

WHAT WE EXPECT FROM EDUCATION

WHAT DO WE REALLY ASK of education? In the United States, we ask the schools to do much that might better be done by other institutions. Not only must they provide general training for adult responsibilities but specific training for work that will match each student's highest expectation. Our colleges and universities rise above the enterprise not as peaks, but as a dominant, accessible massif. None can claim the simplicity or detachment of purpose once given as justification for taking a degree at Oxford: to be able to read the Scriptures in the original and have proper contempt for those who cannot gain emolument in the church. If American education has any central impact, it is that of preparing students to do everything and to be discontented with much of what they do.

What do people expect education to do? Foremost, a man wants work, and asks that education train him sufficiently to give him employment. Second, a man wants some understanding of the world outside and within himself and a sense of control over a portion of it. Third, a man seeks sources of satisfaction of visceral, sensuous, and spiritual desires. If education acts as a restraint upon direct gratification, it tends to increase vicarious pleasures. Fourth, a person wants a variety in life that gives some hope of escaping boredom. Finally, a man wants some encouragement in the face of ultimate darkness.

The list is partial. The order is not necessarily from first to last of importance, nor am I concerned here with the gaining of knowledge that contributes to man's understanding of the universe and to the alleviation of mankind's suffering and toil. In concluding this excursion into a perfect education, I wish to look away from the loftier ends of learning to consider what the individual expects close at hand.

American education—all education—is strongly vocational. The father who schooled his son in the art of hunting or the art of war was preparing him for the most elementary kind of work necessary to his self-preservation. The high school student drawn to electronics or auto mechanics is almost as directly preparing himself for survival. And even the bookish adolescent pursuing Latin probably has some apprehension that beyond mastery of the language lies an occupation that will put his learning to vocational use. Let us be less condescending toward education that aims primarily at utility. The distinction to be made is not between vocational and nonvocational, but rather between the immediately vocational and the distinctly vocational. Short-term goals, like short-term satisfactions, are commonly regarded as less worthwhile, but such regard seldom considers carefully the precise value of the work to be done or the satisfaction it brings.

There is, of course, a rough gradation in the value commonly placed upon work, from the most wearying kind of simple physical labor to the most complex kind of abstract thought. In general, this country honors an education that moves man up the scale. Simply put, a man seeks education to avoid dull, hard work. The more education he gets, the less physical are the demands made upon him. An educated, if elementary, assessment of a man's capabilities over a life span inclines him to this course. Physical prowess declines comparatively early in life. The superiority of the contemplative life is not based on its ability to afford the most intense satisfactions, but on the less exciting appeal that its satisfactions stretch over a longer period of time. Before too long in this country, simple physical work will hardly be feasible as an occupation. The gross muscular movements of lifting, sorting, arranging, and transporting have been taken over by simple and complex machines, and the individual has been made the supervising part of the physical operation. The most important result may simply be that of freeing man from the sweat and strain that exhausts both muscles and mind. The simple machine, which a man was once forced to be, now sits in attendance upon the gears and levers and relays that replace his inferior muscular powers.

The lesson for education in our time is that public school

education need not be seen as the development of the mind to avoid the physical demands made upon the body. With that conflict abated, the social disapproval of the trades and semi-skilled occupations might also diminish. Book learning might be viewed as enhancing everyone's life rather than separating one kind of worker from another. If we are to work toward these ends then, public school education should become more, not less, efficiently vocational, should ask that employers do more to provide specific training for jobs, and should ask that the idea of work be made more appealing to the educated man.

An uneasy relationship still exists between man and the machine, conditioned for over fifty years by man functioning as part of the industrial mechanism and fearing to be displaced by superior machines. For a brief period some years ago, I worked in a box factory, stationed at the final point in a series of mechanical processes that fashioned egg cartons from paper pulp. There, confronting a machine whose physical prowess was greatly superior to mine, I was expected to grab bundles of flattened cartons ten at a time as they came from the machine, turn one bunch one way, the next bunch the other, and stuff them into boxes. The machine had obviously been left unfinished, either because it was cheaper to hire human beings or because the inventor had lost interest. For the first few hours on the job, I was in too desperate a race to keep up with the machine to give the matter much thought. After that, I developed resentment toward asking a human being to do work that could have been done so easily by simply extending a mechanical process. The contest with the machine was all that kept me on the job past the first few hours. When I was sure I could beat it, I quit and took a fairly similar job, sorting mail at a post office. The new job at least involved some sense of serving human activities more exciting than eating eggs, and since it was not automated at all, I could do my work in human company.

Factory work has long stood for work that separates the worker from both the product and his own humanity. But my brief factory experience is surely more related to the past than to the future. The extension of the machine promises to raise the most deadening mechanical work to a human level. The rudimentary tasks of digging holes or laying ties or screwing on nuts are given to the machine, and man enters at a point at which the finished structure can be discerned, the goods moved, and the connection made between product and person. Such a transformation has not been accomplished in up-to-date factories alone. In individual laboring jobs, where the backhoe digs the trench or the fork lift raises the pallet, the human worker is free to take pride in the larger operation of which he is part and to develop interests that his less toilsome work permits him to consider.

Work that is related to varied human desires and that does not deny human association is the kind of work about which public school education could be unashamedly vocational. The increasing automation of the factory has its parallel in every other occupation, from clerical work, where hundreds of mind-numbing tasks are performed by machines, to janitorial service, where even the laborer can take pride in the range of machines at his command. The point is that education need no longer be looked upon as means of escape from physical drudgery. Trades can be given the attractiveness they once had as handcrafts. Those incapable of or uninterested in work which relies to a large degree on some form of abstract thought need not be drummed out of school. Schools must not slight such occupations just because the past has conditioned us to respect only that work associated with formal intellectual training. This is what I mean by asking that the schools become more vocational rather than less.

Education in trades and skills involving machines is expensive because of the equipment necessary to catch the student's interest and develop his competence, and because of the rapid obsolescence of such equipment. In the past, manual training, commercial science, and other vocational courses could provide rudimentary training sufficient to the needs of a large part of the semi-skilled labor force. Even then, the apprentice system was usually superior to formal schooling. Today, the school cannot duplicate the many complex machines that do society's work and cannot be expected to provide adequate training in the use of such machines. With limited resources, a school may be incapable of interesting students in entering a wide variety of semi-skilled occupations. The business and industrial establishments must enter into a more direct educational relationship with the public schools if their interests and the students' interests are to be served.

One cannot help but be optimistic about the amount of repetitive, stupefying, and physically debilitating work that has passed over to machines—beautiful, obliging machines, fortunately incapable of feeling, most easily adapted to simple tasks that need doing over and over again. Placed into machine systems, they do take away many of the handcrafts in which individual men and the guilds they formed once took pride. At the same time, they have also taken away work—like making paper or processing meat—about which only a machine could be enthusiastic. By such means a great deal of the dirty work has disappeared. What is most before us now is making work worth doing, giving value to work that places the worker in the position of operator, inspector, and checker, not the servant of the machine but the keeper of its health. Such positions probably increase the amount of free time on the job. Such time, like the increased leisure hours that are part of the worker's improved condition, is what an education that aims at the development of the individual self, his curiosity, his abilities to observe and relate, to think and feel, is designed to fill. And certainly, as the amount of free time, on the job and off, increases, an education that aims at developing an individual with some means of keeping himself from being bored is the essential education.

If work proposes to interest the educated man, it should involve the worker, however removed his individual job, in the human needs his product serves. In all respects—in making public school education more effectively vocational, in asking places of business to contribute more to actual training, in asking both to enhance to contribute more to actual training, in asking both to enhance the worth of work—a more vital relationship between public schooling and man's work is being asked for, not by sacrificing the academic program, but rather by using specific academic training to better the larger life that specific and effective vocational training makes possible.

If vocational education is to be criticized today, such criticism might well be directed at graduate study. At one time, a critic could be tolerant of the graduate school. It was full of harmless drudges, true, but not in sufficient numbers to make much difference to society. Today, the numbers are much larger, the effects on society much greater, and the impact on education, alone, of a kind and magnitude to arouse concern. The common and most valid criticism of vocationalism in education is that it narrowly trains for work to the exclusion of the large development of the person, which we fondly and rightly expect of a proper education. Almost all of the traditional complaints about advanced study relate to its excessive and narrow vocationalism. Instead of encouraging an intelligent student to feel and think and write, the graduate school asks him to deaden his sensibilities, confine his thought to the specialized research task, and express his findings with no more respect for writing than for thought. Instead of encouraging a student to extend his acquaintance with major human achievements, graduate training encourages a preoccupation with minor work that fits the vocational niche. Instead of asking for the kind of facility in a second language that might make a scholar conversant with another culture, the graduate school sets language requirements as job hurdles or as vocational tools necessary to research. Instead of encouraging breadth and synthesis, the emphasis is all on specialization and analysis. The result is a vocational training not very different in kind from that to be found in any other trade school.

The graduate school has proved immensely successful. Not only does graduate work offer placement in just the kind of job that the course of study has promised, but it escapes the opprobrium attached to technical training by claiming to be the logical extension of undergraduate study in the liberal arts. The large number of students staying on in graduate school are only in part attracted to the life of the mind. Most see clearly that the B.A. degree does not place them in the kind of professional or semi-professional occupation they would like. The indefinite vocational opportunities open to holders of the bachelor's degree are less attractive than the definite vocational placement available to those with the M.A. or Ph.D. degrees. What training could be more specifically and often more narrowly vocational than that which prepares a college professor to fill a specialist's position on the staff of any department in a university? The attraction to college teaching is in part the specific job opportunities that await after one's years of study. What breadth the graduate-school-trained professor achieves, and the real satisfactions he derives from his work, probably develop after his years of pursuing a determinedly vocational objective.

A variety of technical and vocational training disqualified as proper college work flourishes in the graduate school. College students want work as much as non-college students, and society wants well-trained technicians just as it wants doctors and lawyers and engineers and college professors with great technical competence. Yet the demands for specialized technical competence become too great if they must squeeze out the opportunity for enlightenment in matters of general human concern, which the college and university are particularly qualified to provide. Men trained for the professions, men to whom formal study is most fully extended, are commonly expected to and commonly do take a large part in public life. The need for our most educated citizens to possess intellectual breadth as well as depth and to be seriously, joyfully, and intelligently engaged in broad human concerns is a paramount need. Freed from some of the technical tasks that sophisticated machines can perform, the professional man should have an education that aims at developing his full human capabilities.

Even in the undergraduate college, the influence of graduate education has created a suspicion toward involvement in large complex issues, toward anything other than the vocational expertise specialized study creates, and toward studies other than the vocational ones by which graduate students enter their specialized professions. Were the term "research" not so loosely used and applied, more harm would be worked than is. The student is drawn away from a world he wants to understand and explore into a commitment to a field, a department, a concentration that must engage his full interest if he is to keep pace with his fellow students. It is to be regretted that, at a time when higher education has been extended so widely, methods of graduate training have been the model for all education from the early years of public high school on. One of the chief tasks that colleges and universities face is to revitalize general education. Given the vocational needs that could be met before college and the vocational emphasis that prevails in the graduate school, the time is at hand for general education in the colleges to shape a program which can justifiably occupy a larger portion of the undergraduate years.

The length of the foregoing discussion, only preliminary to what needs discussing, testifies to the importance I place upon education's giving a person something to do. The ideal, perhaps, is to bring more and more of us to a condition in which life and work are one. Education moves us toward that realization by opening up a larger range of work and by preparing us for these expanded opportunities. It cannot remove all conflicts between how a man spends his working hours and what he does with his life. Its concern for the one must be matched by a concern for the other.

Among the vague expectations man has from education is the

general hope that it will give him an understanding of himself and the world. A person wants the security of feeling that he understands some corner of his experience. The hostility to facts as constituting a satisfactory education is aroused by the recognition of how little facts mean until they can be meaningfully clustered together. No one remembers very much, but some things stick, and they provide surface for further accumulation. Such gathering is only the means toward understanding. Walking through a strange city and becoming familiar with the names of streets, the location of principal buildings, and the directions in which street numbers run enable a man to find his way from one place to another. But this acquaintance is a long way from the feeling that arises when a person knows a city, cannot only get around in it but is at ease in it, and can live comfortably in it because he is able to understand and control the part of it that means most to him.

To reach that secure understanding, facts not only need to be gathered, but also related to the person. The difficulty in formal education is that one is taken out of contexts that matter most— family, friends, play, sex—and placed in ones that hardly matter at all—the stuff of classroom learning, like history, mathematics, and geography. A teacher constantly struggles to get across the relevance of what he is teaching, and tries to find the frame of reference that will make a new fact a vital part of previous learning or present experience. The feeling that education is worthwhile asserts itself most strongly when one recognizes that isolated facts have grown into a general understanding.

There are many intellectual means by which one gains understanding. Remembering and relating are the ones most involved in my analogy. Continuing attention to cause and effect, particularly if the causes are elusive or complex, surely produces a mind more capable of living with the multiplicity that surrounds it. Practice in weighing evidence to arrive at conclusions is both a natural activity of the mind and one that can be refined by education. Logic, though we come by it obliquely these days, is a practical tool for attaining mastery over the rational processes of thought, and rhetoric in speaking and writing is still a major means by which men understand and exercise control over their experience.

But beyond the rational grasp of the world is the understanding of the self, which seems to be a preoccupation of our time. The easy means to self-discovery and the easy rules for self-mastery are available to every person. Yet such painless familiarity with the self seems offensively smug to the thoughtful man. He rightfully asks that education make clear to him the difficulty of the undertaking, the fitfulness of insight, and the isolation in which man dwells beneath the skin. Man's understanding of himself proceeds by bits and pieces, by making wrong turns and recognizing the mistakes, by coming upon dark corners that need exploring and finding the courage to do it. It is these difficulties that make one ask for sympathy in seeking understanding and hope for the confidence necessary to the search. Without sympathy we cannot enter into a knowing relationship with ourself or with anyone else. Without confidence, the magnitude of knowledge has a way of reducing one's own size, of forcing invidious comparisons between what one can and might do and what has already been done. Sympathy contributes a feeling that is as important to understanding as intellectual comprehension. Confidence is the necessary self-respect that makes the struggle for understanding worthwhile.

Third, a man asks that education be a source of many satisfactions. All of our most satisfying adult acts, muscular, sensory, and sexual pleasures, are in part learned. We learn to play golf, paint landscapes, or make love to immense satisfaction year after year. Education has a legitimate interest in adding to our physical pleasures, though it compromises that legitimacy by insisting upon investing such activities with academic trappings. There is an indisputable satisfaction to be derived from doing any physical activity well. No one need detract from the pleasure of playing a game well by arguing for its intellectual, aesthetic, and moral virtues. Basic instruction in a new skill has justification enough in getting a person beyond the beginning awkwardness that is often the chief cause of discouragement. Less could be said about the values of team sports and a good deal more about the development of physical skills that bring lifelong individual satisfaction.

To acquire skills in sports, as in other activities that bring sensory satisfactions, imitation is essential. This alone gives reason for the high level of performance insisted upon in sports, theater, and the fine arts. But the devotion that leads to professional performance is not what is commonly expected of education. Although a great performer will often acknowledge his debt to a great teacher, he less often singles out an educational institution. His real debt is to the gift and compulsion that drive him to perfect-tion. Education in physical skills should be broader in scope than training for professional performance. What needs cultivating is the amateur who will continue to derive satisfaction from being an imperfect participant rather than a perfect spectator.

Education must provide for spiritual satisfaction as well as physical and aesthetic ones. The secularity enforced upon the schools is a healthy condition insofar as it stands against the divisive effects of religious convictions. There are many reasons for distrusting a religious education, but there are few justifications for an education that does not recognize man's spiritual glimmerings. For man's spiritual nature is involved in the wonder that arises from contemplating the miraculously vast and the miraculously small, and the center, man. It resides in the questions of why we are here and where we are going. It reveals itself in our responses to music and painting and poetry. And it remains stubbornly there even in the existential man, who, having kicked himself free from the universe, nevertheless puzzles over the nature of his own existence. An education that increases our capacity to wonder, shakes us loose from our dogmas, satisfies us as much with questions as with answers, and helps the growth within that brings a man to curse or to pray is necessary to meet this kind of more-than-rational expectation.

It seems to me that variety is a fourth thing we expect of education. Truth itself would pall if it were all one color. Boredom is as much the enemy of man's happiness as vice and need. Of all man's curses, boredom makes its appearance amidst both poverty and plenty, and feeds on both. Boredom, like education, thrives when men have most time. Often, one becomes bored with education itself. The classic Faustian boredom, with its reaction against the rational life, begins in questioning the use of learning and sinks into despair. There is the boredom with that particular direction toward which education inclines us and from which further education makes it difficult to turn away. There is a boredom with the limited achievements that education has brought about. And there is the boredom that a person feels because he is sufficiently educated to have both free time and the inclination to realize he's bored.

But if education cannot provide a sure escape from boredom, it may keep the educated person from being bored with trivial things. Education invites us into more interesting company than that of our actual neighbors. It raises the level of small talk. It encourages great thoughts and great deeds. It pours into the limited span of one person's existence far more than can be easily exhausted. Learning, if it is not a passive experience but a participation of mind and body and heart, is the means by which we find new purposes, set ourselves new directions, and lift our perceptions from our immediate selves and surroundings. The world in its infinite variety is always there to freshen our outlook. Education helps us see it.

Finally, we ask that education keep us alive and hopeful even in the face of ultimate darkness. How brief our time. How vain our strivings. Education may be the master deceiver by keeping those truths away from us and by always asserting that there is something worth finding out even though we will soon know nothing. That is why education should always be joyful, and lead us to laugh in the face of heaven or hell. For serious as our strivings are, they should never be so serious that we cannot lean back and laugh at the absurdity of our being and doing. Education should teach us to play the wise fool rather than turn us into the solemn ass. What if life is but a long day between the play of childhood and the burden of old age, the morning shadowed by the future that must be prepared for and old age by the darkness that is soon to come?

Education cannot change the ultimate facts of decline and death, but it can plunge one into life and keep one there. It can provide that overarching life of a people, a community, a world that was going on before the individual came onto the scene and that will continue on unchecked after he departs. It can provide a larger universal self to which one's passionate ambitions for the limited personal self contribute. Through education we think of ourselves as not only belonging to our kinsmen and friends but to mankind. The importance of a basically literary education is that it extends our physical journeys in this time and place backward to the past that brought us into being and forward to the imaginable future of which we become a part. Such an education, alive to the history of everything around us, fosters the sense of community that, if it cannot seal off the darkness, can widen the cleared area in which we can see.

By such means we come to see the world feelingly and not alone. Our joys are more intense for being shared. Our sorrows are less destructive for our knowing of universal sorrows. Our pride is chastened by an awareness of our betters. Our fears of death fade before the commonness of the occurrence. All humanity argues against our marching blindly toward death. Education, above all, gives value to life. The more we see on the way, the more we feel, the more we ponder over our journey, the more we ask of education, and the more it can give.